Roman Schmidt

Sharing of Probabilistically Correlated Data in Peer-to-peer Networks

Roman Schmidt

Sharing of Probabilistically Correlated Data in Peer-to-peer Networks

Presenting approaches exploiting data correlations on top of the structured overlay network P-Grid

Südwestdeutscher Verlag für Hochschulschriften

Impressum/Imprint (nur für Deutschland/ only for Germany)
Bibliografische Information der Deutschen Nationalbibliothek: Die Deutsche Nationalbibliothek verzeichnet diese Publikation in der Deutschen Nationalbibliografie; detaillierte bibliografische Daten sind im Internet über http://dnb.d-nb.de abrufbar.

Alle in diesem Buch genannten Marken und Produktnamen unterliegen warenzeichen-, marken- oder patentrechtlichem Schutz bzw. sind Warenzeichen oder eingetragene Warenzeichen der jeweiligen Inhaber. Die Wiedergabe von Marken, Produktnamen, Gebrauchsnamen, Handelsnamen, Warenbezeichnungen u.s.w. in diesem Werk berechtigt auch ohne besondere Kennzeichnung nicht zu der Annahme, dass solche Namen im Sinne der Warenzeichen- und Markenschutzgesetzgebung als frei zu betrachten wären und daher von jedermann benutzt werden dürften.

Verlag: Südwestdeutscher Verlag für Hochschulschriften Aktiengesellschaft & Co. KG
Dudweiler Landstr. 99, 66123 Saarbrücken, Deutschland
Telefon +49 681 37 20 271-1, Telefax +49 681 37 20 271-0, Email: info@svh-verlag.de
Zugl.: Lausanne, EPFL, Diss., 2008

Herstellung in Deutschland:
Schaltungsdienst Lange o.H.G., Berlin
Books on Demand GmbH, Norderstedt
Reha GmbH, Saarbrücken
Amazon Distribution GmbH, Leipzig
ISBN: 978-3-8381-0424-9

Imprint (only for USA, GB)
Bibliographic information published by the Deutsche Nationalbibliothek: The Deutsche Nationalbibliothek lists this publication in the Deutsche Nationalbibliografie; detailed bibliographic data are available in the Internet at http://dnb.d-nb.de.

Any brand names and product names mentioned in this book are subject to trademark, brand or patent protection and are trademarks or registered trademarks of their respective holders. The use of brand names, product names, common names, trade names, product descriptions etc. even without a particular marking in this works is in no way to be construed to mean that such names may be regarded as unrestricted in respect of trademark and brand protection legislation and could thus be used by anyone.

Publisher:
Südwestdeutscher Verlag für Hochschulschriften Aktiengesellschaft & Co. KG
Dudweiler Landstr. 99, 66123 Saarbrücken, Germany
Phone +49 681 37 20 271-1, Fax +49 681 37 20 271-0, Email: info@svh-verlag.de

Copyright © 2009 by the author and Südwestdeutscher Verlag für Hochschulschriften Aktiengesellschaft & Co. KG and licensors
All rights reserved. Saarbrücken 2009

Printed in the U.S.A.
Printed in the U.K. by (see last page)
ISBN: 978-3-8381-0424-9

Abstract

The impact of Peer-to-Peer (P2P) networks on the Internet landscape is undisputed. It has led to a series of new applications, e.g., as part of the so-called Web 2.0. The shift from the classical client-server based paradigm of the Internet, with a clear distinction between information providers and consumers, towards consumers sharing information among each other led to the rise of the P2P paradigm. The distributed setting enables users to share their content autonomously and locally, i.e, information remains at computers at the edge of the Internet and is not gathered and organized at central servers. Structured overlay networks were designed to organize the huge quantity of data shared in P2P networks by building a global, though distributed, index of shared information. Whereas the initial aim of these systems was to provide efficient lookup operations for single keyword operations, the need for more complex operations emerged very quickly. Peer Data Management Systems (PDMS) is one such example of application that enables data integration and complex query processing similar to (distributed) database systems on top of structured overlays.

Complex query operators usually require joint access to multiple data entries whereas single key lookups usually only affect a single data entry. The partitioning of the distributed index of standard structured overlays is optimized towards single key lookups and joint data access as required by PDMS was neglected so far. (Distributed) databases have already shown that (index-)data organization supporting correlated data access is necessary and crucial for efficient processing, as network usage is minimized. We aim at applying this insight to structured overlays by clustering correlated data frequently accessed jointly by applications, including PDMS but also other types of applications.

Data correlations can be derived from different sources, data properties, processing properties, users and applications. We study and present solutions for three different types of correlations in the context of different applications: (i) range queries where exploiting the order relationship of data is a fundamental basis for any database-like system; (ii) distributed probabilistic inference where exploiting user-defined complex data correlations gains importance through the Web 2.0; (iii) multi-term queries where exploiting data correlations derived from data access statistics enables simple but powerful keyword search to users. Our approach exploits properties of structured overlays, such as order-preserving hashing, to realize efficient range query processing. We further introduce a distributed clustering algorithm based on the spring relaxation technique to cluster strongly correlated data entries at one node respectively in its proximity. Joint data access is thus performed on a single or few nodes to reduce network bandwidth consumption and therefore to increase system performance.

Our approaches are realized on top of the structured overlay network P-Grid although they are generic enough to be applied to other P2P networks with similar properties. This thesis presents details about the Java implementation of P-Grid, its architectural design and its evaluation on PlanetLab, today's standard testbed for P2P systems. The implementation of P-Grid in a Java application finally enabled us to build a PDMS system on top relying on P-Grid's efficient query processing. We present the UniStore system, a distributed data management system aiming at public data management and support for database-like query operators on heterogeneous data, and its evaluation on PlanetLab.

Keywords: peer-to-peer systems, structured overlay networks, data correlations, peer data management systems.

Contents

Abstract   i

1 Introduction   1
    1.1 Data Oriented P2P Systems 3
    1.2 On Correlated Data 6
    1.3 Scope of Research 7
    1.4 Outline of the Thesis and Contributions 8

I Fundamentals   11

2 Peer-to-Peer Systems   13
    2.1 A Short History 13
    2.2 The Concept of Data Fragmentation 14
       2.2.1 Design Findings for P2P Systems 16
    2.3 Unstructured Overlays 16
       2.3.1 Gnutella 17
    2.4 Structured Overlays 19
       2.4.1 Distributed Hash Tables 20
       2.4.2 Structured Overlays with Order-Preserving Hashing 26
    2.5 PlanetLab 31
    2.6 Conclusions 32

3 The P-Grid Overlay   33
    3.1 Distributed Search Structure 33
    3.2 Basic Search Operation 35
    3.3 Order-Preserving Hash Function 36
    3.4 Overlay Construction 37
       3.4.1 Divide and Conquer 39
       3.4.2 Unstructured Backbone 40
    3.5 Data Correlations in P-Grid 41

	3.5.1 Multi-Dimensional Correlations	41
3.6	Conclusions	43

II Access of Correlated Data   45

4 Range Queries   47
4.1 Algorithms and Complexity Analysis 48
    4.1.1 Min-Max Traversal Algorithm 48
    4.1.2 Shower Algorithm 50
4.2 Related Work 52
4.3 Evaluation 54
    4.3.1 Message Latency and Cost 55
    4.3.2 Query Latency 57
    4.3.3 Success Rate 60
4.4 Completeness Estimation 61
    4.4.1 Completeness on Data vs. Peer Level 62
    4.4.2 Estimating Completeness 62
    4.4.3 Usability in other Overlay Systems 65
    4.4.4 Evaluation 66
4.5 Conclusions 72

5 Distributed Inference   73
5.1 Motivation 74
5.2 Belief Propagation 75
    5.2.1 The Message Passing Algorithm 77
5.3 The Inference Architecture 77
5.4 The Relaxation Algorithm 79
5.5 Evaluation 83
    5.5.1 Network Topologies 83
    5.5.2 Message Reduction 85
    5.5.3 Load Balancing 90
    5.5.4 Reduction Effort 90
    5.5.5 Discussion 96
5.6 Related Work 97
5.7 Conclusions 98

6 Multi-Term Queries   99
6.1 Motivation 100
6.2 Related Work 102

		6.3	Query-Driven Clustering	104
			6.3.1 Architecture	105
	6.4	Evaluation		106
			6.4.1 Probabilistic Networks	107
			6.4.2 Term Posting Lists	107
			6.4.3 Lookup Costs	109
			6.4.4 Relaxation Effort	112
			6.4.5 Load Balancing	113
			6.4.6 Discussion	113
	6.5	Conclusions		115

III From Theory to Practice 117

7 Architecture 121

- 7.1 Overview . . . 121
- 7.2 Routing Layer and API . . . 122
  - 7.2.1 Routing Layer Components . . . 123
  - 7.2.2 Routing Layer Services . . . 124
- 7.3 Indexing Layer and API . . . 125
  - 7.3.1 Indexing Layer Components . . . 126
  - 7.3.2 Indexing Layer Services . . . 127
  - 7.3.3 Data Type Handlers . . . 127
- 7.4 Interaction Diagrams . . . 128
  - 7.4.1 Data Insertion . . . 128
  - 7.4.2 Query Resolution . . . 129
- 7.5 Conclusions . . . 130

8 Implementation 131

- 8.1 Overview . . . 131
- 8.2 Core Package . . . 132
  - 8.2.1 Index Sub-Package . . . 132
  - 8.2.2 Maintenance Sub-Package . . . 133
  - 8.2.3 Search Sub-Package . . . 134
- 8.3 Interfaces Package . . . 134
  - 8.3.1 P-Grid's Routing Interface . . . 134
  - 8.3.2 P-Grid's Indexing Interface . . . 137
- 8.4 Network Package . . . 140
  - 8.4.1 Generic Sub-Package . . . 141
  - 8.4.2 Lookup Sub-Package . . . 141

	8.4.3 Protocol Sub-Package	141
	8.4.4 Router Sub-Package	142
8.5	Util package	143
8.6	Evaluation of P-Grid's Bootstrapping	143
8.7	Load-Aware Message Routing	146
	8.7.1 Routing Strategies	147
	8.7.2 Evaluation	148
8.8	Conclusions	152

9 UniStore — 153

- 9.1 Motivation . . . 154
- 9.2 Challenges . . . 155
- 9.3 Architecture . . . 157
  - 9.3.1 Distributed Storage Layer . . . 157
  - 9.3.2 Triple Storage Layer . . . 158
  - 9.3.3 Schema Mapping . . . 159
- 9.4 Similarity Queries . . . 161
  - 9.4.1 The Query Language VQL . . . 161
  - 9.4.2 Similarity Measures and Processing . . . 163
- 9.5 Physical Operators . . . 164
  - 9.5.1 Similarity Selection . . . 165
  - 9.5.2 Similarity Join . . . 167
  - 9.5.3 Ranking Operators . . . 168
- 9.6 Similarity Operator Costs . . . 169
- 9.7 Evaluation . . . 171
  - 9.7.1 Experimental results . . . 172
- 9.8 Related Work . . . 174
- 9.9 Conclusions . . . 177

10 Conclusions — 179

List of Frequently Used Symbols and Abbreviations — 183

Bibliography — 184

Chapter 1

Introduction

The Internet is nowadays part of our daily life and omnipresent at business and free time. We use it to communicate with friends and colleagues via email, we read the daily news on websites of our favorite newspapers and we inquire about products we consider to buy, compare prices and functionalities on company websites. These services basically represent the core Internet as it was established at its foundation, following the classical client-server paradigm where institutions provide information and services on servers and consumers act as clients. In the last years, this rigid regime was broken up by new technologies and service providers bringing users into the role of information providers. This evolution of the Internet is often referred as part of the "Web 2.0". Web 2.0 includes other important developments such as the Semantic Web aiming at meaningful access to Web data.

The most important new technology in the era of the Web 2.0 are Peer-to-Peer (P2P) systems. This is highlighted by the fact that P2P systems are the leader of overall bandwidth consumption on the Internet for several years already, consuming approximately 74% percent last year[1]. P2P systems enable users to directly share data with other users overcoming the need of expensive central infrastructure for services. The second big advantage of the P2P technology is that these systems do not have and require an administrator, meaning that any content can be shared by any user at all time. This freedom has to be paid by P2P system users as they have to remain online to share their resources with the community and to build and maintain the system. The P2P system itself is responsible to organize the shared data and provide the required functionalities to discover and download shared content. First-generation P2P systems formed loosely coupled unstructured networks of peers where queries by users were resolved by simple message broadcasts. This approach was as successful as simple and used by the first well-know P2P systems such as Gnutella. Technical problems emerged with a growing number of peers and users in the P2P population unveiling scalability limitations in terms of bandwidth consumption, network maintenance and query processing capabilities. The second generation P2P systems introduced

---
[1] http://www.ipoque.com/news_&_events/internet_studies/internet_study_2007

the concept of structured overlay networks and addressed these limitiations by introducing distributed search structures. The basic idea in structured overlay networks is to organize the shared data in a distributed index. The index itself is maintained by peers in the P2P system and enables efficient lookup of all shared data. Maintenance algorithms ensure the consistency of the index and thus reliable data access independent of peer availabilities. In a structured overlay network a hash function is used to map resources and peer IP addresses into a common application-specific identifier space and to bind resources to peers such that peers are responsible for data items with similar hash keys. The hash keys are randomly generated in a way that guarantees that two different data items are mapped to the same hash key only with very small probability.

Distributed Hash Tables (DHT) are one variant of structured overlay networks implementing this idea using a uniform random hash function. The use of a uniform random hash function implies that in general data items are relatively uniformly distributed over peers. A drawback is that relationships among data items are not maintained by the hash function, i.e., related data items are in general mapped to non-similar hash keys. This implies in a distributed setting that related data items are in general not stored at the same or nearby peers as peers are responsible for a short range of similar keys in the hashed key space. As a result any lookup operation beyond single key lookups will therefore lead to potentially inefficient multiple lookup operations involving multiple peers. Thus, a DHT is a solution tailored towards efficient exact key lookups.

Exact key lookups as provided by DHTs are an important way to quickly and efficiently access data in a data management system. But also more complex search predicates are required and provided by such systems. This requires additional access structures depending on the supported query types. For example, range queries are frequently required for structured data access. Obviously a hash table is not an efficient data structure for this type of query as data from a given range is scattered over potentially many peers. Therefore, as alternative, some structured overlay networks consider the use of order-preserving hash functions to build the distributed index. As a result the order of data items is maintained by the hash function and can be exploited during lookups to support more complex search predicates, e.g., range queries. On the downside such an overlay network has to take care of storage load balancing as large data sets can be mapped to a relatively small key range possibly overloading peers in this region, a problem that is avoided when using uniform random hash functions. P2P systems using order-preserving hashing require therefore additional mechanisms to balance the peer distribution with respect to the distribution of keys generated from data items. In the following section we will provide an overview of the issues and solution strategies that have been explored to enable more complex data access functionalities in data-oriented P2P systems, starting from a historical overview of related works in database systems.

1.1 Data Oriented P2P Systems

A database is a collection of structured information organized in such a way that a computer program can quickly select desired pieces of data. The data is stored in a persistent way, e.g., on a hard disk. A database management system (DBMS) is a complex set of software programs that controls the organization, storage, management, and retrieval of data in a database. A DBMS allows users to create new databases and specify their schema (logical structure of data), using a data-definition language (DDL) [UGMW01]. Additionally, a Data Manipulation Language (DML) can then be used to retrieve, insert, delete and update data in a database. The database query language supports users with various operators to access and retrieve data in the database. To speedup data retrieval, databases index stored data and restructure the physical store accordingly. A query optimizer is then responsible for choosing the best access path to access requested data on the disk. An access path refers to the data structures and the algorithms that are used to access the data. Indexes can be used in essentially two different ways. First, they can be used for sequential access to the indexed file – here sequential means Şin the sequence defined by values of the indexed field. Second, indexes can be used for direct access to individual records in the indexed file on the basis of a given value for the indexed field [Dat91]. Indexes can be implemented using a variety of data structures, the most popular ones are B-trees [BM72] and hash indexes. A B-tree is a particular type of tree-structured index storing sorted data for efficient retrieval in a block-oriented storage context. B-trees are therefore efficient for sequential data access as, for example, required by range queries and scans. Hash index is a technique for providing fast direct access to a specific record on the basis of a given value for some field. Therefore, the primary operation it supports efficiently is a lookup: given a key (e.g., a person's name), find the corresponding value (e.g. that person's telephone number).

[OV91] defines a distributed database as a collection of multiple, logically interrelated databases distributed over a computer network. To form a DDBS, files should not only be logically related but there should also be structure among the files, and access should be via a common interface. A distributed database management system (distributed DBMS) is then defined as the software system that permits the management of the distributed database and makes the distribution transparent to the users. In a distributed DBMS, the relations in a database schema are usually decomposed into smaller fragments which might be allocated to different sites. There are two alternatives for this fragmentation, horizontally [CNP82] and vertically [NCWD84] (and using both in a hybrid fashion). In both cases user applications are analyzed for, at least, their most important query predicates ([Wie83] has shown that the most active 20% of user queries account for 80% of the total data access). The distributed DBMS therefore maintains joint access statistics of attributes and their frequencies by user queries. For example, vertical partitioning uses an attribute affinity matrix to represent joint access. This matrix is further used for the fragmentation process by clustering together attributes with high affinity. This process is usually done by a central control unit administering the distributed database and having complete knowledge on the system, or this knowledge is globally available at all nodes, i.e., the DBMS is aware of the partitioning schema and can access the partitioned data directly at successive requests (user queries).

Attempts to overcome the limitation of centralized maintenance were presented in [NDLR00] introducing Scalable Distributed Data Structures (SDDS). The data of an SDDS are partitioned for storage over several servers and SDDS scales transparently for the application to potentially any number of sites. Data access does not require any centralized directory but information on the location of data partitions is eventually distributed over all servers. The partitioning and access scheme depends on the used SDDS. The LH* scheme [LNS93] provides a scalable distributed linear hash partitioning for direct access while the RP* scheme [LNS94] provides scalable distributed range partitioning for parallel range scans. Structured overlay networks go one step further and provide a fully distributed access structure to shared resources using a distributed index without requiring global knowledge at nodes on data partitions in order to maintain scalability with very large numbers of peers. Structured overlays partition data horizontally based on hashed resource identifiers derived from data item properties. Furthermore they deal with the unreliability of peers by providing sophisticated maintenance algorithms. Data partitioning and load balancing are performed in structured overlay networks without exploiting global knowledge on the network and statistical information on data distribution and query access as it is typically exploited in distributed databases. Structured overlay networks can be classified in two types of approaches: distributed hash tables and order preserving structured overlay networks. A Distributed Hash Table (DHT) such as Chord [SMK+01], Pastry [RD01] and CAN [RFH+01] is analogous to an hash index in a database system enabling efficient exact key lookups as known from databases. Overlay networks using order-preserving hashing such as Mercury [BAS04], SkipNet [HJS+03] and P-Grid [Abe01] are analogous to a tree-structured index such as a B-tree supporting efficient range scans.

The first works considering more complex database functionalities for P2P systems were [GHI+01] and [BGK+02]. [GHI+01] focuses on the problem of data placement, i.e., how to distribute data and workload so that cost is optimized under the existing resource and bandwidth constraints. [BGK+02] on the other hand focuses on the problem of data integration, i.e., supporting mappings between P2P databases using different vocabularies to express the same real-world concepts in order to enable query reformulation and answering. Both works have initiated many further works on Peer Data Management Systems (PDMS) such as Piazza [HIM+04] (initiated by [GHI+01]), Hyperion [AKK+03] (initiated by [BGK+02]), PIER [HHH+02, HHL+03] and GridVine [ACMHP04, CMAA07].

Today the notion of PDMS relates mainly to distributed data integration systems providing transparent access to heterogeneous databases without resorting to a centralized logical schema and focus on the problem of data integration, schema mappings and query refor-

1.1. Data Oriented P2P Systems

mulation. PDMS are composed by autonomous databases using local schemas which have to be mapped to each other to enable distributed query processing. This further has to be achieved in a distributed fashion as no central coordination and knowledge is assumed to be available. GridVine [ACMHP04, CMAA07], for example, uses pair-wise schema mappings and query reformulation to form a semantic mediation layer on top of a structured overlay connecting heterogeneous databases. User defined schema mappings are validated by a distributed message passing scheme to automatically detect erroneous mappings [CMAF06]. Piazza [HIM+04] has similar goals as GridVine. It uses a mapping language for mapping between sets of XML source nodes with different document structures (including those with XML serializations of RDF). The system uses the transitive closure of mappings to answer queries and is able to follow mappings in both forward and reverse directions. RDFPeers [CF04] is a scalable and distributed RDF triple repository and self-organizes peers into a multi-attribute addressable network (MAAN) which extends Chord to efficiently answer multi-attribute and range queries. The system's query processing capabilities are very similar to the ones of GridVine as it supports triple pattern queries, disjunctive and range queries and conjunctive multi-predicate queries using RDQL. The recent rise of triple-based data models such as RDF [W3C] led to several examples where structured overlays support vertical partitioning of databases [CF04, KSHS06]. Proper partitioning strategies for triple-based data are also the focus of research for Semantic Web data management with centralized DBMS [AMMH07].

PIER [HHH+02, HHL+03] has a slightly different focus on P2P data management supporting Internet-scale querying. It is built on top of the Bamboo DHT [RGRK04], aiming for large-scale data and peer distribution beyond the usual scale of distributed databases. It supports massively distributed, database-style data-flows for snapshot and continuous queries as known from distributed DBMS. PIER provides a full degree of data independence, including a relational data model, and a full suite of relational query operators and indexing facilities that can manipulate data without regard to its location on the network. PIER maintains several different index structures to speedup query operations executed by query plans passed along peers in the system. PIER's query operators are very similar to those offered by traditional (distributed) database systems.

Other approaches to P2P query processing are PeerDB [NOTZ03, OTZ+03] and IrisNet [GKK+03]. PeerDB is a database application implemented on top of BestPeer [NOT02] enabling SQL query processing on heterogeneous databases. Schema relations are annotated with descriptions and keywords used during a two-phase query processing strategy to select candidate relations in the first phase, before a query is finally submitted to promising peers. BestPeer can be reconfigured accordingly to keep promising peers in the proximity to reduce network costs. The IrisNet system uses a hierarchical data model (XML) and a hierarchical network overlay (DNS) to route queries and data. As a result, IrisNet shares the characteristics of traditional hierarchical databases: it is best used in scenarios where the hierarchy changes infrequently, and the queries match the hierarchy.

P2P data management systems such as PIER and GridVine rely heavily on the availability of structured overlay networks to achieve Internet scalability. As we have further seen, structured overlay networks, in particular DHTs, were mainly designed for supporting efficient exact key lookups. Efficient range scans are supported by those structured overlay networks using order-preserving hashing. Beyond that, little attention has been devoted so far to the implications of the data access patterns in structured overlay networks induced by P2P data management systems and the influence on data processing performance. In particular different forms of correlations among data items implied by data access patterns have so far not been considered in the design and use of structured overlay networks. This thesis studies the problem of considering joint data access on correlated data in structured overlays and provides novel solutions for optimizing fragmentation/partitioning of the distributed access structure and algorithms using the distributed access structure to reduce network utilization. We therefore discuss now in more detail the issues on accessing correlated data in structured overlay networks.

1.2 On Correlated Data

P2P applications, such as peer data management systems, frequently use structured overlay networks as distributed index to efficiently access data. Access is not only limited to single data entries, e.g., for retrieving an entry by its identifier, but can involve a set of data entries. Joint access to data entries induces a correlation relationship among data entries. The strength of the correlation among a set of data entries corresponds to the probability that those data entries are accessed jointly by an application.

In a distributed system data is distributed over different nodes and data access implies consumption of network resources to retrieve data entries. Joint data access to a set of data entries can therefore require to access multiple nodes to retrieve them all. The number of nodes required to access depends on the distribution of the data in the network. Network access is still the most expensive resource in distributed systems and an important design goal in distributed systems is thus to minimize bandwidth consumption and reduce communication latency. In the case of joint data access this implies in particular that the number of nodes accessed when retrieving a set of data entries should be minimized. This can in particular be achieved if correlated data, i.e., data that is processed frequently jointly, is stored at the same or nearby nodes. In order to achieve this goal existing data correlations to estimate joint data access of applications need to be exploited when partitioning data among nodes.

Data correlations can be obtained in several ways. First, correlations can be derived from inherent properties of the data domains, in particular from known relationships among different data values. The knowledge of the nature of the relationship and the possible types of queries allows to derive that certain sets of data entries are more likely to be jointly accessed than others. A simple example of such a data value property is the order relationship among data values in an ordered domain. Since structured query languages support range queries, neighboring data values are likely to be jointly accessed and therefore should be stored together. Another example of this type are similarity relationships among text data values. Since queries typically retrieve the most similar text values to a given query text it is advantageous to jointly store similar text values.

Secondly, data correlations can be derived from relationships among data entries which are explicitly represented in the database. Such relationships are particularly rich in PDMS as data is provided and maintained by a community of users integrating and relating heterogeneous information to common knowledge. Examples of such relationships are schema mappings in PDMS, relating a local schema to other schemas in the system, and Friend-of-a-Friend (FOAF) networks relating persons and documents in the Semantic Web. The Semantic Web and itÕs modeling languages enable to define a variety of relationships with the aim to support their automated processing. In this context we find new types of relationships which go beyond standard structured data representation, for example distributed probabilistic inference networks. For performing probabilistic inference, inference algorithms require access to the inference network. Due to the nature of these algorithms neighboring data entries in the probabilistic inference network have a higher probability to be accessed jointly during inference inducing higher correlation of data access amongst them.

Finally, joint access statistics can be used to obtain data correlations between data entries. A system can monitor queries and their predicates to identify access patterns of applications. These can be maintained in access statistics which are used to derive data correlations for frequently jointly accessed data entries. An example for such a correlated data access are multi-term queries, i.e., queries for multiple keywords. Multi-term queries access all data entries matching all/any keywords and therefore induce a data correlation among frequently jointly queried keywords and their corresponding data entries.

Different sources of information on data correlation can also be combined. For example, joint access statistics can be further refined with data correlations derived from the order relationship of data values. While the order relationship enables to estimate joint access, statistics can highlight frequently queried ranges and therefore refine data placement.

1.3 Scope of Research

In this thesis, we investigate the problem of optimizing joint data access in structured overlay networks. We present algorithms to partition the distributed index of overlay networks among nodes exploiting data correlations. We derive and use data correlations from data properties,

properties of data processing algorithms and joint access statistics of applications. We present for each of these cases a concrete example of a problem based on a data processing problem in structured overlay networks. The common objective of all solutions is to cluster correlated data on nodes to reduce communication cost for joint access as required by the specific applications.

For concrete description of our solutions and implementation we rely on P-Grid, a structured overlay network using order-preserving hashing, although our findings can be generalized to other systems with similar properties as discussed for each presented solution in the corresponding chapter. We describe the implementation and evaluation of our approaches into the P-Grid system, and show how a peer data management system can be built on top of our work.

1.4 Outline of the Thesis and Contributions

This document is divided into three parts. The first part, *Fundamentals*, provides an overview of P2P systems and a more detailed description of P-Grid basics we use in the remainder of this thesis. *Access of Correlated Data*, the second part, presents algorithms to efficiently partition the distributed index of correlated data to improve joint access to it. The third part, *From Theory to Practice*, shows how some of these algorithms are realized in a Java application and finally used by a peer data management system to ensure scalability, reliability and efficiency.

Part I: Fundamentals

This thesis starts with an overview of the best-known P2P systems in Chapter 2. In our overview we focus on structured overlay networks and their way of data placement, i.e., how data is partitioned among peers and how data correlations are considered during this process. We further present PlanetLab, a distributed P2P system testbed which is used to evaluate some of our approaches and implementations. The first part finishes with a more detailed description of the structured overlay network P-Grid in Chapter 3. The algorithms we present in the second part of this thesis are based on P-Grid.

The main contributions of this part are:

- a detailed survey of the most popular structured overlay networks and a discussion of their way to consider data correlations

- a precise overview of P-Grid basics including its structure, search algorithm, hash function and construction

Part II: Access of Correlated Data

Chapter 4 presents two algorithms suitable for P-Grid to efficiently resolve range queries in a structured overlay. Range queries rely on the order relationship which can be derived from data properties. Although the algorithms were designed for P-Grid, they are also suitable for other structured overlays with similar properties. The next chapter, Chapter 5 targets the problem of more complex data correlations provided by users and/or applications. We consider data correlations derived from probabilistic inference networks, e.g., to perform reasoning in the domain of the Semantic Web. While range queries are naturally supported by P-Grid, this type of data correlations requires an additional index re-partitioning algorithm to improve joint data access. Our approach is based on the spring relaxation technique enabling distributed clustering by autonomous peers. The last Chapter 6 tackles the problem of data correlations derived from access statistics induced by applications. Structured overlay networks were originally designed for efficient single-term lookups given a single key. We propose to apply our spring relaxation algorithm already used in Chapter 5 to improve lookup efficiency in case more than one keyword is present. Our aim is to cluster frequently jointly queried keywords together to reduce network communication and thereby joint data access.

The main contributions of this part are:

- an approach for range query processing in structured overlay networks
- an algorithm to estimate the number of replies by range queries together with a completeness estimation during range query processing
- a decentralized clustering algorithm for multi-dimensional correlation graphs on top of structured overlay networks
- an architecture for distributed inference on Bayesian networks on top of structured overlay networks
- an approach to efficiently support multi-term queries in structured overlay networks

Part III: From Theory to Practice

The previous part presented algorithms and their analytical and practical evaluation based on simulations and an implementation of the P-Grid system. This part presents details about the P-Grid system itself. Chapter 7 presents the architectural design and provides a high-level overview of our system. P-Grid's implementation is divided into two parts, a routing layer and an indexing layer, which both have a defined API for applications. Our intention was to provide a P-Grid independent API for P2P systems which can be used by other P2P system developers at will. Interaction diagrams show how these two layers interact and how data can be inserted and queried by applications. Chapter 8 provides details about the Java implementation following the architectural design. The code is divided into several packages and sub-packages of which the most important classes are described briefly. Finally, we present an evaluation of P-Grid's unique bootstrapping capabilities and a query load balancing solution representative for the enhancements implemented in the course of this thesis. The last chapter of this thesis presents an application based on P-Grid and benefiting from the designed and implemented algorithms in P-Grid. Chapter 9 presents UniStore a large-scaled but still light-weight distributed data management system on top of P-Grid. The main motivation for UniStore is the idea of public data management, where a large amount of independent users provide and/or look for information structured in any conceivable way. The focus of UniStore lies on efficient query processing, which involves the choice of distributed indexes, cost-based optimizations and the application of Multiple Mutating Query Plans (M2QP). We present UniStore's approach to efficiently process similarity queries on top of P-Grid and provide a PlanetLab evaluation of various similarity operators.

The main contributions of this part are:

- an extensible two-layered architecture for P-Grid enabling applications to tailor P-Grid's behavior towards application-specific needs

- a high-level overview of P-Grid's implementation, its main components and services and their internal interaction

- a stable API for P2P systems enabling applications to interchange the underlying P2P system implementation at will

- an overview of P-Grid's Java implementation listing all packages and their core classes and functionalities

- a simple though effective way of query load balancing implemented and tested on PlanetLab

- an overview of the UniStore application based on P-Grid including its architecture and query language

- an approach to efficiently process string similarity queries in structured overlays

Part I

Fundamentals

Chapter 2

Peer-to-Peer Systems

The concept of Peer-to-Peer (P2P) systems is to share resources such as data, storage, CPU and bandwidth in a cooperative way. Peers provide a small fraction of their resources to build a distributed system of larger capacity than any of the peers alone would be able to provide. As a result, the system is able to provide better scalability for their services than a centralized solution. All peers are treated equally and autonomously, i.e., no central coordinator is in control of other peers.

The most common service provided by current P2P systems is the distributed management of large sets of files. Examples are the well-known file-sharing networks where individual autonomous users collaborate to share their files. The data is provided by the users and remains under their control. This paradigm is recently more and more adopted by so-called peer data management systems aiming at providing Internet-scale database systems supported by autonomous users. The functionalities offered by these new P2P systems go beyond simple file-sharing applications and aim at advanced services like distributed query processing and data integration.

This chapter briefly presents the history of P2P systems and their evolution over the last years resulting in a variety of systems adjusted for different needs of applications. We then present the most well-known P2P systems and discuss their differences with a focus on how these systems organize shared data and exploit data correlations.

2.1 A Short History

The history of P2P systems in the Internet is not even 10 years old but their impact was noticeable from the beginning on and their success is nowadays undisputed. The development started with the Napster [Nap] system released June 1, 1999 and used by millions of users all over the world to share music files. The concept was so simple and the system so easy to use that its success caused its shutdown already two years later by injunction for facilitating the transfer of copyrighted material. From that point on, P2P was mainly associated by the public with pirate-to-pirate although P2P systems were used in earlier days by the scientific community, e.g., Seti@Home [ACK+02], almost unnoticed by the public though. But the financial impact of Napster on the music industry and its attention in the global news caused the breakthrough for P2P on the Internet leading to a variety of P2P applications nowadays used by almost every Internet user.

The variety of applications also strongly influenced the evolution of P2P systems as new applications had new requirements on data processing leading to new infrastructures and designs. Napster had a central server to index all shared files which was soon recognized as single-point of failure and bottleneck for P2P systems as data was only processed at the central server. Later systems were aiming at complete decentralization of data processing lacking any central coordination. These fully decentralized networks can be categorized in unstructured and structured overlay networks. The most successful unstructured overlay is the file-sharing network Gnutella [Gnua]. Its decentralization and simplicity still guarantees its survival although several protocol revisions have already been implemented. For example, Gnutella introduced the concept of SuperPeers, a hierarchical overlay of inter-connected peers (SuperPeers) responsible for query routing and "normal" peers connecting to SuperPeers. This hierarchical architecture was later adopted by many other overlay systems, e.g., KaZaA [KaZ]. Nowadays, P2P systems are omnipresent in our daily life and responsible for almost three-fourths of todays' Internet traffic[1]. Most modern systems are based on structured and/or hierarchical overlays. The most popular P2P systems nowadays are BitTorrent [Bit] and Skype [Sky]. BitTorrent is a file-sharing network enabling fast downloads of large files by splitting files in smaller chunks and downloading them from multiple nodes in parallel. Skype is a distributed Voice over IP (VoIP) application allowing users to communicate (audio-visually) over the Internet. Skype currently counts approximately 276 million users with already 100 billion call-minutes, according to Skype.

2.2 The Concept of Data Fragmentation

The idea of partitioning data and distributing it among several peers is not new and was already introduced in the area of distributed databases [OV91]. The main difference between distributed database systems and P2P systems is the autonomy of peers. Nodes in a distributed database are under the control of a central database management system (DBMS) organizing the storage devices located in the same physical location or distributed over a network of interconnected computers. The data stored in the database is fragmented/partitioned and distributed across the multiple physical locations in the network, while under the control of the central coordinator. Database nodes get assigned a partition of the data they are responsible for. Like in P2P systems, data can be replicated to increase reliability and

---

[1] http://www.ipoque.com/news_&_events/internet_studies/internet_study_2007

2.2. The Concept of Data Fragmentation

fault-tolerance, depending on business needs, and the distribution of data is transparent to users, i.e., a user does not have to know where data is stored or retrieved from.

An interesting problem in both distributed databases and P2P systems is how to partition and fragment data among peers. An approach used by some of the early structured overlay networks is random uniform distribution using a hash function such as SHA-1. Data fragments are randomly assigned to peers and an index has to be kept to retrieve them later. While this achieves good storage load-balancing, one of the important criteria for distributed systems, it lacks performance for more complex distributed data processing operations beyond simple lookups retrieving a single data fragment. Two approaches to tackle this problem in distributed database systems, where more complex data processing is common, are horizontal [CNP82] and vertical [NCWD84] fragmentation. Both have the aim to partition data into smaller fragments of correlated data which can then be stored at different physical locations.

Horizontal partitioning partitions a relation in a database into subsets of tuples. This is useful if certain value ranges are often processed together. For example, students with ZIP codes less than 5000 are stored in Students_South, while students with ZIP codes greater than or equal to 5000 are stored in Students_North. The two partition tables are then Students_South and Students_North, while a view with a union might be created over both of them to provide a complete view of all students.

Vertical partitioning partitions a relation in a database by partitioning the attribute sets and projecting the tables onto the attribute set partitions. Normalization is a process that inherently involves vertical partitioning. A common form of vertical partitioning is to split (slow to find) dynamic data from (fast to find) static data in a table where the dynamic data is not used as often as the static. Creating a view across the two newly created tables restores the original table with a performance penalty, however performance will increase when accessing the static data, e.g., for statistical analysis.

A hybrid approach combines both horizontal and vertical partitioning. Which method is used in the end mainly depends on the queries posed against the database and the performance requirements. Horizontal partitioning is advisable if mainly all or most columns of a table are requested for certain parts of a table, e.g., for all students with a ZIP code lower than 5000. On the other hand, if two attributes are frequently processed together, not requiring other attributes of a table, then vertical partitioning provides better performance. To choose a partitioning schema, the query history can be analyzed to identify dependencies between data entries if they are not already known in advance. The partitioning aims at storing highly correlated data at the same physical device to provide the best performance.

2.2.1 Design Findings for P2P Systems

The previous section has shown that the idea of data partitioning is not new and has been studied for a long time in the field of distributed databases. P2P systems implement the same concept of data sharing and data partitioning as distributed databases but without central control and with autonomous peers. Nevertheless, data has to be organized in a certain way to provide efficient lookup and database-like lookup guarantees for performance and completeness. Structured overlay networks achieve this by building a decentralized index of all data shared in their system. The index is fragmented and partitioned among participating peers similar to horizontal data fragmentation in distributed databases. An important question that remains is which peer holds which index entries.

Section 2.4 will present some of the most prominent structured overlays with a specific focus on their strategies of data respectively index partitioning. We distinguish between two types of systems: (i) systems using a uniform hash function and (ii) systems using a order-preserving hash-function. Why is this an important criterion for us? Distributed databases have shown that data partitioning according to data correlations is important to achieve good performance. They therefore store correlated data on the same physical location. We think that this is also an important requirement for P2P systems if they are supposed to perform efficiently for more complex operations beyond single key lookups.

For completeness before discussing structured overlay networks, we will present the concept of unstructured overlays as they are currently very widespread for P2P file-sharing applications and well-known. Their design is usually very simple to provide stable large-scale networks with best-effort lookup operations. These networks are very well suited for file-sharing applications as highly requested files are usually also strongly replicated in the network and therefore very likely be found. Rare content is however more difficult to find and no guarantees can be given that it will be found at all. Some unstructured networks therefore already consider a hybrid approach to overcome this shortcoming by combining the benefits of structured and unstructured networks [HK07]. The next section will present the basic concept of unstructured networks and in more details the most prominent representative, Gnutella.

2.3 Unstructured Overlays

Unstructured overlays organize peers in a random graph and use flooding, random walks or expanding-ring Time-To-Live (TTL) search, etc. to query content stored at overlay peers. Using an unstructured topology implies to involve all peers in data processing if the processing has to be complete. As both data and index items remain locally at peers each query is only evaluated against the local index. Data is therefore not reorganized in the network and no global structure is maintained. No central coordinator has knowledge of all the shared

2.3. Unstructured Overlays

data. Therefore no data correlations can be exploited as peers are not aware of other peers' data respectively index. Thus, unstructured networks are of minor interest for us as we aim at reducing lookup costs (the number of involved peers) by exploiting data correlations between data items shared in a P2P system. We will nevertheless present the first and probably most famous unstructured P2P system Gnutella for completeness. Other prominent systems are FastTrack [Fas], eDonkey [eDo], BitTorrent [Bit], and Freenet [CSWH00]. A detailed description of them and a discussion can be found in [LCP+04].

2.3.1 Gnutella

Gnutella [Gnua] is a decentralized protocol for distributed search on a flat unstructured network of so-called servents (peers). Peers are called servents as they act as servers (serv-) and clients (-ents) at the same time according to the P2P paradigm that all peers are equal and share their resources among each other. The original Gnutella protocol supported only a flat hierarchy-less topology soon leading to performance and scalability problems as described in [Rit01]. The scalability problem arises from the flooding based resource location algorithm as shown in Figure 2.1.

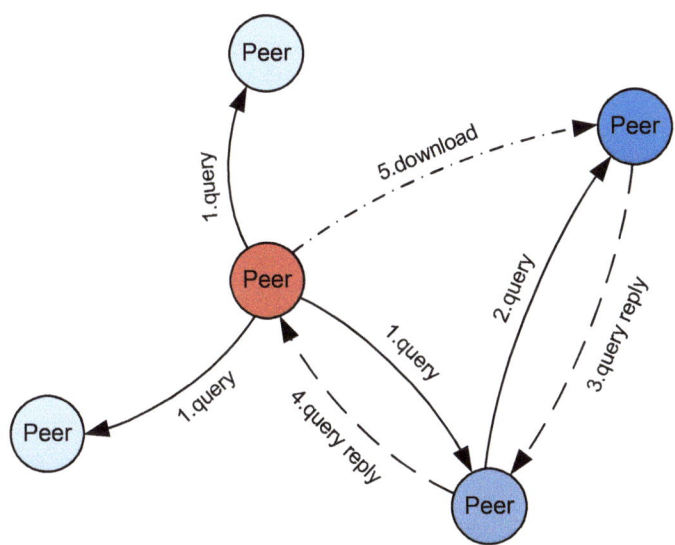

Figure 2.1: Gnutella architecture and content location

All communication is entirely pair-wise between two servents and peers only know their shared content, their neighbors and a set of recently received peer addresses. Gnutella is therefore purely P2P as there is no central coordination or control and peers only interact locally with their environment. Peers further only decide based on local information and do not have influence on other peers as others can refuse connections and ignore messages at will. These properties enable peers to create ad-hoc networks in a fast way and to remain operational even in very dynamic environments with frequent peer joins and leaves. The simple protocol consists of only 5 messages: ping, pong, query, query response, and push on top of TCP/IP connections. Ping and pong are required to maintain the network structure, query and query response to locate content and announce matching items, and push is used for downloads from firewalled servents. Peers not behind a firewall wishing to download content using the standard HTTP protocol [HTT] can request to "push" a file from a firewalled peer to them by sending a push message to these peers. The firewalled peer in response opens a TCP/IP connection to the requesting peer which can now initiate the standard HTTP download protocol.

Queries are flooded by peers to all their neighbors in a certain radius defined by a Time-To-Live (TTL) of a query. The usual TTL is 7 meaning that a query is forwarded 7 times to all neighbors a peer has, i.e., generating multiple queries with the same TTL. This design is extremely resilient against peers leaving and joining at any time but can generate high network traffic reducing the overall performance of the system or even cause its breakdown. Each peer receiving a query evaluates its shared content against the query and returns all matching items to the peer it received the query from. Thus, a query reply traverses the same path back a query came from. Downloads are afterwards handled directly between two peers.

The network structure to locate content is maintained in a similar way as query resolution. Peers periodically send out so-called ping messages to all their neighbors which are then again flooded to all their neighbors, of course reducing the TTL by one. Peers receiving a ping message respond with a pong message containing addresses of overlay peers. In this way, peers get to know more and more peers in the network enabling them to open further connections if desired or repairing broken connections to other peers. The simplicity of this protocol makes Gnutella networks very stable against node churn, i.e., peers joining and leaving the network at any time, and they remain operational even if a large number of overlay peers become unavailable. New peers willing to join the network require only to know one peer of the network, usually a so-called bootstrap peer provided by the network administrator. A new peer simply sends a ping message to the bootstrap peer or any other peer in the network and it receives as response a list of participating overlay peers it can connect subsequently.

Due to the aforementioned scalability problems, the latest protocol [Gnub] includes support for a two-layered SuperPeer architecture. SuperPeers are called UltraPeers in the Gnutella network and improve the scalability of the network as messages are only broadcasted in the UltraPeer network and "normal" peers only connect to (one or more) UltraPeers to advertise their shared content and issue queries. UltraPeers perform query processing on

2.4. Structured Overlays

behalf of their leaf peers shielding them from most of the network traffic. As the bandwidth and processing requirements are higher for UltraPeers, only peers meeting certain requirements can become UltraPeers, e.g., fast peers with a good network connection remaining online for most of the time. The two-layered architecture therefore also increases the fault-tolerance against node failures and communication errors as only reliable peers can become SuperPeers to form a stable network backbone more dynamic nodes can connect to at will. Figure 2.2 shows a two-layered P2P infrastructure using SuperPeers.

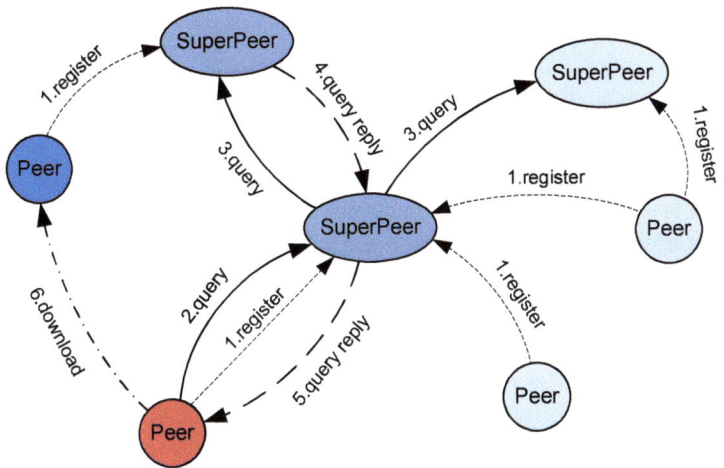

Figure 2.2: SuperPeer architecture

2.4 Structured Overlays

Structured overlays provide a distributed index structure across multiple physical devices for efficient location of resources, avoiding some of the scalability problems of unstructured overlay networks. The efficient resource location service enables applications to realize different application services on top such as data management (search, insert, update, etc.). Application specific identifiers are used on top of the physical networking layer for managing resources and addressing peers in the overlay network. While applications could also use physical identifiers of peers directly, e.g., the IP address, application specific identifiers enable semantic routing and generic services for network maintenance, authentication, trust, etc., which would be difficult to integrate into and support at the networking layer. Additionally, the independence of application specific identifiers of peers from their physical identifier (IP address) enables peers to change their physical address while remaining addressable and reachable in the overlay network.

In any structured overlay network, a set of peers provides access to a set of resources. Both, peers and resources, are mapped to an (application-specific) identifier space using a hash function, associating resources and peers with application specific identifiers, so-called keys. Resources are assigned to peers using a closeness metric on the identifier space, e.g., resources are assigned to the peer with the closest identifier to the resource identifier. To enable access from any peer to any resource a logical network is built, i.e., a graph is embedded into the identifier space. The structure of the graph depends on the type of overlay network and peer identifiers determine the position of peers within the structure, e.g., on a ring, in a tree, etc..

We classify in the following structured overlays by the hash function used to map peers and resources into an identifier space. Initially, structured overlays were designed for efficient single key lookups, i.e., retrieving resources based on their application specific identifier. Chord [SMK+01] uses uniform hashing to map peers and resources on a ring, i.e., the identifier space. The uniform hashing produces random keys on the identifier space for peers and resources, leading to a uniform distribution of resources on peers. Structured overlays using uniform hashing are also called Distributed Hash Tables (DHT) and we will present their most prominent representatives, Chord, Pastry [RD01] and Tapestry [ZHS+04]. We will finally present the initial design of CAN [RFH+01] originally using uniform hashing of which today variants exist using order-preserving hash functions.

Structured overlays with order-preserving hashing represent our second category. The difference to DHTs is that they preserve the semantic relations of resources in the identifier space, e.g., if a resource r_1 is "smaller than" resource r_2 in an ordered domain then the identifier of the resource $key(r_1)$ is also "smaller than" $key(r_2)$ in the identifier space. Preserving semantic relations of resources enables the implementation of efficient lookup services relying on these correlations, e.g., range queries exploiting the order relationship of resources. Examples of systems exploiting this feature are Mercury [BAS04] and SkipNet [HJS+03], which we will present in the following, and P-Grid [Abe01] which will be presented in more detail in Chapter 3.

2.4.1 Distributed Hash Tables

Distributed Hash Tables (DHT) are structured overlay networks using uniform hashing to map peers and resources uniformly and randomly on the identifier space. As a consequence, resource identifiers are uniformly assigned to peers. Peers are responsible for resource identifiers close to their own identifier in the identifier space. The uniform distribution of resource identifiers on peers leads theoretically to a uniform storage load for peers, i.e., all peers are responsible for approximately the same number of resource identifiers. Even in the case of a homogeneous system where all nodes have the same capacity, DHTs can exhibit a substantial load imbalance due to a natural variance of the randomized hash-

2.4. Structured Overlays

ing [SMK+01]. [GS05, BKadH05] have presented approaches to tackle this problem as load balancing is one of the main objectives of structured overlay networks and was the main incentive for early systems to apply uniform hashing. The disadvantage of uniform hash functions is that they do not preserve semantic relationships of resources, as illustrated by Figure 2.3. The data fragments $a - z$ are mapped to the key space $0 - 9$. The figure shows how the hash function approximately uniformly distributes data fragments on the key space while destroying the lexicographical order of the data fragments. In the end, all fragments are spread out on the key space and each peer $A - D$ holds approximately the same amount of data falling into the key range it is responsible for. In the following we will present several systems using such a uniform hash function in more details.

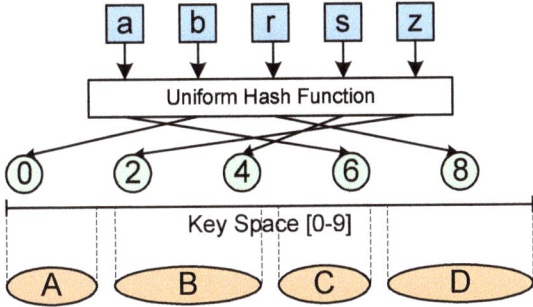

Figure 2.3: Uniform Hashing

Chord

Chord [SMK+01] is a ring-based DHT using consistent uniform hashing [KLL+97] to assign peers and resources an m-bit identifier, using SHA-1 as the base hash function. The peer identifier defines the peer's position on the ring and is obtained by hashing the peer's IP address. A resource identifier, also called key, is obtained by hashing a data value of the resource. The length of the identifier m must be large enough to make the probability of peers and resources hashing to the same identifier negligible. Identifiers are ordered on an identifier circle modulo 2^m. The key k of a resource is assigned to the first peer whose identifier is equal to or follows k in the identifier space. This peer is called the successor peer of key k, denoted by *successor(k)*. If identifiers are represented as a circle of numbers from 0 to $2^m - 1$, then *successor(k)* is the first peer clockwise from k. The identifier circle is called the Chord ring. To maintain consistent hashing mapping when a peer n joins the network, certain keys previously assigned to n's successor now need to be reassigned to n. When peer n leaves the Chord system, all of its assigned keys are reassigned to n's successor. Therefore, peers join and leave the system with $(log N)^2$ performance, where N

is the number of peers in the system. No other changes of key assignments to peers need to occur. In Figure 2.4 the Chord ring is depicted with $m = 6$. This particular ring has ten peers and stores five keys. The successor of the resource identifier 10 is peer 14, so key 10 will be located at peer 14. Similarly, if a peer were to join with identifier 26, it would store the key with identifier 24 from the peer 32. Each peer in the Chord ring needs to know how to contact its current successor peer on the identifier circle. Each peer n further maintains a routing table with up to m entries, called the finger table. The ith entry in the table at peer n contains the identity of the first peer s that succeeds n by at least 2^{i-1} on the identifier circle, i.e., $s = successor(n + 2^{i-1})$, where $1 \leq i \leq m$. Peer s is the ith finger of peer n ($n.finger[i]$). A finger table entry includes both the Chord identifier and the IP address (and port number) of the relevant peer. Figure 2.4 shows the finger table of peer 8. The first finger entry for this peer points to peer 14, as it is the first peer that succeeds $(8+1) \bmod 26 = 9$. Similarly, the last finger of peer 8 points to peer 42, i.e., the first peer that succeeds $(8+32) \bmod 64 = 40$. In this way, peers store information about only a small number of other peers, and know more about peers closely following it on the identifier circle than other peers. Such networks are also called Small-World networks [Kle99]. Also, a peer's finger table does not contain enough information to directly determine the successor of an arbitrary key k. For example, peer 8 cannot determine the successor of key 34 by itself, as successor of this key (peer 38) is not present in peer 8's finger table. Queries are therefore resolved in multiple hops using always the longest finger possible reaching a peer with a smaller or equal identifier. For example a query lookup at peer 8 for the identifier 34 would be forwarded first to peer 32 present in peer 8's routing table and closest to the destination. Peer 32 will then be able to forward the query to the responsible peer 38 holding key 34.

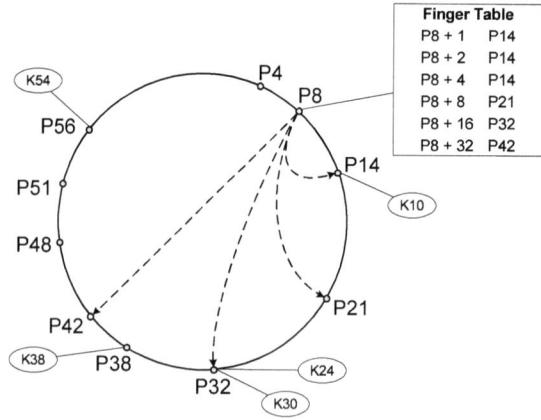

Figure 2.4: A Chord ring

As the fingers are only shortcuts to route messages in less hops to a destination, the

2.4. Structured Overlays

successor pointers are essential for the Chord network to remain operational. Therefore the Chord protocol periodically runs a stabilization protocol in the background to update these pointers. The frequency of these corrections depends on the frequency of peers joining and leaving the network, invalidating pointers in peers' routing tables. The correctness of the Chord protocol relies on the fact that each peer is aware of its successor, otherwise lookup operations cannot be guaranteed. When peers fail, it is possible that a peer does not know its new successor, and that it has no chance to learn about it. To avoid this situation, peers maintain a successor list of size r, which contains the peer's first r successors. When the successor peer does not respond, the peer simply contacts the next peer on its successor list. Assuming that peer failures occur with a probability p, the probability that every peer on the successor list will fail is p^r. Increasing r makes the system more robust. By tuning this parameter, any degree of robustness with good reliability and fault resiliency may be achieved though at the cost of maintaining more pointers in the routing table.

Pastry

Pastry [RD01] is a DHT similar to Chord. Although the functionality of Pastry is almost identical to other DHTs, what sets it apart is the proximity-based routing built into the DHT concept. This allows Pastry to realize the scalability and fault tolerance of other DHTs, while reducing the overall cost of routing a packet by choosing the "nearest" node from where the message originates, in terms of the proximity metric. The proximity metric is supplied by an external program based on the IP address of the target node and can be easily switched to shortest hop count, lowest latency, highest bandwidth, or even a general combination of metrics. This proximity-based routing has the advantage that messages are forwarded to close neighbors or well connected peers reducing routing latency. In other DHTs not considering this aspect, messages can travel around the globe several times before the destination peer is hit though it could be very close to the original sender. This is avoided in Pastry.

As mentioned already before, Pastry is very similar to Chord using uniform hashing to distribute peers and resources uniformly on a circular index space. It therefore shares the same properties as discussed earlier for Chord. Additionally to the ring structure known from Chord, Pastry nodes further maintain a routing table forming a tree. The binary tree structure is probably the first routing geometry that had been proposed for DHTs [PRR97]. In the tree approach, the leaf nodes of the tree correspond to the node identifiers that store the keys to be searched. The height of the tree is $log(n)$, where n is the number of nodes in the tree. The search proceeds down the tree by doing a longest prefix match at each of the intermediate nodes until the target node is found. Therefore, in this case, matching can be thought of as correcting bit values from left-to-right at each successive hop on the tree.

Tapestry

Tapestry [ZHS+04] resembles Pastry by its hybrid ring and tree structure and proximity-aware routing using the same uniform hash function SHA-1 mapping peers and resources uniformly on an identifier space. The difference between Pastry and Tapestry is the handling of network locality and data object replication. Tapestry's architecture uses a variant of the Plaxton [PRR97] distributed search technique, with additional mechanisms to provide availability, scalability, and adaptation in the presence of failures and attacks. Plaxton [PRR97] proposes a distributed data structure, known as the Plaxton mesh, optimized to support a network overlay for locating named data objects which are connected to one root peer. Tapestry uses multiple roots for each data object to avoid single points of failure. It uses local routing maps at each peer, to incrementally route overlay messages to the destination ID digit by digit, for instance, $***7 \Rightarrow **97 \Rightarrow *297 \Rightarrow 3297$, where '*' is the wildcard. The lookup and routing mechanisms of Tapestry are based on matching the suffix in peer identifiers as described above. Routing maps are organized into routing levels, where each level contains entries that point to a set of peers closest in distance that matches the suffix for that level. Also, each peer holds a list of pointers to peers referred to as neighbors. Tapestry stores the locations of all resource replicas to increase semantic flexibility and allowing the application level to choose from a set of resource replicas based on some selection criteria, such as date. Each shared resource may include an optional application-specific metric in addition to a distance metric; e.g. OceanStore [KBC+00] global storage architecture finds the closest cached document replica which satisfies the closest distance metric. These queries deviate from the simple "find first" semantics, and Tapestry will route the message to the closest k distinct resources.

CAN

The Content Addressable Network (CAN) [RFH+01] uses a hyper-dimensional Cartesian coordinate space on a multi-torus to organize peers and map resources onto peers and partitions. This d-dimensional coordinate space is dynamically partitioned among all peers in the system such that every peer possesses its individual, distinct zone within the overall space. A CAN peer maintains a routing table that holds the IP address and virtual coordinate zone of each of its neighbor coordinates. A peer routes a message towards its destination using a simple greedy forwarding to the neighbor peer that is closest to the destination coordinates. Figure 2.5 shows a 2-dimensional CAN network and illustrates the query routing among neighbors till the destination area respectively peer is reached. The query is initiated at peer X and peer X's coordinate neighbor set contains the peers A, B, C, D. CAN's greedy routing algorithm aims at selecting the neighbor closest to the destination coordinate of a query. Therefore peers compare the coordinates of their neighbors with the destination coordinate and select the peer which is closest to the destination. This is done till the query

2.4. Structured Overlays

hits the peer responsible for the destination coordinate. In our example, peer X first forwards its query to peer D which is the closest neighbor to peer E, the destination coordinate. CAN has a routing performance of $O(d \cdot N^{\frac{1}{d}})$, N being the number of peers, and its routing state is of $2 \cdot d$ bound.

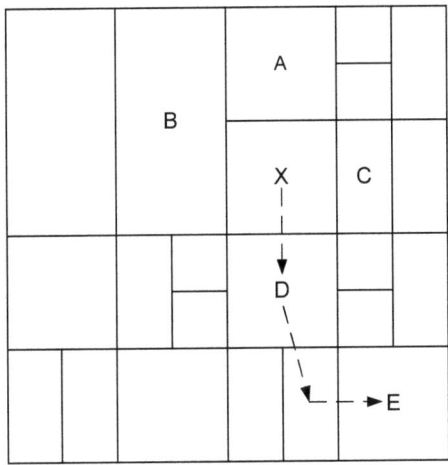

Figure 2.5: Query routing in CAN

The virtual coordinate space is used to store $\{key, value\}$ pairs by applying a uniform hash function to the content to obtain a key mapped deterministically onto a point P. The $\{key, value\}$ pair is then maintained by the peer responsible for point P. To retrieve a certain value, a peer applies the same hashing function to obtain the destination coordinates of the key. These coordinates are included into a query and routed along neighbors till the responsible peer is reached.

Peers partition the virtual space during the join process. A new peer first contacts one of the well-know bootstrap peers to obtain an IP address of a random peer of the CAN network. The new peer further choses a random point P in the CAN coordinate space and requests the route to this point from the random peer retrieved before. Using CAN's routing technique, the new peer will eventually get in contact with the peer responsible for the point P. The current peer in zone P will then split the zone in two equal halves and hand over one half to the new peer. In a 2-dimensional space, zones are first split along the X dimension, then the Y, and so on. The new peer takes over the neighbors from the previous peer of point P and both peers add each other to their neighbors. Further all $\{key, value\}$ pairs falling in the zone of the new peer are handed over by the previous peer. A takeover algorithm handles peers leaving the network and ensures that all areas of the coordinate space are covered by peers. If a peer leaves the network, its neighbor takes over its half and informs all neighbors about the change to update their neighboring sets.

CAN is able to route messages even if several peers are temporarily unavailable by picking the next closest peer in the neighbor set. To improve data availability, CAN can maintain multiple independent coordinate spaces with peers being assigned different zones in each space, so called *reality*. For a CAN with r realities, a single peer is assigned r coordinate zones, one on each reality available, and this peer holds r independent neighbor sets. The contents of the hash table are replicated on every reality, thus improving data availability. For further data availability improvement, CAN could use k different hash functions to map a given key onto k points in the coordinate space. This results in the replication of a single $\{key, value\}$ pair at k distinct peers in the system. A $\{key, value\}$ pair is then unavailable only when all the k replicas are simultaneously unavailable. Thus, queries for a particular hash table entry could be forwarded to all k peers in parallel thereby reducing the average query latency, and reliability and fault resiliency properties are enhanced [LCP+04].

Discussion

All structured overlay networks using uniform hashing resemble the hash table concept and are therefore so-called Distributed Hash Tables (DHTs). DHTs further resemble the hash index known from databases to efficiently lookup resources given their identifier. Independent of the used network topology, resources are hashed to random identifiers which are scattered uniformly around the network. Although this leads to good load balancing, i.e., all peers hold approximately the same number of resource identifiers, it does not preserve semantic relations. DHTs are therefore mainly suitable for exact-key lookup operations, retrieving resources based on their identifiers, as their counterparts in database systems.

Tapestry provides semantic flexibility to applications to select resource replicas based on application-specific metrics, e.g., the freshest copy. To support more complex lookup services, DHTs were adopted to meet according requirements. For example, [GAE03, SGAE04] use CAN with an order-preserving hash function to hash ranges of values and to support range queries in CAN. We will discuss this approach in more details in Chapter 4 and now present structured overlays based on order-preserving hashing.

2.4.2 Structured Overlays with Order-Preserving Hashing

Structured overlays with order-preserving hash functions preserve the order relationship of resources while mapping them onto the identifier space, i.e., the generated identifiers of neighboring resources in a set of ordered resources are also neighbors in the identifier space. The order relationship is the natural relationship to be preserved as one-dimensional key spaces are predominant in structured overlay networks. Peer identifiers have to be distributed according to the distribution of resource identifiers to meet the load balancing re-

2.4. Structured Overlays

quirement, i.e., that all peers are responsible for approximately the same number of resource identifiers. The partitioning of the identifier space depends on the distribution of resource identifiers respectively the distribution of resources.

Figure 2.6 shows how data fragments are mapped on a key space using order-preserving hashing. The hash keys of lexicographically ordered data fragments are in the same order as the original data fragments. This leads to the same distribution in the key space as in the data domain possibly leading to a load-imbalance among peers responsible for partitions. The advantage is that similar content is now stored at the same peer, or at least in the proximity, e.g., data fragments a and b are mapped to key 0 respectively 1 and therefore maintained by the same peer A. The remainder of this chapter will present two structured overlays based on order-preserving hashing. Chapter 3 will present P-Grid, also using an order-preserving hash-function, in more details.

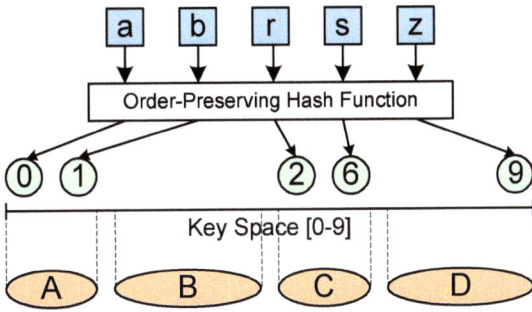

Figure 2.6: Order-Preserving Hashing

Mercury

The design focus of Mercury [BAS04] was to support multiple-attribute range queries. Peers are organized in multiple routing hubs, one for each indexed attribute. A routing hub is a circular overlay of peers and places data contiguously on this ring, i.e, each node is responsible for a range of values of a particular attribute. In contrast to DHTs distributing data randomly and uniformly on the ring, Mercury's order-preservation causes the data being populated contiguously on the ring. A range query can therefore simply be answered by finding the lower or upper bound and traversing all peers along the ring until the other bound is reached. Exact lookup operations for a single key are of course further supported with logarithmic effort as know from other DHTs.

Figure 2.7 illustrates an example Mercury network consisting of two routing hubs H_x and H_y (also called attribute hubs) indexing values of x and y coordinates of objects. The minimum and maximum values for the x and y attributes are 0 and 320 respectively. Accordingly, the ranges are distributed to various nodes. The data-item with x-coordinate 100 and y-coordinate 200 is sent to both H_x and H_y, where it is stored at nodes b and e, respectively, as node b is responsible for all x-coordinates between 80 and 160. A query as shown in Figure 2.7 is first routed to the more selective routing hub, in this example hub H_x, and then forwarded along neighbors till the queried range is covered. As this can lead to high query latencies, long-distance links, so-called fingers in Chord, are used to provide a more efficient routing mechanism.

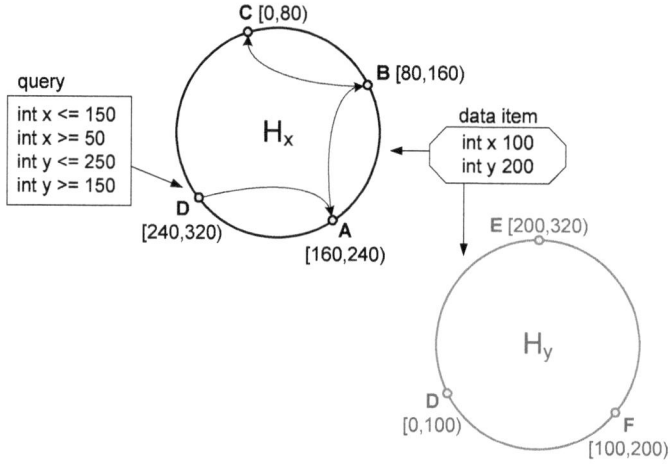

Figure 2.7: A Mercury network

Since there are likely to be particular ranges of an attribute that are more popular for queries and data-records, nodes responsible for these ranges will be unfairly overloaded with both routing and computation tasks. Mercury performs explicit load balancing by moving around nodes and changing their responsibilities according to the loads. This enables the combination of good load-balancing with support for range predicates. However, one important side effect is that the distribution of range sizes is no longer guaranteed to be uniform. Peers in popular areas are responsible for smaller ranges than peers in less popular areas. Range queries with equal range size will therefore involve more peers in popular areas than in less popular areas, leading to higher lookup costs/delays in the first case as more peers are involved. Load balancing is performed by a join-leave protocol populating overloaded areas of a routing hub and requesting peers in lightly loaded areas to leave the network and re-join it. Over time these leaves and re-joins cause a shift in the peer distribution. The load distribution is sampled periodically by peers and represented by approximate histograms.

SkipNet

SkipNet [HJS+03] is a scalable overlay network that supports traditional overlay functionality as well as *content locality* and *path locality* based on Skip Lists [Pug90]. Content locality refers to the ability to either explicitly place data on specific overlay nodes or distribute it across nodes within a given organization. Path locality refers to the ability to guarantee that message traffic between two overlay nodes within the same organization is routed within that organization only. Content and path locality provide a number of advantages for data retrieval, including improved availability, performance, manageability, and security. For example, nodes can store important data within their organization (content locality) and nodes will be able to reach their data through the overlay even if the organization becomes disconnected from the rest of the Internet (path locality). Storing data near the clients that use it also yields to performance benefits.

SkipNet supports efficient message routing between overlay nodes, content placement, path locality, and constrained load balancing. It does so by employing two separate, but related address spaces: a string name ID space as well as a numeric ID space. Node names and content identifier strings are mapped directly into the name ID space, while hashes of the node names and content identifiers are mapped into the numeric ID space. A single set of routing pointers on each overlay node enables efficient routing in either address space and a combination of routing in both address spaces provides the ability to do constrained load balancing.

Figure 2.8 shows the routing infrastructure for a 8 node system labeled A, D, M, O, T, V, X, and Z. The nodes are organized in a ring structure ordered by their name, their name ID. All nodes are connected by the *root ring* formed by each node's pointers at level 0. The pointers at level 1 point to nodes that are 2 nodes away and hence the overlay nodes are implicitly divided into two disjoint rings. Similarly, pointers at level 2 form four disjoint rings of nodes, and so forth. Note that rings at level $h+1$ are obtained by splitting a ring at level h into two disjoint sets, each ring containing every second member of the level h ring.

Each node can randomly choose a ring membership encoded as unique binary number, the node's numeric ID. As illustrated in Figure 2.8, the first h bits of the number determine ring membership at level h. For example, node X's numeric ID is 011 and its membership at level 2 is determined by taking the first 2 bits of 011, which designate Ring 01. As described in [SMK+01], there are advantages to using a collision-resistant hash (such as SHA-1) of the node's DNS name as the numeric ID. The SkipNet design does not require the use of hashing to generate nodes' numeric IDs; they only require to be random and unique. Because the numeric IDs of nodes are unique they can be thought of as a second address space that is maintained by the same SkipNet data structure. Whereas SkipNet's string address space is populated by node name IDs that are not uniformly distributed throughout the space, SkipNet's numeric address space is populated by node numeric IDs that are

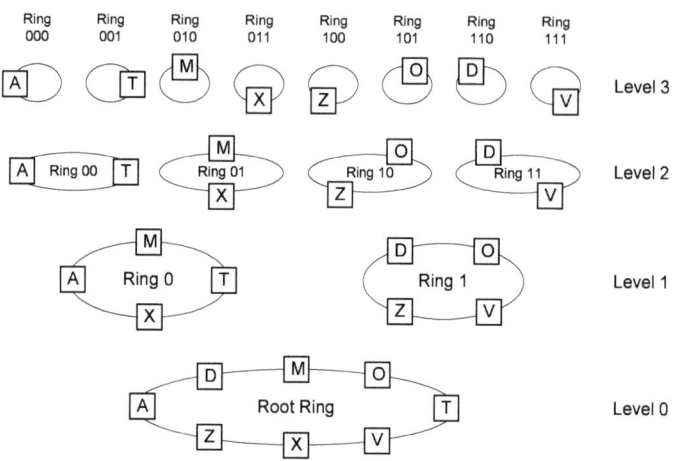

Figure 2.8: The SkipNet network structure

uniformly distributed. The uniform distribution of numeric IDs in the numeric space is what ensures that the routing table construction yields routing table entries that skip over the appropriate number of nodes.

SkipNet supports Constrained Load Balancing (CLB). To implement CLB, a data object's name is divided into two parts: a part that specifies the set of nodes over which load balancing should be performed (the CLB domain) and a part that is used as input to the hash function (the CLB suffix). In SkipNet the special character '!' is used as a delimiter between the two parts of the name. For example, suppose the document using the name *msn.com/DataCenter!TopStories.html* is stored. The CLB domain indicates that load balancing should occur over all nodes whose names begin with the prefix *msn.com/DataCenter*. The CLB suffix, *TopStories.html*, is used as input to the hash function, and this determines the specific node within *msn.com/DataCenter* on which the document will be placed. Storing a document with CLB results in the document being placed on precisely one node within the CLB domain (although it would be possible to store replicas on other nodes). If numerous other documents were also stored in the *msn.com/DataCenter* CLB domain, then the documents would be uniformly distributed across all nodes in that domain. To search for a data object that has been stored using CLB, we first search for any node within the CLB domain using search by name ID. To find the specific node within the domain that stores the data object, we perform a search by numeric ID within the CLB domain for the hash of the CLB suffix.

Discussion

The aim of structured overlay networks with a order-preserving hash functions is to retain the order relationship among resources. These systems resemble, independent of their network structure, the idea of B-trees used in databases to support efficient range scans on the index. Range queries are therefore only supported by structured overlays with order-preserving hashing. DHTs, such as Chord, using uniform hashing were extended with, for example, a Prefix Hash Tree (PHT) [RRHS04] to support similar functionality. This system implements multiple indexes optimized for different lookup operations as also used in centralized databases.

The real advantage of traditionally using a hash index/table in main memory is the constant time of lookup, insert, and delete operations. But to facilitate this, a hash table sacrifices the order-relationship of the keys. However, over a network, where only parts of the hash table are stored at each location, these operations need multiple overlay hops anyway. For most conventional DHTs the number of hops is logarithmic in the network size. Thus the main advantage of constant time access no longer exists in DHTs. This makes overlay networks with order-preserving hashing a natural choice since they provide normal key search for the same order of message complexity as a DHT and efficiently support range queries.

2.5 PlanetLab

PlanetLab is a global platform for deploying and evaluating Internet-scale network services such as overlay networks. It was launched in 2002 with 100 machines distributed to 40 sites. Currently, about 800 nodes spread over around 400 sites form an Internet-scale testbed used by researchers all over the world to evaluate their developments. Further, a longer-term goal of PlanetLab is to support continuously running services that potentially serve a client community. In other words, PlanetLab is not only designed as testbed but also to support the seamless migration of an application from early prototype, through multiple prototype design iterations, to a popular service that continues to evolve. In the long term, PlanetLab could serve as a microcosm for the next generation Internet [PACR02]. We use PlanetLab as testbed for evaluating most of our algorithms we will present in the remaining of this thesis. This section therefore briefly describes the architecture and use of PlanetLab.

The centerpiece of the PlanetLab architecture is a *slice* (a horizontal cut of global PlanetLab resources). Each *service* (a set of distributed and cooperating programs delivering some higher-level functionality) runs in a slice of PlanetLab. A slice encompasses some amount of processing, memory, storage, and network resources across a set of individual PlanetLab nodes distributed over the network. A slice is therefore more than just the sum of the distributed resources, it is more a network of *virtual machines* with a set of local resources bound to each virtual machine.

A virtual machine is the environment where the program that implements some aspects of a service runs. Each virtual machine runs on a single node and is allowed to consume some fraction of that node's resources. In addition to being bound to a set of resources, a virtual machine also defines the execution environment for which programs are written. Multiple virtual machines run on each PlanetLab node, where a virtual machine monitor arbitrates the node's resources among them [CCR+03].

From a users point of view, PlanetLab provides a large set of servers distributed all over the world available any time for testing developments. All nodes can be accessed by SSH connections using a private/public key pair created during user registration. This allows users to use scripts accessing hosts to deploy and start their prototypes as well as monitoring application status or retrieving log files for later local analysis.

The popularity of PlanetLab in the last years had led to several problems making evaluations on it sometimes difficult and not reproducible. As resources are shared among all slices at a node and users cannot reserve resources nor time slots for their experiments, the behavior of PlanetLab can be unpredictable sometimes, especially at high seasons of conference deadlines. As a consequence less resources are available for each user and node and network failures are more likely. The high load at some nodes further leads to higher response times as somebody would expect from "normal" computers as multiple processes share one or two CPUs at the same time.

Nevertheless, PlanetLab is the state-of-the-art evaluation platform for real Internet-scale developments all implemented system have to be tested on. Even though its performance may be unpredictable it just reflects the real-world distributed systems have to be able to deal with anyway. We therefore evaluated most of our algorithms on PlanetLab using a Java implementation of P-Grid we will present in more details in Chapter 7 and Chapter 8.

2.6 Conclusions

This chapter introduced various types of P2P systems with a focus on structured overlay networks. Structured overlay networks provide access to shared resources through a distributed index structure. Peers storing a fraction of the distributed index maintain routing information to other peers to enable efficient lookups for any resource identifier. We categorized structured overlay networks by their hashing function. DHTs use uniform hashing to achieve load balancing and are mainly suitable for exact key lookups, i.e., retrieval of resources by their identifier only. Structured overlay networks with order-preserving hashing retain the order relationship among resources to additionally support efficient range queries.

Chapter 3

The P-Grid Overlay

The overview of P2P systems presented in the previous chapter has shown that structured overlay networks using order-preserving hashing are the natural choice if both, single key lookups and range queries, should be supported efficiently. This chapter will present P-Grid, a trie-based structured overlay using order-preserving hashing, in more details. As the advantage of constant time for lookup, insert and delete operations in a classical hash index does no longer exist in DHTs, a distributed trie structure can provide the same logarithmic access guarantees as DHTs while retaining the order relationship of data.

We will present P-Grid's distributed virtual binary trie to partition peers and to assign them a small portion of the distributed index. The lookup operation based on greedy prefix-routing implements single key lookups on top of this access structure. Its construction and required load balancing is further briefly described although not the focus of this chapter. These functionalities are the base for the remainder of this thesis. An evaluation of P-Grid's construction and single-key lookup mechanism will be presented in Chapter 8. At the end of this chapter, we discuss P-Grid's extensions for sharing correlated data.

3.1 Distributed Search Structure

P-Grid's virtual binary trie is used to partition peers and to assign them a small portion of the distributed index. The index is mapped onto a key space represented by binary strings. Without constraining general applicability P-Grid uses binary keys. This is not a fundamental limitation as a generalization of the P-Grid system to k-ary structures is natural, and exists [AP03]. Each peer is associated with a leaf of the tree and a so-called *path*. Each leaf corresponds to a binary string, the so-called *key-space partition*.

Each peer $p \in P$ is associated with a leaf of the binary trie, i.e., a key space partition, which corresponds to a binary string $\pi(p) \in \Pi$ called the peer's *path*. For search, the peer stores for each prefix $\pi(p,l)$ of $\pi(p)$ of length l a set of references $\rho(p,l)$ to peers q with property $\overline{\pi(p,l)} = \pi(q,l)$, where $\overline{\pi}$ is the binary string π with the last bit inverted. This means that at each level of the trie the peer has references to some other peers that do not pertain to the peer's sub-trie at that level which enables the implementation of prefix routing. The cost for storing the references and the associated maintenance cost scale as they are bounded by the depth of the underlying binary tree. More details and an example of the search algorithm are presented in Section 3.2.

Each peer stores a set of data keys $\delta(p)$. Binary keys are calculated using an order-preserving hash function presented in Section 3.3. For $d \in \delta(p)$ $key(d)$ has $\pi(p)$ as prefix but it is not excluded that temporarily also other data keys are stored at a peer, that is, the set $\delta(p, \pi(p))$ of data keys whose key matches $\pi(p)$ can be a proper subset of $\delta(p)$. Moreover, for fault-tolerance, query load-balancing, and hot-spot handling, multiple peers are associated with the same key-space partition (structural replication), and peers additionally also maintain multiple references $\sigma(p)$ to peers with the same path (data replication), i.e., their replicas, and use epidemic algorithms to maintain replica consistency [DHA03].

Figure 3.1 shows a simple example of a P-Grid tree consisting of 6 peers (peer A - F) responsible for 4 partitions (00, 01, 10, 11), e.g., peer F is responsible for the partition 00 and therefore peer F's path is 00. As mentioned before, peers have to maintain references at multiple levels to other parts of the tree. The number of references is equal to the length of a peer's path. As the path of peer F is 00, its routing table consists of two levels. Level 0 holds references to peers of the right side of the tree with no common path prefix, e.g., peer E with path 11. Level 1 holds references to peers of the neighboring sub-tree 1∗ with peers having the first bit in common, e.g., peer B with path 01. The example shows that peers have to maintain at least one reference per level to be able to route to all parts of the tree, i.e., to all sub-trees seen by a peer, but it is not necessary to maintain references to all partitions of the key space. Further, as multiple peers are assigned to partitions they also maintain multiple references per level for the same reasons, i.e., fault-tolerance, query load-balancing and hot-spot handling. Finally, each peer stores keys having a prefix with a peer's path, e.g., peer B maintains all data keys with prefix 01.

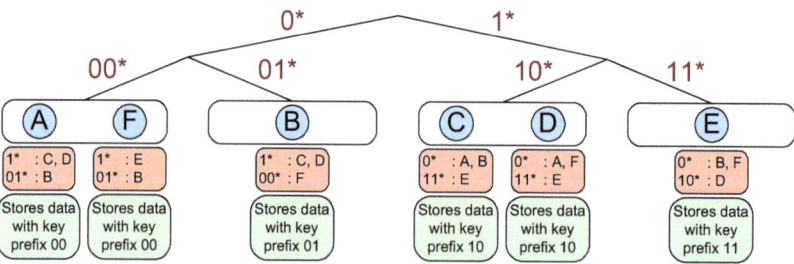

Figure. 1: An examplary P-Grid overlay network

There are several other structured overlays which topologically resemble P-Grid and use prefix-based routing variants, for example, Pastry [RD01] and particularly Kademlia [MM02] whose XOR distance metric results in the same tree abstraction and choice of routes from all peers in complementary sub-trees as in P-Grid. Important distinguishing features of P-Grid include the bootstrapping algorithms for the P-Grid network based on randomized algorithms, support for substring queries, and the adaptive, structural replication (multi-faceted load-balancing of storage and query load) [ADHS05].

There is another motivation for having a trie-structured overlay network instead of a standard distributed hash table: The real advantage of traditionally using a hash table in main memory is the constant time of lookup, insert, and delete operations. But to facilitate this, a hash table sacrifices the order-relationship of the keys. However, over a network, where only parts of the hash table are stored at each location, we need multiple overlay hops anyway. For most conventional DHTs the number of hops is logarithmic in the network size. Thus the main advantage of constant-time access no longer exists in DHTs. P-Grid provides normal key search for same order of message complexity as a DHT, but in addition can be naturally extended to support more complex queries such as range queries.

3.2 Basic Search Operation

The virtual binary trie of P-Grid now allows us to route queries to responsible peers to resolve user queries. This is achieved by an eager prefix-routing algorithm presented in Algorithm 3.1. The algorithm recursively resolves the query for the given key k whereas p denotes the peer that currently processes the request. The key is a binary string created by hashing the keyword s with the same hash function used to index data at insertion. The key is only used to identify the peer responsible for the query, i.e., the peer whose path is a prefix of the query key. Once the responsible peer is reached, the keyword is used to find and return all matching index items. If the current peer is not responsible for the query, i.e., its path is not a prefix of the query key, it forwards the query to one peer of its routing table for further processing. The query is therefore forwarded to a peer with the longest prefix match. For example, if the current peer has two bits in common with the query key, it will select randomly a peer of the routing table level two. Any peer at this level has to have at least three bits in common with the query key. Therefore a query is resolved bit-wise till the responsible peer is reached. Since P-Grid uses a binary tree, its basic search operation is of complexity $O(\log |\Pi|)$, measured in messages required to resolve search requests, in a balanced tree, i.e., all paths associated with peers are of equal length. Skewed data distributions may imbalance the tree, so that it may seem that search cost may become non-logarithmic in the number of messages. However, in [Abe02b, Abe02a] it is shown that due to the randomized choice of routing references from the complimentary sub-tree, the expected search cost remains logarithmic ($0.5 \log n$), independently of how the P-Grid is structured. The intuition why this works is that in search operations keys are not resolved bit-wise but in larger blocks thus the search costs remain logarithmic in terms of messages. This is important as P-Grid uses order-preserving hashing to compute keys which may lead to non-uniform key distributions.

Algorithm 3.1 Basic search in P-Grid: Retrieve(p, k, s)

1: **if** $\pi(p) \subseteq k$ **then**
2:    return$(d \in \delta(p) \mid key(d) = k, \ w \subseteq d)$;
3: **else**
4:    determine l such that $\pi(k,l) = \overline{\pi(p,l)}$;
5:    r = randomly selected element from $\rho(p,l)$;
6:    Retrieve(r, k, s);
7: **end if**

The algorithm always terminates successfully, if the P-Grid is complete (ensured by the construction algorithm) and at least one peer in each partition is reachable (ensured through redundant routing table entries and replication). Due to the definition of the routing table and the search algorithm it will always find the location of a peer at which the search can continue (use of completeness). With each invocation of $Retrieve(p,k,s)$ the length of the common prefix of a peer's path and the query key increases at least by one and therefore the algorithm always terminates. Note that, while the network has a tree/trie abstraction, the system is hierarchy-less, and all peers reside at the leaf nodes.

The search algorithm presented in Algorithm 3.1 resolves queries by first determining the peer responsible for the query and then matching all index items against a given keyword. The query key is generated by the same hash function used to index data. Therefore a query will locate the same peer for a given key that has been located while storing the key. Substring search can be supported by simply indexing not only the full string but also the substrings and by adding them to the index. P-Grid is therefore able to support any sort of substring search depending on the granularity of indexing, which can be chosen by the application/user using P-Grid.

3.3 Order-Preserving Hash Function

P-Grid's hash function maps application data to binary strings. In the reference implementation we assume application data to be strings for simplicity, but in fact any data type can be used. The hash function is order-preserving, i.e., it satisfies the following property for two input strings s_1 and s_2:

$$s_1 \subseteq s_2 \Rightarrow key(s_1) \subseteq key(s_2)$$

where $\subseteq$ means *is-prefix-of*. To enable this mapping, a balanced trie is constructed from a sample string database consisting of unique, lexicographically sorted strings of equal length (sample string databases can be provided by the user for different applications). Providing an application-specific sample database enables applications to perform an implicit load balancing, independent of P-Grid's load balancing mechanism, as application-specific knowledge about expected data distribution is used to achieve a preferably uniform key distribution. The database is recursively bisected into equally-sized partitions until each partition is smaller than a threshold. The keys P-Grid uses are then calculated by using the application data to "navigate" character-wise through this trie and appending '0' to the generated key for each "left-turn" or '1' otherwise. Algorithm 3.2 illustrates the hashing of a string representing application data. The function requires the trie root as initial input to recursively build the binary hash string.

Algorithm 3.2 Hashing in P-Grid: Hash(trie_node, data_string, key)
1: **if** $trie\_node$ == null **or** $data\_string$ is prefix or equal to $trie\_node$ **then**
2:     return key;
3: **else**
4:     **if** $data\_string$ is lexicographically smaller than $trie\_node$ **then**
5:         return Hash($trie\_node$.left, $data\_string$, key + '0');
6:     **else**
7:         return Hash($trie\_node$.right, $data\_string$, key + '1');
8:     **end if**
9: **end if**

3.4 Overlay Construction

So far we were assuming a constructed binary trie to route queries to responsible peers partitioned according to the load present in the system. The construction of an Internet-scale overlay network requires an algorithm to partition the key space by local interactions between autonomous peers. In principle a construction of an overlay network can also be achieved by the standard maintenance model of sequential node joins and leaves. However, this approach encounters two serious problems:

- The peer community will have to decide on a serialization of the process, e.g., electing a peer to initiate the network. Thus in principle the peer community has to solve the leader election problem, which might turn out to be impossible to solve for very large peer populations without making strong assumptions on coordination or limiting peer autonomy.

- Since the process is performed essentially in a serialized manner it incurs a substantial latency. In particular it does not take any advantage of potential parallelization, which would be a natural approach.

The need for an efficient and fast bootstrapping algorithm for structured overlay networks emerged with their increasing adoption for data-oriented applications. Resources in such networks are identified by dynamically changing predicates. Many different overlay networks can be used simultaneously, each of them indexing a specific attribute value of shared resources. Creating a distributed index for an attribute value requires to build a new structured overlay network from scratch. The insertion of large document sets can further lead to a reconstruction of an overlay network, considering the new distribution of resources leading to better load balancing in the system. Due to catastrophic network failures the standard maintenance mechanisms no longer can reconstruct a consistent overlay network. Thus the overlay networks needs to be constructed from scratch. This scenario applies of course generally in any application, but becomes more probable when multiple overlay networks are deployed in parallel.

P-Grid uses a fully parallel approach involving all peers simultaneously. In data-oriented applications there exists an additional factor that adds to the difficulty of finding a solution to the construction problem: load balancing. When using overlay networks for semantic processing of keys (range queries being a popular example) the canonical method of uniform hashing of keys to remove skew in the key distribution is no more applicable. This has led to substantial research on including load balancing features into overlay networks [ADH05, GBGM04, Man04]. During construction this has to be taken into account, thus the construction approach has also to solve load balancing problems. In fact, P-Grid addresses two types of load balancing problems simultaneously, the balancing of storage load among peers under skewed key distributions and the balancing of the number of replica peers across key space partitions. The first is important in order to balance workload among peers and is solved by adapting the overlay network structure to the key distribution. The second is important to guarantee comparable availability of keys in unreliable networks where peers have potentially low availability. This is a classical Şballs into binsŤ load balancing problem. P-Grid's approach is based on a key-space bisection process which is a completely decentralized, parallel and randomized algorithm for assigning peers to key space partitions in proportion to the key distributions of the partitions. By recursively applying key-space bisection, peers can incrementally construct the overlay network while maintaining load balance. More details about load-balancing aspects in the process of the overlay construction can be found in [ADHS05].

3.4. Overlay Construction

3.4.1 Divide and Conquer

The process of constructing an overlay network from scratch should require low latency, i.e., be highly parallel and require minimal bandwidth consumption. At the same time the following load balancing criteria should be achieved:

1. The partitioning of the key space should be such that each partition holds a constant number of data keys, i.e., the load of peers is approximately the same.

2. Each resulting partition should be associated with a constant number of peers such that the availability of the different data keys is approximately the same.

In a decentralized process peers do not have precise information on the number of peers and keys present in a partition and cannot know which decision the other peers in a partition take with respect to associating themselves with a partition. The only available information is on the set of locally stored data keys and information gathered from local interactions with other peers. The decentralized process of P-Grid is based on random peer encounters and a set of basic local interactions. The random encounters can be initiated by performing random walks on a pre-existing unstructured overlay network. The interactions peers can perform in their encounters can be classified in three categories, as shown in Figure 3.2.

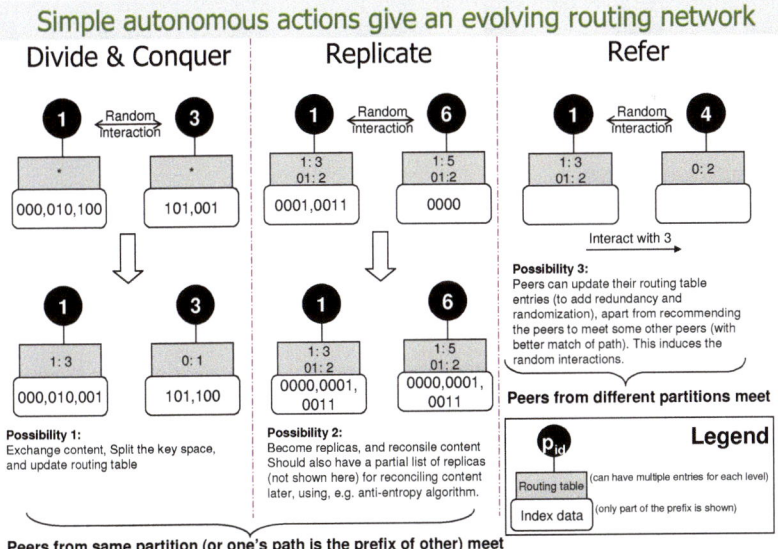

Figure 3.2: Network evolution

If peers belong to the same partition they can either *repartition* the present partition (a divide-and-conquer strategy) or *replicate* the data keys they currently hold. If they do not belong to the same partition, they can *refer* each other to other peers using their routing table entries and thus route to a peer that belongs to the same partition. If peers from the same partition meet, they may decide to *repartition* in case the current partition contains a sufficient number of data keys to justify a further split, i.e., the partition is overloaded. They can coordinate locally their decision. In addition, peers keep a reference to the peer encountered after a split, and thus incrementally construct their routing tables.

We will present an evaluation of P-Grid's bootstrapping algorithm in Section 8.6, showing the required bandwidth consumption to build a P-Grid network from scratch for about 300 PlanetLab nodes.

3.4.2 Unstructured Backbone

P-Grid is known as structured overlay network based on a binary trie to route messages with logarithmic effort to responsible peers. But P-Grid also maintains an unstructured network for maintenance and fault-tolerance reasons. The two networks thereby do not co-exist next to each other with individual maintenance strategies but both are tightly coupled and maintained at the same time. P-Grid's construction and maintenance algorithm of divide and conquer requires a random subset of peers to meet randomly and on a periodic basis. This subset is called *fidget list* in P-Grid and basically resembles the host cache in Gnutella keeping recently met or received hosts in cache. Fidget lists are exchanged frequently between P-Grid peers and peers select a random subset to keep in cache locally. The frequent exchange guarantees that these lists are fresh and mainly contain online peers.

The unstructured network is not only used for fault-tolerance reasons but is also used to resolve queries at the beginning of P-Grid's lifetime or if P-Grid is restructured and its trie is temporarily not usable for lookups. This allows P-Grid to be operational and resolve queries from the beginning on, even if no structured overlay has been formed yet. Since this as a short period at the beginning of the overall lifetime of a P-Grid network, broadcasting as presented for Gnutella is a tolerable approach for searching. The same holds for situations where the P-Grid structure might collapse if a large population of peers leaves at the same moment and a complete restructuring is necessary.

Apart from these scenarios, P-Grid's unstructured backbone offers support for more ad-hoc networks which are formed for a shorter time and probably do not require a structured overlay as they likely be of smaller nature. Again, their short lifetime and limited number of nodes makes a flooding based lookup approach tolerable as building a structured overlay for such a short period might exceed overall search efforts.

3.5 Data Correlations in P-Grid

So far we have introduced the basic concepts of P-Grid and its support for simple key lookups as also provided by other structured overlay networks. Further, P-Grid uses a order-preserving hash function to map data keys to binary index keys distributed among participating peers to retain the order relationship among hashed keys. Figure 3.3 illustrates how such one-dimensional correlations can be mapped onto a P-Grid network of peers by P-Grid's order-preserving hash function. The network layer at the bottom reflects the P-Grid structure seen from a networking side, i.e., how peers are connected physically. Each peer requires at least three connections for the given P-Grid example to resolve queries. The data layer shows data fragments indexed in P-Grid and their static order correlations, i.e., lexicographical correlations. Their order retains while assigned to peers in the P-Grid network. Therefore P-Grid naturally supports range queries on the same distributed index already used for single key lookups. Even though P-Grid naturally supports range queries by its hash function, the algorithmic realization of query resolution is still non-trivial and several solutions are feasible. We present two approaches and their comparison in Chapter 4. We further provide an approach for completeness estimation during range query processing. Range queries exploit the order relationship of shared data and their induced data correlations. These data correlations can be seen as one-dimensional as they can be represented by an ordered list.

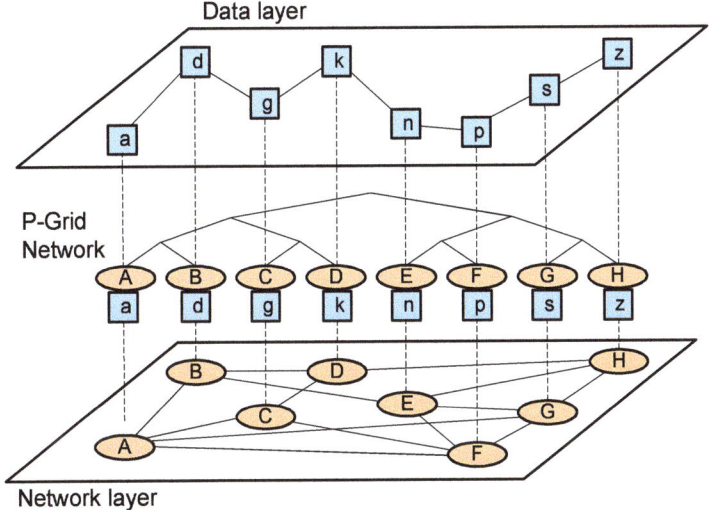

Figure 3.3: One-dimensional correlations in P-Grid

3.5.1 Multi-Dimensional Correlations

More complex data correlations can be modeled with probabilistic networks forming random graphs in multiple dimensions. Such multi-dimensional correlation graphs can usually not simply be mapped by a hash function to a one dimensional key space. Further, such data correlations can change over time and require an adaption of the data mapping. Order relationships and their mapping are static and cannot change over time. Therefore, structured overlays using order-preserving hashing require explicit load-balancing mechanism to compensate possible imbalances.

This thesis shows how data with multi-dimensional correlations can be mapped on structured overlays using a one-dimensional key space, such as P-Grid. The mapping should cluster correlated data on one peer, or if this is not possible, in the proximity to improve joint data access imposed by applications. Figure 3.4 illustrates the problem based on the example already used in Figure 3.3. Again, we have the organization of peers in the P-Grid structure and some data fragments on the data level. Unlike for one-dimensional correlations, these data fragments are now correlated in a multi-dimensional probabilistic network which can be defined by users or gathered by observations. A relation between two fragments indicates that these two fragments are likely to be accessed together, e.g., be returned by a query. It is therefore beneficial if strongly correlated fragments are maintained close to each other to reduce processing costs.

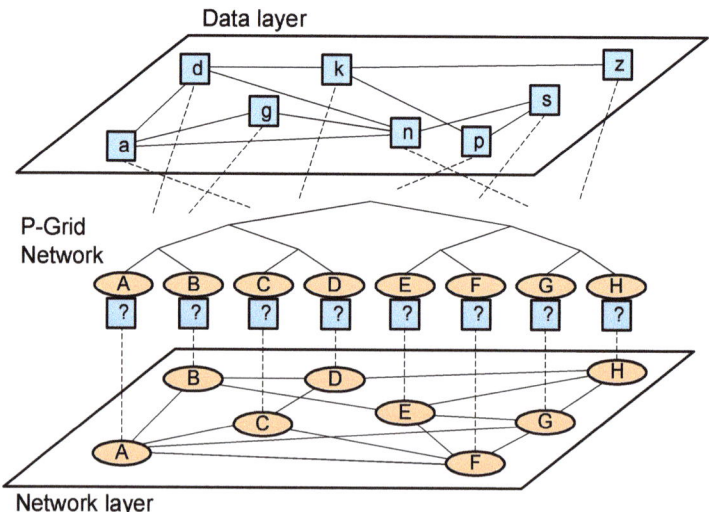

Figure 3.4: Probabilistic Correlations in P-Grid

We already introduced two examples of multi-dimensional data correlations and outlined their solution in Section 1.2. The concrete and detailed description for distributed inference is presented in Chapter 5 whereas an extension of P-Grid for multi-term queries can be found in Chapter 6.

3.6 Conclusions

P-Grid is a structured overlay network using an order-preserving hash function enabling efficient exact key lookups based on prefix-based greedy routing. P-Grid's overlay construction is based on pair-wise autonomous interactions between peers which can be performed in parallel leading to an efficient and fast construction algorithm. The algorithm has shown to achieve good load balancing even for skewed data distributions.

The design of P-Grid further allows efficient support for more complex lookup operations benefiting from data correlations in the shared data set. One-dimensional data correlations, e.g., derived from order relationships, are supported by design and only require an efficient algorithm to execute range queries on top of them.

Multi-dimensional data correlations are less straightforward to be supported by P-Grid. The problem of mapping them in a similar manner onto the one-dimensional key space of P-Grid, and other structured overlay networks, will be shown in the following chapters of this thesis. The aim is to use an additional overlay network on top of P-Grid which clusters these probabilistically correlated data on peers and in the proximity to increase processing efficiency.

Part II

Access of Correlated Data

Chapter 4

Range Queries

Range queries are a common lookup operation to retrieve all matching data in a given range and are supported by most (distributed) information systems. The processing of range queries causes a joint data access on data items in the range. To improve the performance of such lookups, systems exploit the order relationship among data entries and arrange them according to their lexicographical order. Range queries are therefore an example application for distributed systems to exploit data properties for correlated data access. We can estimate data correlations based on existing data relationships derived from data properties, such as the order relationship. Related data items, i.e., neighboring data items in lexicographical order, have a higher probability to be jointly accessed and therefore also a stronger data correlation. Preserving the lexicographical order of data entries in a structured overlay exploits these data correlation and enables efficient range query lookups in such systems.

P-Grid's data access structure, a virtual binary trie, and its order-preserving hash function fulfill this requirement and therefore naturally support the execution of range queries. A trie is a standard database structure to support range queries and was adapted by P-Grid for structured overlay networks to efficiently support exact lookups and range queries in the same overlay topology. This chapter shows how range queries can be efficiently executed on top of the P-Grid structure, respectively any other structured overlay resembling P-Grid. We present two approaches and compare their performance analytically, and additionally present their evaluation on PlanetLab. The first algorithm is the simple approach of traversing all neighbors along the queried range starting from the lower, respectively the upper, bound. This approach is easy to implement in most structured overlay networks but has several drawbacks such as high latency and poor fault-tolerance. The second approach, a shower algorithm, uses the tree structure of P-Grid to resolve a range query in parallel leading to low query latencies and higher fault-tolerance against lost messages for the cost of more messages sent.

As the shower algorithm is executed in parallel involving possibly multiple messages, a requesting peer will also receive multiple query replies containing partial result sets. Detecting the completeness of a query is therefore non-trivial as the number of messages to expect as result is not known a-priori to a query initiating peer. We present an approach at the end of this chapter to estimate the completeness of a range query executing the shower algorithm. We are able to recognize completeness when the last reply message was received. This information can be used to start post-processing of the final result set or to simply notify the user respectively an application.

4.1 Algorithms and Complexity Analysis

A range query retrieves all data items within a given range R defined by a lower and upper bound b_l and b_u. Assuming all data items are ordered according to the desired criteria, the simplest approach is to skip to the lower respectively upper bound of the range query and then proceed and return all data items till the upper respectively lower bound is reached. P-Grid's order-preserving hash function guarantees that all data items are ordered and distributed among neighboring peers, i.e., a correlated data item is either on the same peer or a neighboring peer. The sequential *min-max traversal* we will present and discuss next uses these properties whereas the following parallel *shower* algorithm makes additional use of P-Grid's trie structure which parallelizes the execution of range queries.

4.1.1 Min-Max Traversal Algorithm

Range queries can be processed sequentially by starting from a peer holding data items belonging to one bound of the range and forwarding the query to a peer responsible for the next partition of the key space, until a peer responsible for the other bound of the range is encountered. This strategy is called *min-max traversal*. The underlying data structure itself does not always have the information about peers belonging to the next neighboring key space partitions. However, such routes can be established either during the construction of the P-Grid overlay structure (algorithmically trivial), or at run-time using the existing routing information at the peers. Figure 4.1 shows the min-max traversal algorithm graphically.

First peer A initiates the range query by querying P-Grid for the lower bound of the range which is peer C in this example. Steps (1) and (2) denote standard P-Grid routing and in step (3) the result is returned to peer A, i.e., peer C. Then in step (4) peer A sends the range query request to peer C and peer C sends its data pertaining to the interval to peer A (in the implementation steps (3), (4), and (5) are actually done in one step). Concurrently the range query is forwarded to peer D using the "next" pointer. Peer D checks whether it is in the queried range, and if yes, peer D sends its data pertaining to the interval to peer A, and concurrently forwards the range query to peer E which repeats the same operations

4.1. Algorithms and Complexity Analysis

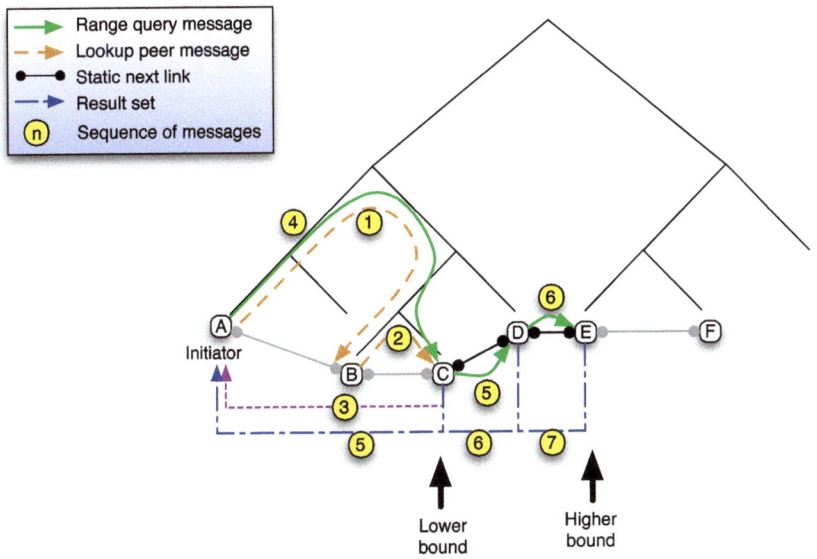

Figure 4.1: Min-max traversal range query strategy

as peer D except that it does not forward the query to another peer as it has checked that it is a peer responsible for the other bound of the queried range. Algorithm 4.3 shows this algorithm in pseudo code.

Algorithm 4.3 Sequential range queries: minmax(R, p)
1: **if** $\pi(p) \subseteq R$ **then**
2:     return($d \in \delta(p) \mid key(d) \in R$);
3:     determine a peer r responsible for the next key space partition;
4:     minmax(R, r);
5: **end if**

For simplifying the analysis we assume that the algorithm starts at the lower bound of the range R (the routing of the query to the lower bound is not shown here, but is algorithmically trivial in P-Grid). It is assumed that the neighbor links are cached at each peer during the construction of the trie (this is also algorithmically trivial). In the complexity analysis of this algorithm we can assume storage load-balancing (which is achieved stochastically by the P-Grid base system) and that on average there exist M data items per key space partition. Then, if there is a range query for the range R, such that there are D data items in the given range, search cost and latency using min-max traversal (assuming "next" links have been established during construction) is $O(\log_2 |\Pi|) + |\Pi_R| - 1$, where $|\Pi_R|$ is the number of partitions over which the whole range is stored in P-Grid and $|\Pi|$ is the total number of leaf-nodes in the complete P-Grid tree (total number of key space partitions). The search cost and latency using min-max traversal is dependent on the size of the answer set D for the range query, but independent of the size of the range R of the query. This is because $|\Pi_R|$ has an expected value of D/M, and in particular, using Markov's inequality, $Pr[|\Pi_R| \geq cD/M] \leq \frac{1}{c}$ for any positive c thus giving a weak bound on the deviation. We do not consider the trivial case $D \leq M$ as this would only affect 1 or 2 peers and concentrate on the more general case of $D > M$.

As already mentioned, establishing and maintaining "next" pointers in P-Grid is algorithmically trivial and most other DHTs pro-actively maintain it as well. Without them, an additional small overhead of $|\Pi_R|O(\log_2 |\Pi|)$ would have to be included. Note that this is an upper bound, as part of the routing does not have to be repeated for the peers in the interval.

4.1.2 Shower Algorithm

The other variant for processing range queries is to do them concurrently. Here, the range query is first forwarded to an arbitrary peer responsible for any of the key space partitions within the range, and then the query is forwarded to the other partitions in the interval using this peer's routing table. The process is recursive, and since the query is split in multiple

4.1. Algorithms and Complexity Analysis

queries which appear to trickle down to all the key-space partitions in the range, we call it the *shower algorithm*. The intuition of the algorithm is shown graphically in Figure 4.2.

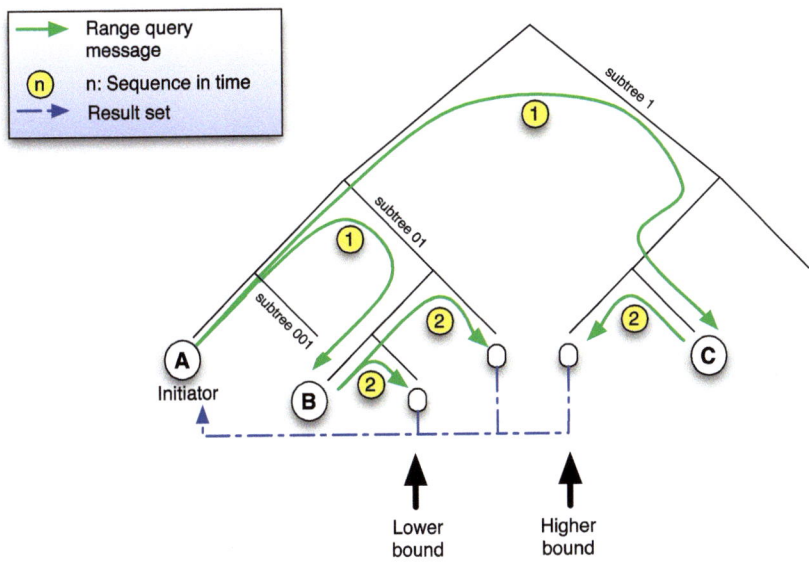

Figure 4.2: Shower range query strategy

In the course of forwarding, it is possible that the query is forwarded to a peer responsible for keys outside the range. However, it is guaranteed that this peer will forward the range query back to a key-space partition within the range. Moreover, the P-Grid routing ensures that no key space partition will get duplicates of the range queries. Algorithm 4.4 gives the pseudo code for the *shower* algorithm.

The search cost (in terms of messages) of this variant is lower bounded by $O(x)+|\Pi_R|-1$. Since every message created in the range sub-space reaches a different leaf node (since the sub-spaces are exclusive), and there are expected D/M such sub-spaces, the upper bound is $O(x) + min(2O(|\Pi_R|), 2^{Depth-x})$ where $Depth$ is the maximum path length of any partition in the range. Thus the complexity of the shower algorithm is again dependent only on the size of the answer set D for the range query, but independent of the size of the range R of the query.

The upper bound for latency is $O(x)+O(Depth-x)$. In particular, unlike in the sequential variant, the latency of the parallelized shower algorithm is independent of the number of data items in the range R, but depends on the distribution of the data items (which determines the $Depth$). Note that the issuer of the query will start getting responses for part of the range

Algorithm 4.4 Parallel range queries: shower(R, $l_{current}$, p)
1: **if** $\pi(p) \subseteq R$ **then**
2:     return($d \in \delta(p) \mid key(d) \in R$);
3: **end if**
4: determine l_l such that $\pi(min(R), l_l) = \overline{\pi(p, l_l)}$;
5: determine l_u such that $\pi(max(R), l_u) = \overline{\pi(p, l_u)}$;
6: $l_{min} = max(l_{current}, min(l_l, l_u))$;
7: $l_{max} = max(l_l, l_u)$;
8: **if** $l_{current} < l_{max}$ **then**
9:     **for** $l = l_{min}$ to l_{max} **do**
10:         r = randomly selected element from $\rho(p, l)$;
11:         shower(R, l+1, r);
12:     **end for**
13: **end if**

with a minimum latency of $O(x)$, since it will already encounter some peer responsible for part of the range.

The expected value of x is $0.5 \log(nM/D)$. The intuition for the value of x is that, if we increase the average memory of each logical partition to D instead of M, there will be $\frac{n}{D/M}$ key space partitions in total, otherwise retaining the routing network's properties, and since first the query needs to reach any arbitrary peer within the range, this translates into reaching this virtual partition of average size D, and hence x is the expected search cost in this new network, which has the same topological properties, but fewer (nM/D) partitions.

4.2 Related Work

Traditional database research has shown that tries are among the most practical data structures to support range queries. The work on prefix hash trees (PHT) superimposes a P-Grid-like trie onto an arbitrary structured overlay network [RRHS04]. The advantage of PHT is thus its universal usability on top of any DHT, however, it is considerably less efficient. Using a native trie structure as is done in P-Grid makes range queries more efficient in terms of both message cost and latency. Note that the analysis we showed before gives the costs in terms of the total number of overlay network messages. The analysis of PHT provides the number of DHT searches for answering a range query, and each of these DHT searches for a typical DHT (like Chord [SMK+01]) involves logarithmic number of messages in terms of the key space partitions (alternatively peer population). This is due to the fact that semantically close data items are not necessarily stored close to each other in the overlay network (high fragmentation), and hence, multiple overlay network queries are required to

4.2. Related Work

locate all the content. In contrast, tries cluster semantically close data items which in turn enable efficient range access. Another recent approach [LNS+04] uses a hierarchical tree structure but because of the hierarchy, it inherently has poor fault-tolerance and poor query load-balancing characteristics.

To support approximate range queries, locality-preserving hashing to hash ranges instead of keywords is used in [GAE03]. An improvement of this approach to support exact range queries is proposed in [SGAE04]. The fundamental problem of these approaches is that the ranges themselves are hashed, and hence, simple key search operations are not supported or are highly inefficient. Since both key and range queries are needed, it is desirable to have one mechanism supporting both, instead of maintaining separate hash tables for keys, and separate hash tables for ranges, because such a strategy fails to reuse the resources of the peers. These approaches [GAE03, SGAE04] lead to very bad fragmentation even for related ranges, and can result in either poor storage-load balancing or inefficient access. Moreover, since they use CAN as the underlying network, the search efficiency guarantees hold only for uniform partitioning of the space, which conflicts with storage load which is arbitrarily distributed, as will be the case for caching range queries, more so because queries will also be non-uniformly distributed.

In terms of key search efficiency, support for range queries and storage load-balancing, there are some interesting novel structured overlay network abstractions which exhibit performance comparable to our trie-structured proposal: Skip Graphs [AKK04, AS03] which are based on skip lists [Pug90], and Mercury [BAS04] which is based on small-world routing. Skip Graphs can be viewed as a trie of skip lists that share their lower levels. As Skip Graphs preserve the ordering relation among keys they also support range queries. Similar to the shower variant of P-Grid, range queries are resolved by finding any node in the interval ($O(\log n)$ messages) and then broadcasting the query through the m nodes in the interval which requires $O(m \log n)$ messages. In total this is still of logarithmic complexity but quite a bit higher than the effort (in terms of messages) incurred by our approach. Mercury, on the other hand, retains the data sequentially, dynamically assigns the range for which individual peers are responsible in order to provide good load-balancing, and uses small-world routing among the peers. Multiple-attribute range queries by using an individual index for each attribute as proposed in Mercury can be done based on any indexing scheme, including ours. The important and unaddressed issue in all existing literature on multiple-attribute range queries is the issue of efficient joins. Though Skip Graphs and Mercury offer comparable complexity characteristics in terms of search and range queries as our approach, these systems have so far only been evaluated with simulations, and no real implementations or experimental evaluations in a real-world networking scenario exist. For our approach, however, we do not only provide the theoretical study of the performance, but also report on deployment and experimentation of a fully implemented overlay network.

There exist many other range query proposals, which are of lesser relevance than the approaches discussed above. A detailed survey of search mechanisms in P2P systems, including range queries can be found in [RM04].

4.3 Evaluation

The two range query algorithms were implemented on top of the Java-based P-Grid implementation and we performed a number of large-scale experiments on PlanetLab to validate the analytical results presented in Section 4.1 in a practical setting.

Experimental setup In the experiments we used a network of 250 peers each running on a dedicated physical PlanetLab node. We inserted 2500 unique data items into the system and required an average replication factor of 5 which is necessary in any overlay network to compensate for node and communication failures. Thus initially we would have a total of $5*2500 = 12500$ data items in the system and each peer would be responsible for $5\frac{2500}{250} = 50$ data items. The real number of data items in the system in fact was higher as for load-balancing each peer was required to manage a minimum of 50 and a maximum of 100 data items, and given the randomized construction approach of P-Grid, each peer would thus hold on average 75 data items, i.e., the total number of data items in the system was $250*75 = 18750$.

To show that the algorithms basically work for any data distribution, we used two different data sets, one uniformly distributed and one Pareto distributed (with a probability density function of $\frac{a \, k^a}{x^{1+a}}$ and parameters $k = 1$ and $a = 2.0$) as shown in Figure 4.3.

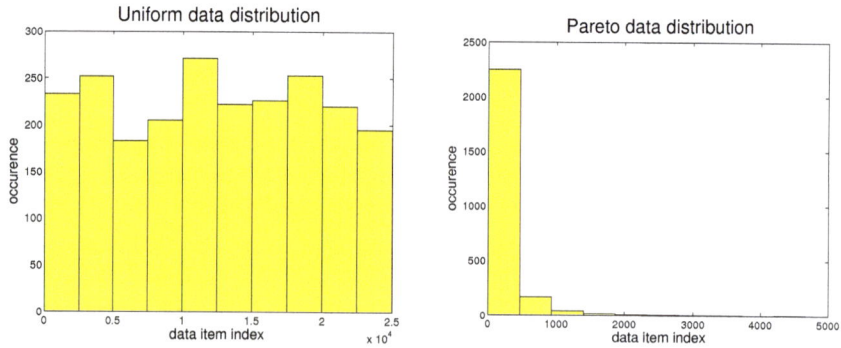

Figure 4.3: Data set distributions

Pareto is a typical long-tail distribution which occurs frequently. We will see in the experiments that P-Grid is insensible to such distributions due to the efficiency of the underlying

4.3. Evaluation

load-balancing algorithm which balances both storage and replication load. We can thus safely infer that if the results are good for a Pareto distribution, the system will perform equally well for other frequent long-tail distributions, e.g., Zipf.

In the experiments each peer selected randomly 10 data items of a global data set according to one of these distributions. The peers then constructed a P-Grid which had an average height of $\log_2 \frac{2500}{10*5} = 5.6$. Then range queries which affected data from all partitions of the data sets were issued. The queries were started from randomly chosen peers with random lower range bounds, and were constructed in a way, such that they would return 50, 100, 150, 200, 400, and 800 data items. For each of the six answer set sizes, each of the two distributions, and each of the two algorithms, one query was issued by each of the 250 peers, i.e., a total of $6*2*2*250 = 6000$ queries resulting in 250 values per data point in Figures 4.4–4.7.

Experimental results There are several performance metrics of interest to evaluate the system as well as the algorithms for their suitability to support range queries. This includes load-balance characteristics (storage, replication, and query load), data fragmentation, as well as message costs and latency for various data distributions. Chapter 3 and [ADHS05] have shown P-Grid's efficient multi-faceted load-balancing characteristics and that the use of order-preserving hashing ensures low data fragmentation, while the dynamic construction of the trie structures ensures storage-load balancing.

The main objectives of our experiments in this section were to demonstrate the cost/latency trade-off of the range query algorithms, and to show that because of the use of a load-balanced trie-structured overlay network, the cost of range queries is independent of the data distribution and the size of the range, but only dependent on the used algorithm and the size of the answer set which we expected from the theoretical analysis of Section 4.1. From the experimental results presented in the following, we can observe that the cost and latencies are indeed independent of the distribution and indirectly prove that the overlay network has good storage-load balancing characteristics.

4.3.1 Message Latency and Cost

Figure 4.4 shows the costs incurred by range queries in terms of message latency (hops), i.e., the maximum number of messages required to hit each sub-partition of the range, i.e., one peer in each sub-partition. Figure 4.4(a) shows a direct comparison of the experimental results and Figure 4.4(b) gives the standard deviations of each of the four types of experiments as error bars.

On average we need 3 hops to reach a responsible peer for both types of algorithms, but the min-max algorithm then suffers from the sequential traversal of the range to reach all sub-partitions after reaching the lower bound. This leads to increasing hop counts with increasing

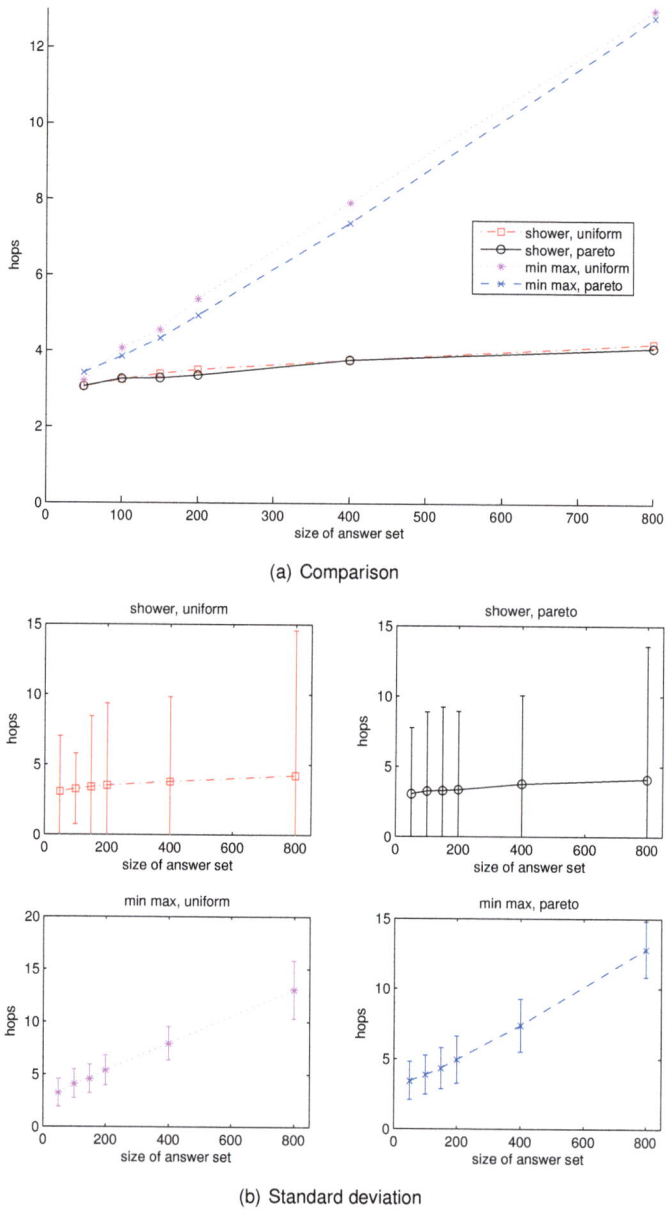

(a) Comparison

(b) Standard deviation

Figure 4.4: Message latency (hops)

4.3. Evaluation

range sizes whereas for the shower algorithm the number of hops remains constant, i.e., it is rather insensitive to the size of the answer set as an increase in the number of hops for this algorithm basically means that the range has exceeded one level in the tree and an additional hop is necessary as the "shower" has to start at the next higher level. However, this benefit comes at the cost of an increase in the overall messages as shown in Figure 4.5. Figure 4.5(a) shows a direct comparison of the experimental results and Figure 4.5(b) gives the standard deviations of each of the four types of experiments as error bars.

The shower algorithm requires a slightly higher number of messages but improves latency as it sends them to the responsible peers in parallel. Therefore all peers responsible for a range section are reached after 3 hops (in the experiment's setup) independent of the range size. Range queries with an answer set size of 50 are answered mostly by one peer because peers on average are responsible for 75 data items. It can further be seen that both algorithms perform equally well for both data distributions and scale well as expected. An increase of the answer set size by a multiplicative factor of the average peer storage size yields an additional message on average which is the best possible result achievable with limited storage available at the peers and again indirectly proves the optimal behavior of the underlying load-balancing algorithm.

Figure 4.5 also shows the total number of peers involved in a range query, i.e., the number of peers forwarding or replying to a range query. For the min-max algorithm this number is equal to the number of messages because only one message is first routed to the lower bound and then forwarded to the higher bound. Therefore the number of peers forwarding a query to a peer of the desired range is smaller than for the shower algorithm. More peers are involved during the shower algorithm because messages are sent in parallel to reach desired peers (partitions).

4.3.2 Query Latency

In terms of query latency, it is interesting to see that the shower algorithm is almost insensible towards answer set sizes. As can be seen in Figure 4.6 the latency is nearly constant.

This can be explained by the fact that a considerable number of data items would have to be added before the trie increases its height which is the major contribution to the latency for this algorithm. For the min-max case the latency increases for obvious reasons as messages are forwarded sequentially which increases the latency. Here an increase of the height of the trie has a much more dramatic influence as the min-max algorithm heavily depends on the width of the interval. While increasing the height of the trie means only an additional hop for the shower-algorithm which is processed largely in parallel, for the min-max algorithm the number of sequential messages increases by a factor of 2 on average. Note that this is expected from theory, since the height of the tree will increase by 1 only if approximately twice the data items are in the same range, and in the min-max algorithm, both latency and

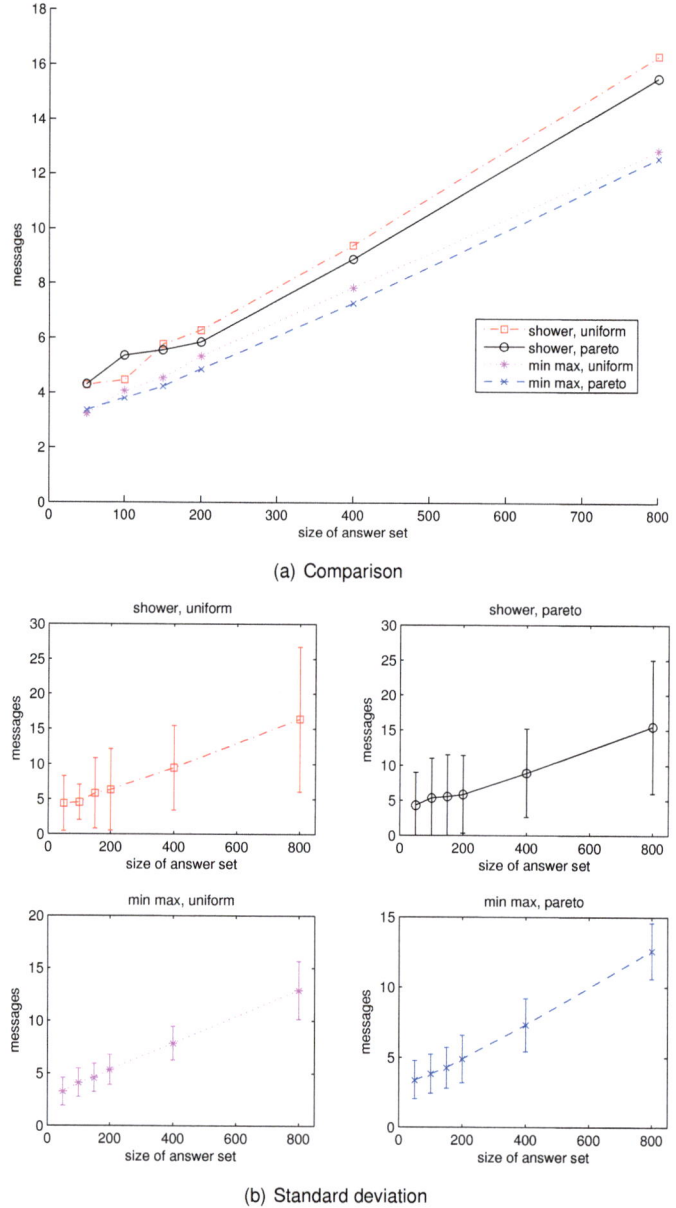

(a) Comparison

(b) Standard deviation

Figure 4.5: Message cost

4.3. Evaluation

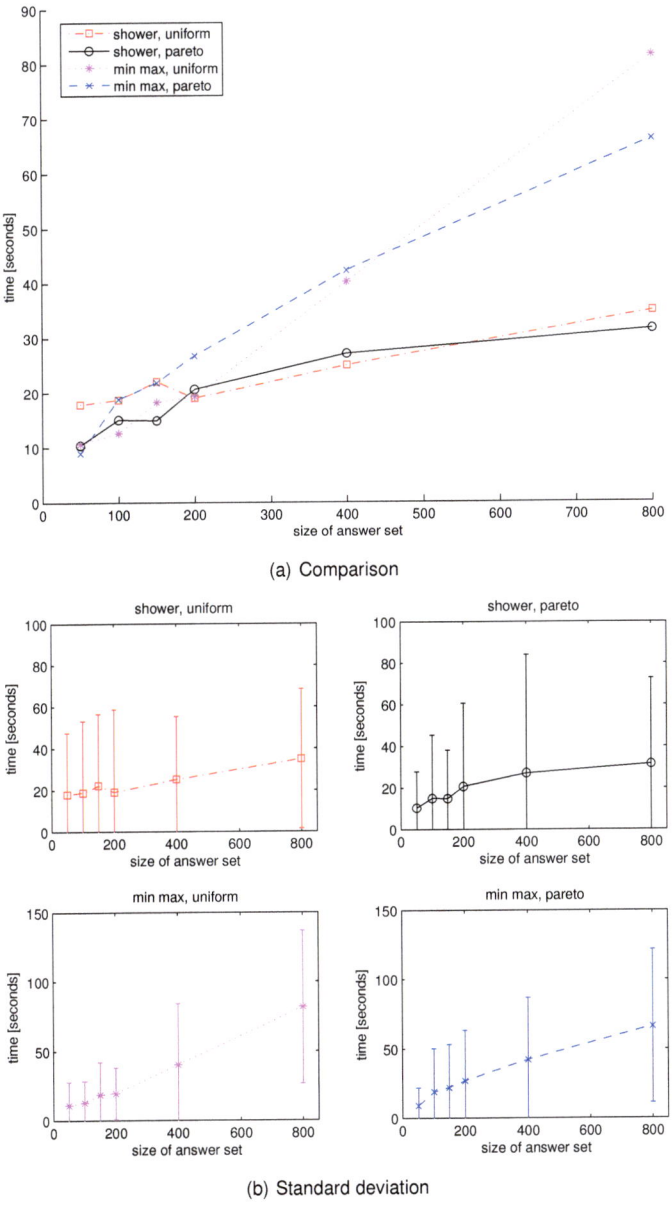

(a) Comparison

(b) Standard deviation

Figure 4.6: Query latency (time)

message cost is proportional to the number of data-items in the answer-set.

A side result which can be inferred from these plots is that the smallest range queries involving 3–5 peers take approximately 10–20 seconds on average. Larger range queries using the min-max algorithm take a multiple of that. This can be explained by the success of PlanetLab as an experimental test-bed, since a large number of experiments are conducted concurrently which considerably slows down PlanetLab's overall performance.

4.3.3 Success Rate

Finally, in Figure 4.7 we show what level of result completeness we could achieve by our range queries.

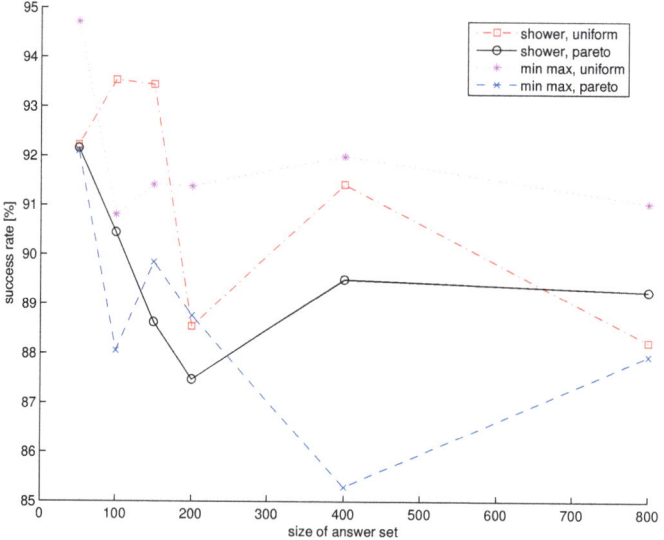

Figure 4.7: Result completeness

This measure represents the percentage of received data items as answers to a range query with respect to the actual number of data items inserted (present) in the specific range. The result completeness is around 90% and is mainly independent of the range sizes and the data distributions. We observed several problems during our experiments in respect to the PlanetLab environment, for example, communication problems and crashes of PlanetLab nodes (not of the tested P-Grid system but the physical PlanetLab nodes), which explain the non-exhaustive results. Note that, while it is an issue that is beyond the scope of this evaluation (such failures because of unreliable peers are characteristic of any deployed P2P system, the relatively high success rate in fact demonstrates the robustness of P-Grid under churn. Smaller scale experiments in a local environment with lower numbers of nodes and node failures have proved the functional correctness of our implementation and provided a 100% success rate. To increase the success rate on PlanetLab we could increase the replication factor, i.e., data is replicated more often, and thus node failures could be possibly compensated better. This will increase the maintenance overhead but should provide better results. However, due to the duration of the experiments and the lack of possibility to assess the conditions on PlanetLab that caused a certain experimental result and behavior, we have no experimental evaluation of this strategy yet. In the experiments discussed above we used a replication factor of 5 on average (in fact, each data item was replicated between 1 and 10 times). Taking this into account and the very dynamic situation on PlanetLab a success rate of 90% seems reasonable. In future work, we will explore the possibility to adapt replication to the dynamic situation on the physical network to improve on the result completeness.

4.4 Completeness Estimation

Section 4.1 presented range query algorithms for the P-Grid overlay using parallel multi-cast protocols. A main challenge remaining is to estimate the progress of query processing, i.e., to answer the question which fraction of the total query result is already received. The difficulties are due to the purely decentralized nature of the structured overlay, the lack of global knowledge (no peer knows how many peers are responsible for the queried key range), the dynamics of the network (peers may leave the network during processing a query), as well as the often used best-effort strategy for query routing and answering.

However, estimating the completeness of a query result is not only a helpful information for the user issuing the query, but it is also needed for processing complex queries. For instance, query operators like aggregation or ranking-based queries (e.g., skyline queries [BKS01, KMS07]) require to know when all input data is arrived in order to calculate the aggregate value or to sort the input.

The objective of this section is to estimate the completeness of range queries as a fundamental operator for more complex query operators and to give guarantees on the quality of this estimation. The idea is to map the completeness on data level to a completeness on peer level, thus, estimating a number of replies expected for each query. Though it is guaranteed by the shower algorithm that all peers receive exactly one range query message, it is currently not possible for the initiating peer to estimate the number of peers concerned by a range query, i.e., estimating the number of response messages it has to expect. For keyword based queries, a peer receives only one query response by one peer in a structured overlay network as only one peer (or any of its replicas) is responsible for the given keyword. A peer is therefore able to determine when a query finished and when it received all matching items to either inform a user, start post-processing or initiate subsequent queries. This is currently not possible for range queries in structured overlay networks as the number of response messages depends on the number of peers in the target range, which is usually not known for a peer. We will present an approach to estimate this number based on the local information available in a peer's routing table and corrected by intermediate peers forwarding range queries or peers responding to range queries. We thereby assume a load-balanced system where each peer holds approximately the same amount of data as shown for P-Grid in [ADHS05]. Hence estimating the number of responding peers is equivalent to estimating the number of query hits expected to be retrieved by a range query.

4.4.1 Completeness on Data vs. Peer Level

Estimating the completeness of queries should intuitively be bound to the data level: the user is interested in what fraction of all expected result hits she/he already received. This also holds for subsequent processing steps following the execution of range queries. As briefly mentioned in the last section, predicting completeness on data level is almost impossible without enormous costs. Fortunately, in a load-balanced overlay system this completeness can be mapped to completeness on reply level, because each reply should deliver approximately the same number of results. This is especially true for range queries, because no filtering steps are applied – if a peer is responsible for a part of the range, it will return all of its local data items. Moreover, we will show that we are able to guarantee to identify the last query reply when actually receiving it. Thus, a completeness of 100% on reply level corresponds to a guaranteed completeness of 100% on data level. So, for subsequent operations that rely on complete range query replies estimation on reply level is absolutely satisfying. In order to show its applicability for other situations, in Section 4.4.4 we show that completeness on data level and reply level almost match. Note that, due to the characteristics of sophisticated overlays, the majority of queries will be answered completely.

4.4.2 Estimating Completeness

We focus on the shower algorithm implemented in P-Grid. In Section 4.4.3 we discuss the possibilities for other systems to provide completeness estimation for range queries and the applicability of our approach to them.

A peer initiating a range query starts this query by providing the interval bounds of the desired range. Afterwards, each intermediate peer responsible for routing the query, forwards it to one or more sub-trees, depending on its own path, the paths of peers from its routing table, and the paths of the queried range. Thus, the crucial point is to estimate the number of peers responsible for a certain key range. But, due to load-balancing aspects, this is quite difficult. The idea is to use all available path information in order to build an estimated P-Grid

4.4. Completeness Estimation

trie. Based on this tree, we can determine a minimal number of replies expected.

In the following we will explain, how we can determine the minimal number of replies from an estimated P-Grid trie. Let

$$b_1 b_2 b_3 \ldots b_x$$

denote the x bits that form the binary path of such a peer. From this path, we can deduce the existence of at least x other peers: Let $\bar{b}_i$ denote the inverted bit b_i. For each path

1: $\bar{b}_1$

2: $b_1 \bar{b}_2$

3: $b_1 b_2 \bar{b}_3$

...

x: $b_1 b_2 \ldots b_{x-1} \bar{b}_x$

there must exist *at least one* responsible peer. Knowing about several paths from peers in a range, the initiator can deduce a minimal number of peers in that range. In order to achieve this, the initiator builds a tree from those paths and reflects to the minimal number of peers.

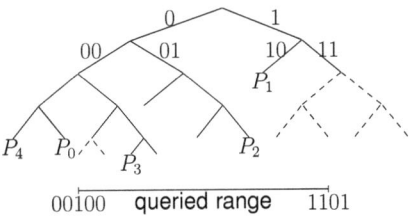

Figure 4.8: Estimating the P-Grid trie

Figure 4.8 illustrates this. The figure shows an example P-Grid tree. Assume a query for the range $00100 - 1101$ was initiated. Further, the initiator P_0 knows about four peers, where the paths from P_1, P_2 and P_3 are in the range. As every peer has at least one reference to another peer for each of the positions of its path, P_0 must at least know about four peers, each located in a different sub-tree. The part of the tree the initiator can deduce from its local routing information is shown in solid lines. The dashed lines indicate that part of the tree not known to the initiator, which results in a small error in this first estimate. The minimal number of peers in the range estimated in this situation is 8, the correct value is 10.

Estimation Refinement

The first estimation performed by the query initiating peer is solely based on the routing information available at that peer. This information consists of at least one reference per level respectively one peer of each sub-tree a range query is sent to. For fault-tolerance and load-balancing reasons structured overlays usually keep multiple references at each level to remain operational during peer churn or to select the least loaded peer for query load balancing. Therefore, the information a query initiating peer has about the structure and peers in a sub-tree increases with the number of references per level.

But, the information gathered like this is still not complete and the estimation might still be too small as some peers remain "invisible" from the local point of view. Therefore, initiating peers piggy-back with each query sent to a sub-tree the estimate of peers considered in a sub-tree. For example in Figure 4.8, the range query sent from peer P_0 to peer P_3 also contains the estimate that three peers build the sub-tree $001*$. As P_0 only knows that P_3 has path 00110, it knows that there must be a peer 00111 and at least one peer for 0010, though P_0 does not know that the sub-tree $0010*$ actually consists of two peers. P_3 is aware of this fact, because P_3's routing table must contain at least one of the peers from sub-tree $0010*$, and can return the correct number of peers in sub-tree $001*$ with its query reply to peer P_0. P_0 can then correct the estimate of query replies expected for the initiated range query. Peers receiving a range query with correct information do not have to "correct" the initial estimate.

The required message overhead for our completeness estimation is therefore minimal as no additional messages have to be sent and only small information are piggy-backed with sent query and query reply messages. In case a range query hits a peer outside the target range with an incorrect estimate, the receiving peer can either react by replying with a short acknowledgment message correcting the initial estimate, or it forwards the incorrect estimate to target peers in the range and the correction will be returned in the query reply messages. In the first case, the query initiator can sooner correct the estimated completeness at the cost of a small extra message, whereas in the second case the correction is done at a later time with the reception of query results without additional messages.

Applying the method as described above, we will never over-estimate the number of expected replies. Moreover, when a query is finished, we will always recognize this for sure. This is possible because the paths of the replying peers are analyzed. Thus, receiving these replies, we always know for sure the actual size of the corresponding sub-tree.

Further Improvements

There was much research spent on designing overlay systems as much stable and reliable as possible. Thus, we can even cache estimated trees once they are built. These cached trees can later be used for subsequent queries. The trees should then be adapted

4.4. Completeness Estimation

to changes in the overlay structure registered – which may, of course, occur, but are expected to be rather rare. In this way, we achieve a quite accurate and satisfyingly exact completeness estimation, which is automatically maintained with each query initiated.

The task of achieving complete query results is due to the used overlay system, in this case the P-Grid overlay. Nevertheless, incomplete results may occur in rather unstable and unreliable large-scaled systems. This also effects the completeness estimation, as, for instance, we will experience a difference in the *static* completeness concerning all data that should be available, and the *dynamic* completeness based on the results actually received. This should be involved into completeness considerations. A nice aspect of the method proposed here is that it allows for estimating the size of results missing in this case.

4.4.3 Usability in other Overlay Systems

Our approach is based on a parallel resolution of range queries in a binary trie similar to a prefix hash tree, whereby in the case of P-Grid the depth of each sub-tree can be estimated by the known nodes of this sub-tree stored in the local routing table. To the best of our knowledge no other system can already provide completeness estimation for range queries. In this section, we briefly discuss the possibilities for other systems to estimate the number of query replies and the usability of our approach for them.

The approach for range queries in SkipGraphs [AS03, AKK04] is the most similar one to the one of P-Grid as peers also maintain routing information at multiple levels. Our proposed method can also be used by SkipGraphs to estimate the number of peers in other sub-trees. The only problem is the number of peers remaining in the bucket layer below the lowest interconnected skip-list level. But, as load-balancing is in place, this number should be similar to the number of buckets the current node is in.

Mercury, the second structured overlay network using order-preserving hashing, uses long-range links within the Chord-based attribute hubs to implement a similar range query algorithm as P-Grid's shower algorithm. Based on the information available we assume that Mercury can estimate range query completeness in a similar way than we have shown here for P-Grid if adequate routing information is available and cached.

Approaches like [RRHS04] and [LNS+04] are based on a prefix hash tree where peers remain at each level of the tree, unlike in P-Grid where peers only remain at the leaf level. The routing in this tree starts at the root level and trickles down the tree from nodes to their children until all nodes in the target range are reached. As we assume that nodes do not know the exact number of their children, it is not possible for them to estimate how many nodes will return results for a range query. If this number can be estimated, the technique presented in this paper can also be adapted for completeness estimation in systems based on prefix hash trees.

Finally, approaches forwarding a range query sequentially along neighbors cannot estimate the final number of nodes involved in a range query, e.g., CAN-based systems presented in [GAE03, SGAE04].

4.4.4 Evaluation

The focus of the following evaluation is to show the applicability, exactness and quality of the proposed completeness estimation. These aspects are not directly depending on the size of the network, but rather on the size of the constructed overlay trie. This, in turn, also but not exclusively depends on the network size. We created a local and reliable but real environment consisting of 61 nodes. These nodes were physically distributed over 20 machines, each running up to 4 instances listening on different ports. As the environment was stable, we were able to use a low replication factor, lowering the number of replicas responsible for one path in the P-Grid trie. This resulted in a wider and deeper tree. Thus, the results are also significant for larger scaled networks, where usually a higher replication factor is used. We used two environments, the first with a replication factor of 2, the second with a factor of 1. In unreliable systems, this factor will be set to 5 or higher compensating frequent joins and leaves by peers. Our evaluation focuses on the completeness estimation of range queries and we assume that P-Grid guarantees the availability of at least one peer per partition even in very dynamic or unreliable setups like PlanetLab.

We inserted 48 data items from each of the peers, resulting in a total of 2928 data items. The used string data represents information about movie titles and was taken from IMDB[1]. The average number of leafs, maximal path length and the average path length were 32, 8 and 5 for a replication factor of 1. For a factor of 2, the values were 19, 6 and 4.5, respectively. The resulting P-Grid trie was not balanced. Almost 40% of the leafs were located under key prefix 0 and the tree was deeper and wider under key prefix 1.

In order to evaluate the influence of the number of references for one level of the local routing table we built three environments, using a maximal number of references of 1, 3 and 5. A query mix of three different range queries, involving different parts of the trie and therefore resulting in a different number of replies, was run. Each query was initiated 10 times, each time on a randomly chosen node. In the following, we present and discuss the results of the described experiments.

Completeness on Data Level

The first figure shows the correspondence between completeness on data level and on peer level. Figure 4.9 shows the percentage of the final result received with respect to the number of replies received. We exemplary chose one of the described network environments (replication factor 2, maximal references 5) – in the other settings results look similar. The

---
[1] http://www.imdb.com/

4.4. Completeness Estimation

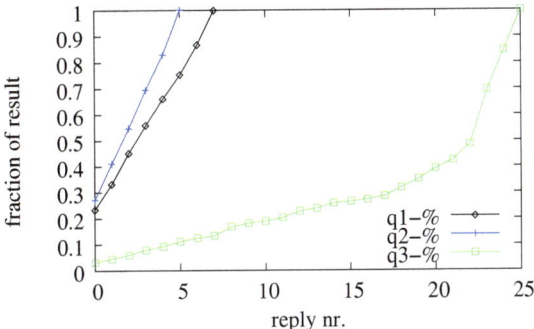

Figure 4.9: Completeness on data level

plot shows that especially for the two queries resulting in less answers the development of the result size is almost linear. For the query involving the whole P-Grid trie there is a higher increase in that size with the last query replies. Even if P-Grid implements a sophisticated load-balancing, there might exist keys a particular high number of data items is mapped to. P-Grid's load-balancing technique splits high frequented key space partitions more finegranular than others, but does not "split" single keys. Thus, some peers are still responsible for a higher number of items than others. Due to the locally used storage system, the answer time correlates to the amount of data to be processed locally. Therefore, replies from these peers arrive at the end, resulting in a higher increase of the result size with the final answers. A perfect mapping would be indicated by a straight line. The figure shows that the mapping from completeness on data level to the completeness on reply level is satisfyingly realistic in load-balanced overlay systems.

Estimate Number of Replies

Figure 4.10 shows the number of replies we estimated using the proposed technique with each reply received. Additionally, the straight line represents the actual completeness on reply level. The figure clearly shows that our method always estimates the number of replies correctly at the end. Moreover, it gets evident that only a small number of first replies is needed in order to determine a correct value in the end. As expected, the higher the number of references for each level of the routing table, the more exact the initial estimation and the less corrections are needed. The figure also shows that in this case the size of the temporary errors is smaller than with lower references per level. The differences in the number of replies for equal queries are due to the need for starting networks with different parameters from scratch every time. By this, and the application of a random-walk strategy in order to build the P-Grid trie, this results in, only slightly, different overlay trees.

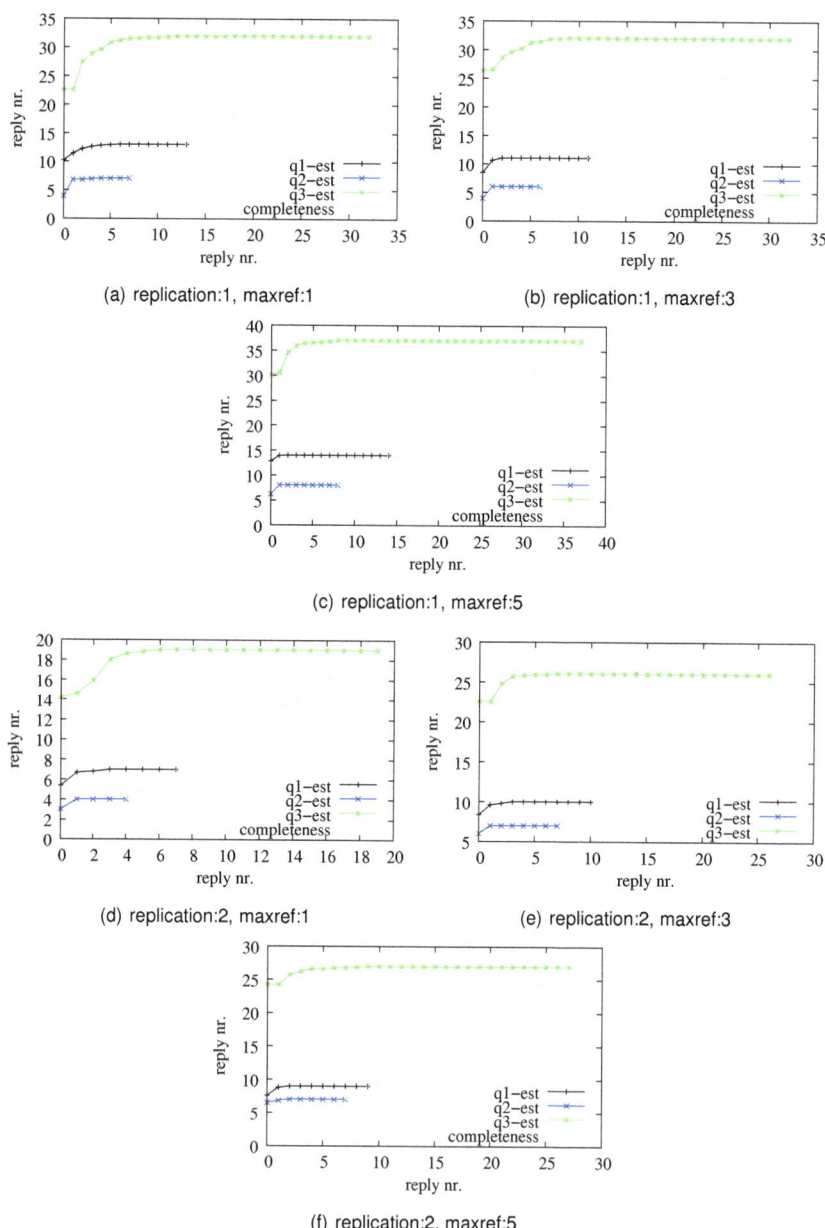

Figure 4.10: Estimated number of replies with corrections

4.4. Completeness Estimation

The smaller the part of the trie involved into range query processing the less information is needed in order to achieve exact estimations. For the first two queries, even the settings using a replication factor of 1 and/or a maximal number of references per level of 3 and 1 are quite satisfying. As it is more probably that sub-trees are queried than the whole tree, this shows that the proposed method provides quick and exact estimations even with low information. This also shows the effectiveness for larger scaled and unreliable systems where, in turn, more information shall be contained in the local routing tables.

Summarizing, we can state that for each of the considered cases we only need a fraction of replies in order to achieve an exact completeness estimation. As the method goes along with very low additional effort, this proves its powerfulness for trie structured overlays in general.

Relative Estimate

The last figures show the relative completeness ($\frac{estimatedreplies}{finalreplies}$) estimated with each reply. Thus, it illustrates the ratio of error correction. Moreover, this time the queries were run on two different networks for each setting, each of them run for a different time before starting queries. Results from the hence four runs were averaged. Thus, effects of slightly different overlay tries are eliminated. Figure 4.11 shows that the ratio of correction is always almost equal for each of the used environments. Following, independent from the query actually initiated, completeness estimation is comparably good and corrections provide equally good improvements with respect to the size of the final result. The figures also show that the initial estimate is good for all tests, but it is better if more references are stored at each routing table level. As expected, the reduction in the error is visible only for the first query replies and converges to 0 for the later replies. Another important observation is that the estimation for the queries with less replies are very exact with little information and that the corresponding plots approach each other with rising numbers of references.

Estimation on PlanetLab

Finally we ran some experiments on PlanetLab. In each run, we involved as many nodes as were available in the tests. This always involved nodes spanning the whole globe. At the time of our experiments, for each run there were between 382 and 390 peers available in our slice. Every time a new experiment was initiated, we built a P-Grid network from scratch. After a certain waiting time for establishing a suitable overlay trie we initiated range queries. The inserted data was again randomly chosen from a set of top-frequent entries from the IMDB, resulting in a total of about 16,000 index entries. The set of all generated keys shows a skewed heavy-tail distribution (power-law like), as shown in Figure 4.12 (all keys that were inserted more than one time, log-log scale). We used a value of 5 for P-Grid's replication

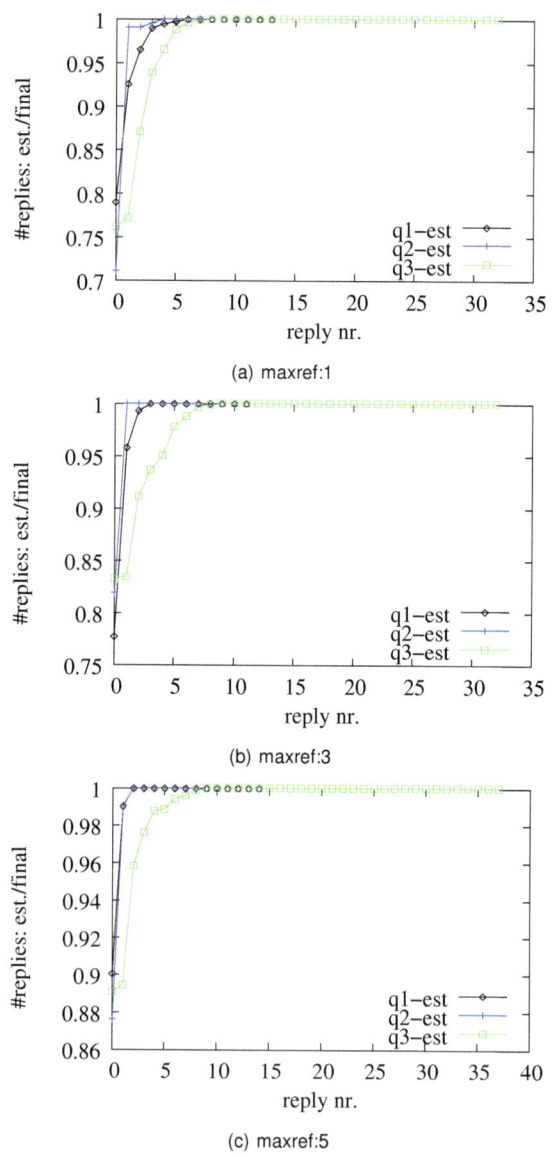

Figure 4.11: Estimated relative number of replies with corrections

4.4. Completeness Estimation

factor as well as the maximal number of references per routing level. The resulting P-Grid trie was not balanced. Almost 40% of the leaves were located under key prefix 0 and the tree was deeper and wider under key prefix 1. The average number of leaves, maximal path length and the average path length were 35, 7 and 5, respectively. The average number of single entries each peer was responsible for was approximately 5,000.

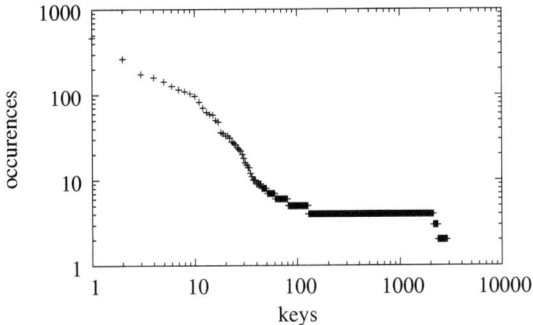

Figure 4.12: Key distribution

Figure 4.13 shows the number of estimated replies with respect to the number of already received replies and reveals that completeness estimation is quite exact in this case, even with the very first replies. Additionally, the figure shows the number of actually received replies averaged over all queries. We only need a small fraction of all replies in order to achieve almost exact correctness. This result therefore confirms our findings presented in Figure 4.10.

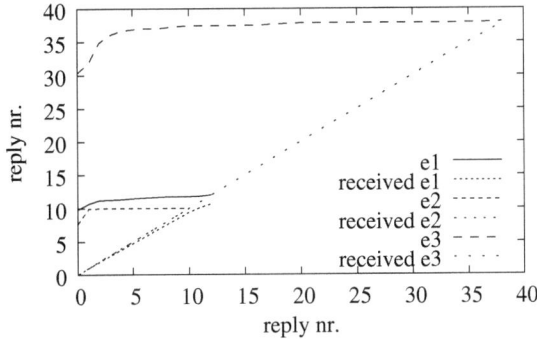

Figure 4.13: Completeness estimation on PlanetLab

All in all the proposed method for completeness estimation is absolutely satisfying. The initial estimation, based on no further knowledge than the local one, is quite good for any type of query and environment. Even if this first estimate is erroneous, only a small amount of replies is needed in order to determine an exact estimate.

4.5 Conclusions

This chapter has shown how range queries can efficiently be implemented in structured overlay networks using order-preserving hashing. Whereas the min-max traversal approach is basically supported by any structured overlay as it only requires neighboring links between peers usually already required for system maintenance. The shower algorithm on the other hand benefits from P-Grid's trie structure to process range queries in parallel using multiple messages at the same time trickling down the tree till all queried partitions are reached. As multiple query messages result in multiple query reply messages, we provide a range query completeness estimation for users and applications to estimate the number of reply messages to expect, even before the first message is issued. We can further identify the completeness of a query, i.e., the event of receiving the last reply, on data and peer level.

The evaluation of the range query implementation in the P-Grid application has shown that both algorithms perform well even in a realistic environment such as the PlanetLab testbed. The applications part at the end of this thesis will show how applications can benefit from a structured overlay network providing efficient range queries to enrich the applications functionalities, making the support for range queries indispensable in any P2P system.

Chapter 5

Distributed Inference

Structured overlay networks enable applications to share large data sets in wide-area networks and to efficiently locate shared information. The previous chapter has shown how range queries can be implemented in these systems exploiting data properties to estimate correlated data access. There, data correlations are derived directly from data properties. A second way to obtain data correlations is by applications and their users, providing additional information to set their data entries into a relationship, i.e., also into a relationship with other users' data. This annotation of data with metadata is common practice in PDMS and the Semantic Web as data is provided and maintained by a community integrating and relating new information to existing knowledge.

The Semantic Web community has developed a number of languages (RDF, RDF Schema, OWL) that deploy logic for automatic reasoning of shared data. The database community supports this new trend with efficient inference support for semantic web data in their central databases. Inference is the act or process of deriving a conclusion based on data available in an information system. Inference is studied and applied within several fields such as logic, statistics and artificial intelligence. It enables applications to draw conclusions from a collection of data and relationships between data and potential conclusions. This has the advantage that data can be processed system internally and that large amounts of data do not have to be exposed to the application. A system enabling inference operations can therefore optimize its internal structure accordingly to more efficiently process reasoning requests. For a P2P system supporting inference, data does not have to be retrieved from several peers and returned to an application, but instead can be processed in the P2P system itself and only return a final, probably relatively small, result. This in-network processing can thereby be optimized by the P2P system and is orthogonal to classical lookup operations presented so far.

This chapter shows how distributed inference can be supported on top of a structured overlay network such as P-Grid. By distributed inference we understand the reasoning about data shared in a distributed system such as an overlay network. We show how the shared data is reorganized to more efficiently process reasoning requests, i.e., to optimize in-networking processing. We base our approach on Bayesian networks and Bayesian inference, representing one of many inference methods. However our approach of restructuring shared data is not limited to Bayesian networks. Our data reorganization approach is based on the spring relaxation technique already successfully used for other purposes in P2P systems, such as proximity routing. The spring relaxation technique allows us to cluster correlated data on peers and their proximity. Data correlations are derived from user annotations and used during the inference process to draw conclusions. Clustering correlated data therefore has the advantage of reducing messaging costs for distributed inference. This chapter presents our variant of the spring relaxation algorithm to cluster correlated data for efficient distributed inference, and its extensive evaluation in a simulation.

5.1 Motivation

Recently, inference found a new field of application in the context of the Semantic Web as description logics, such as OWL, can be automatically processed using automatic reasoners. The Web Ontology Language (OWL) is a language for authoring ontologies and OWL ontologies are written in RDF/XML to aid automated parsing. For example, consider the terms 'professor' and 'staff' in an ontology for universities, with the relation of 'professor' being a subclass of 'staff'. Then we can deduct by inference that all professors are also staff members at the university. This knowledge can now be used for query resolution or query reformulation to improve the quality of the result set. OWL is an important part of the Semantic Web, and has attracted both academic and commercial interest. Centralized databases optimized for RDF such as Sesame[1] and Jena[2] offer efficient reasoning capabilities on the locally stored data as required by Semantic Web applications built on top of them. Efforts of the P2P community to provide a distributed version of such an RDF store are the systems GridVine [CMAA07] and UniStore [KSR$^+$07]. They provide lookup operations on shared RDF data using RDF Schema/RDQL queries respectively a variant of SPARQL, the query language of the Semantic Web, named VQL. Chapter 9 will present more details about UniStore, its internal data organization and data processing support. The storage of semantic data in a distributed system hamper reasoning as all the required data is not available locally anymore. To support similar inference capabilities as in centralized systems, a distributed system either first collects the required data to perform inference, or uses distributed inference. The collection of data for local inference can become expensive if the reasoning involves large data sets spread around the globe. Distributed inference has the advantage that no data has to be gathered first and data is processed locally at nodes in the network.

---

[1] http://www.openrdf.org/
[2] http://jena.sourceforge.net/

To derive conclusions, intermediate results have to be exchanged in-between involved data sets, requiring to send messages across the network if parts of the data are not available locally. This inference method is called message-passing and a standard technique to perform probabilistic inference, in a local and distributed setup. GridVine already applied reasoning internally to analyze the correctness of schema mappings as shown in [CMAF06]. The message passing technique applied in [CMAF06] motivated us to provide a distributed inference architecture on top of P-Grid supporting the reasoning on shared data in P2P systems.

Distributed probabilistic inference is also already applied for various applications in sensor networks [PGM05] where network limitations are probably more obvious than in classical P2P networks. Sensor networks provide data streams and it is sometimes too expensive to ship all the generated data over the network, especially in outdoor settings consisting of nodes running on battery power. In such a scenario, network communication is the most expensive operation and has the strongest limiting influence on the life-time of these networks and should therefore be avoided [HSPM06]. In-network processing as for example by distributed inference is therefore a good solution to avoid unnecessary network communication as data can remain at the nodes. To minimize network communication induced by reasoning over facts stored at network nodes, data required for this operation should be available at one node or preferably in the neighborhood of the node. The data reorganization requires to cluster correlated data accordingly.

5.2 Belief Propagation

Pearl's belief propagation [Pea88] enables distributed inference by a simple message-passing algorithm between nodes in a Bayesian network modeling correlations between variables. A node can represent any kind of probabilistic variable, be it an observed measurement, a parameter, a latent variable, or a hypothesis. Belief propagation was first successfully applied in the domain of error correcting codes (Turbo Codes [BGT93]), speech recognition, image processing and medical diagnosis. Recently, it was used in P2P systems in the context of content distribution [BMR04] and in sensor networks [IJWFMW04]. The simplicity of the message-passing algorithm holds the risk of being not scalable towards large-scale networks because many small messages have to be sent between nodes. Approaches to reduce communication costs such as Generalized Belief Propagation [YFW00] cluster nodes and build a hierarchy based on common variables of clusters. The message reduction comes with the drawback that the size of sent messages increases exponentially ($number\ of\ states^{nodes\ in\ the\ cluster}$) because the exchanged messages now contain the joint probabilities of all nodes and states in the cluster. An open problem is how nodes are clustered in a distributed way requiring no global knowledge and coordination so that the communication costs are minimized.

The belief propagation algorithm, also known as the sum-product algorithm, is an iterative algorithm for computing marginal probabilities, "beliefs" about possible diagnoses, of nodes on a probabilistic graphical model such as Bayesian networks. A Bayesian network is a directed acyclic graph of nodes representing variables and edges representing dependence relations among the variables. If there is an edge from node A to node B, then node B's state depends on node A's state. This is specified by a conditional probability distribution for node B, conditioned on the state of node A. A Bayesian network is a representation of the joint distribution over all the variables represented by nodes in the graph. We assume that the joint probability distribution factors into a product of terms involving node pairs and single nodes. These factors are called edge potentials $\psi_{ij}(x_i, x_j)$ and local potentials $\phi_i(x_i)$. Evidence nodes are nodes with a known value. A node can represent any kind of variable, e.g., an observed measurement, a parameter, a latent variable, or a hypothesis. For example, consider the simple Bayesian network in Figure 5.1 consisting of 3 variables OS1, Driver1 and App1. The dependencies are as follows: if the hardware driver Driver1 is installed on the operating system OS1, the application App1 is likely to run smoothly with 90% probability. If the driver is missing, the application runs only to 40% and if OS1 is not installed, then the application does not run at all independent of the driver. If it is known that OS1 is installed, then its probability would be set to 1 and the probabilities for App1 to run would only depend on Driver1 thereafter.

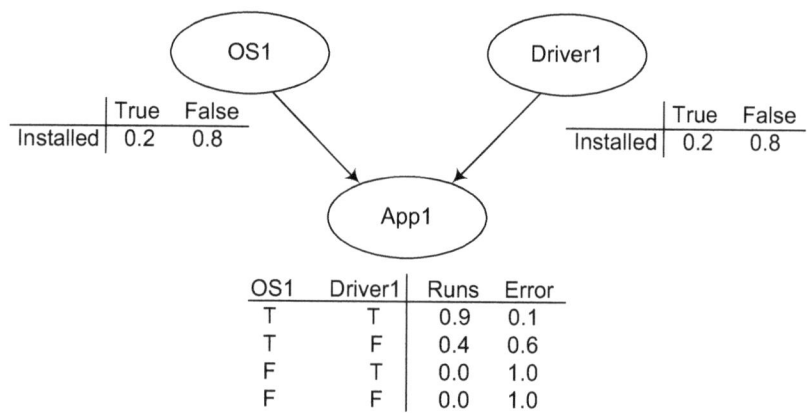

Figure 5.1: Bayesian network example

The belief propagation algorithm is provably efficient on trees and experiments demonstrate its applicability to arbitrary network topologies using loopy belief propagation for loopy networks [Wei00], which we will present in the following. The algorithm is currently used with success in numerous applications including low-density parity-check codes, turbo codes, free energy approximation, and computer vision.

5.2.1 The Message Passing Algorithm

The algorithm passes messages across the edges in the graphical model, i.e., in each iteration, a node sends a message to an adjacent node if it has received messages from all of its other adjacent nodes at the previous iteration. In the first iteration, nodes send an initial message, usually set to 1, to all adjacent nodes. In subsequent iterations, messages passed from node x_i to node x_j are updated using the following rule:

$$m_{ij}(x_j) = \sum_{x_i} \phi_i(x_i)\psi_{ij}(x_i, x_j) \prod_{k \neq j} m_{ki}(x_i)$$

where $\phi_i(x_i)$ are the local potentials of node x_i and $\psi_{ij}(x_i, x_j)$ are the edge potentials. The product of messages excludes the message received in the previous iteration from node j, the node we are passing the message to. The messages $m_{ij}(x_j)$ and the local potentials $\phi_i(x_i)$ are vectors whose length corresponds to the number of states a node x_i can be in. The edge potentials $\psi_{ij}(x_i, x_j)$ are N x M matrices where N is the number of states node x_j can be in and M is the number of states for node x_i.

Finally, the marginal probabilities of nodes, called the beliefs, can be computed by multiplying all received messages by the local potentials:

$$b_i(x_i) = \alpha \phi_i(x_i) \prod_k m_{ki}(x_i)$$

The beliefs are normalized by α to avoid numerical underflow. The algorithm converges if none of the beliefs in successive iterations changes by more than a small threshold. For singly connected graphs, it is proved [Pea88] that beliefs at nodes converge to the marginal probability at that node, which is:

$$b_i(x_i) = \alpha \sum_{x_j/x_i} p(x) = p_i(x_i)$$

In networks with loops, evidence is counted multiple times. As all evidence is double counted in equal amounts, Pearl's belief propagation also provides good approximations of the marginal probabilities in loopy networks.

5.3 The Inference Architecture

Our idea of providing a generic distributed inference system is based on two fundamental design decisions: (i) no central coordination of the variables in the system and their dependencies; (ii) no global knowledge and only pair-wise interactions between nodes. Both requirements are satisfied by the P-Grid overlay infrastructure and Bayesian networks together with belief propagation. P-Grid is used to store the structure of the Bayesian network by indexing all variables of the probabilistic network and all dependencies between them. This is achieved by indexing the following information tuples:

- $(\#(v_i), P(v_i))$: enables applications to find all variables of the Bayesian network as the variable identifier (v_i) is hashed by P-Grid's hash function($\#()$). It further contains the information on which peer $P(v_i)$ the value of variable v_i is currently maintained for inference. The value of $P(v_i)$ can change over time and has to be updated every time variable v_i is moved to a different peer to improve reasoning performance.

- $(\#(v_i), v_j)$ and $(\#(v_j), v_i)$: represents the edge e_{ij} required to find all correlated variables of v_i respectively v_j. As the edge is non-directional, an edge has to be indexed twice.

The advantage of storing a Bayesian network in a distributed infrastructure is that any user of the system can add variables and edges to the probabilistic network. Thus, the Bayesian network can be maintained by a user community and is not subject to supervision by a single authority, i.e, administrator.

Learning a Bayesian network structure and probabilities from distributed data is studied in various papers [Yam97, Hec95, CSK04]. In this thesis we assume an existing Bayesian network stored in P-Grid and do not further study the possibility of Bayesian learning. Belief propagation requires multiple message-passing iterations between all nodes of the Bayesian network which are stored at physical P-Grid nodes. P-Grid's index structure allows to locate all correlated variables by simply performing a lookup. If correlations (v_i, v_j) and variable locations $P(v_i)$ do not change frequently, these system lookups can be economized by local lookups in a cache, holding the necessary information. This means that peers responsible for a variable cache the location of correlated variables for direct communication during the reasoning process. This avoids repetitive lookup operations during distributed inference to locate the current peer responsible for a variable and all correlations of a variable. To keep the cached information up-to-date, a peer should periodically query for the latest set of correlations for its locally maintained variables to be aware of the latest updates. The second cached information, the current peer responsible for a variable value $P(v_i)$, can be obtained on demand. If a peer p_i during the reasoning process contacts a peer $P(v_i)$ for the value of a variable v_i, and $P(v_i)$ is no longer responsible for v_i, then p_i can lookup the current location $P(v_i)$ using P-Grid's index.

On a global scale, this can still lead to scalability problems for our system as distributed inference requires to send messages between all correlated variables located at different peers. To reduce network access and thereby processing delays, we uncouple variable values, the local potentials, from the P-Grid index and allow them to be stored at different physical P-Grid nodes to improve the efficiency of belief propagation. This relocation of variable values is stored in the index by the reference to $P(v_i)$, the currently responsible peer for v_i's local potential. An open problem is how those local potentials are stored close to each other, in the best case even on the same physical P-Grid node, without central coordination and knowledge, to achieve the desired network access reduction.

5.4 The Relaxation Algorithm

In this section we describe the relaxation algorithm based on the spring relaxation technique that we developed. We assume that Bayesian variables are connected by springs and the Bayesian network forms a spring network which has to be relaxed, i.e., the network has to be in a state requiring least possible energy. The energy a spring requires is directly proportional to the distance between the two P-Grid nodes the Bayesian variables are stored at. In P-Grid, the distance between two nodes can be defined by which routing table level has to be used to reach a peer. For example, Table 5.1 shows the distance to several peers based on the peer's routing table.

Table 5.1: P-Grid distance for a peer with path 010

Level	Prefix	Peers	Distance
0	1*	1010, 110, 111, ...	3
1	00*	000, 0010, 0010	2
2	011*	00110, 00111	1
Replicas	010	010	0

The distance between two nodes is indirectly proportional to the level of the routing table as the expected routing cost (hops) to lower levels is higher than to higher levels, i.e., closer levels. Peers have proportionally more references to closer levels and can therefore route to peers in these levels with less hops. The spring between two variables remaining at the same node requires no energy. Therefore, the optimal solution of the spring relaxation algorithm would be to place all variables at one node. This is of course not desirable because P2P systems are based on the idea of load sharing which is in contradiction with the optimal solution mentioned before. Thus, the spring relaxation algorithm also has to consider load balancing of variables among participating nodes. P-Grid provides already heuristic statistics about the current load of each level of the trie represented by a peer's routing table. These statistics are required by P-Grid itself to provide load-balancing of stored index information and are used in the following for our approach too. The statistics are based on periodic interactions with random peers of the routing table to sample the current load distribution. The periodic sampling enables peers to estimate the current load of a routing table level and the global average load.

Figure 5.2 illustrates our idea for the example presented in Figure 3.4. The data layer shows correlated variables (data items) connected by springs representing the attractive force between these items. The strength of the force is thereby proportional to the distance among data items, i.e., the distance of the peers in the P-Grid network as shown above. The relaxation algorithm presented in this section aims at relaxing all springs between correlated variables to map them in a way onto the P-Grid network leading to a minimum remaining energy in the spring network. A spring network with minimal stored energy also represents the optimal solution for our initial aim to minimize in-network processing costs of distributed inference. The reasoning costs are minimal as the number of variables at the same peer was maximized by the relaxation algorithm, leading to a minimal number of physical messages required to send across the network. The number of inference messages sent between probabilistic variables thereby remains the same as before the relaxation step. We are only interested in reducing the number of physical messages sent between peers, i.e., between variables stored at different peers.

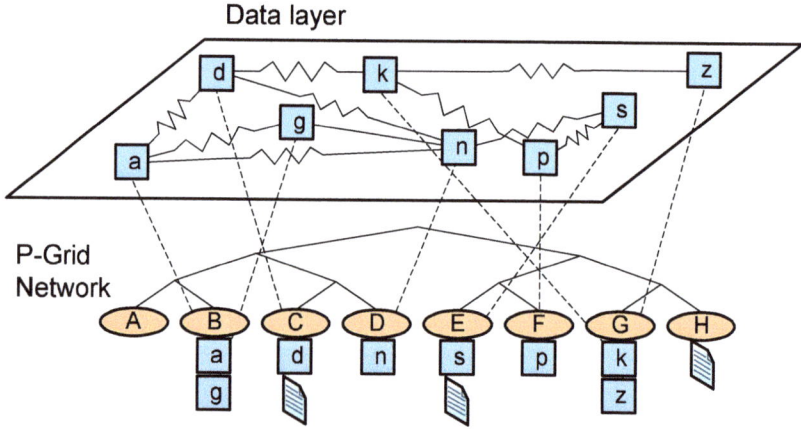

Figure 5.2: Illustration of the spring relaxation approach

The algorithm used to relax the Bayesian network is shown in Algorithm 5.5. The algorithm is executed by each node iteratively till no improvement is achieved anymore, i.e., if the tension a node observes for its variables increases between two steps, or a maximum number of iterations is reached. The algorithm obviously also terminates if no node has variables to move anymore, i.e., the load is balanced among all nodes. The following list provides an overview of the used variables in the algorithm:

5.4. The Relaxation Algorithm

- **localVars**: list of variables the local node maintains
- **avgLoad**: local estimate of the global average load
- **currentLoad**: the current load of the local node
- **routingTable**: the routing table of the local node
- **routingTable.levels**: the number of levels in the local routing table
- **candidate(j).tension(i)**: the tension at level i for candidate variable j
- **candidate(j).tension**: all tensions at all levels for candidate variable j

First, in line 1 to 4, each node checks if it has "free" variables it can move to other nodes or not. Currently, nodes are allowed to move variables as long as they have more than $avgLoad/2$ variables. The limit was chosen by us to ensure that all peers contribute a minimum amount of storage to the system to share the storage load collaboratively amongst all peers in the network. P-Grid obtains an estimate for the current average load in the system but the accuracy of this estimate is not crucial for the algorithm. In line 5, nodes determine those local variables which have a tension to other nodes remaining at the same level of the local routing table leading to one tension at one level. Ideally, variables have a tension to only one node and not to different nodes at the same level. If the local node can move variables and it found such unidirectional variables, it moves them directly to the corresponding level or node (line 6 to 10). Nodes can refuse to maintain new variables if their load is already greater or equal to twice the average load. In such a case, the variable is moved to another node at the same level. Moving a variable always requires only one message between the two involved peers.

A node can try to balance the load in the system if it maintains above average many variables. It therefore uses all non-unidirectional variables, i.e., variables which have tensions at multiple levels (line 12 and 13). Next, the node tries to balance each level of its routing table, starting with the highest level, i.e., its closest neighbors (line 14). Starting with the closest neighbors allows nodes to balance load first locally before they try to balance load on peers further away from them, i.e., on peers stored in lower levels. If a level is underpopulated (line 15), i.e., a level maintains below average many variables, then the node first selects candidate variables out of its local variables (line 16). Candidates are all variables which have a tension at the current level. Next, starting from line 17, the node checks if the tension at the current level for the candidate variable is the strongest tension the variable has considering all levels. This ensures that variables are moved to levels with their strongest tension. This process continues as long as candidates are available and the node has enough variables to move.

Algorithm 5.5 The spring relaxation algorithm

1: $freeVars = length(localVars) - avgLoad/2$;
2: **if** $(freeVars <= 0)$ **then**
3: return;
4: **end if**
5: $undirVars$ = variables having a tension only at one level;
6: **while** $((freeVars > 0)$ **and** $(length(unidirVars) > 0))$ **do**
7: move variable to a peer from the level with the tension;
8: removeFirst($unidirVars$);
9: $freeVars = freeVars - 1$;
10: **end while**
11:
12: $multidirVars$ = variables having tensions to multiple levels;
13: **while** $((currentLoad > avgLoad)$ **and** $(length(multidirVars) > 0))$ **do**
14: **for** $i = routingTable.levels$ to 1 **do**
15:   **if** (level i is underpopulated) **then**
16:    $candidates$ = variables having a tension at level i;
17:    **for** $j = 1$ to $length(candidates)$ **do**
18:     **if** $(candidate(j).tension(i) >= max(candidate(j).tension))$ **then**
19:      move variable to a peer from level i;
20:      remove($multidirVars, candidate(j)$);
21:      $currentLoad = currentLoad - 1$;
22:      **if** $(currentLoad <= avgLoad)$ **then**
23:       break;
24:      **end if**
25:     **end if**
26:    **end for**
27:   **end if**
28: **end for**
29: **end while**

5.5 Evaluation

The presented relaxation algorithm was implemented in Matlab and evaluated with diverse Bayesian networks. We present results for Bayesian networks resembling the topology of random networks, binary trees and scale-free networks with up to 2048 variables, stored in P-Grid networks with up to 512 nodes. As the ratio between number of variables and number of P-Grid nodes is the most dominant factor for the achieved performance, we will present results for 2048 variables in a P-Grid network of 64, 128, 256 and 512 nodes. Considering the motivating scenarios we have in mind for our system, tree-based belief networks and scale-free networks are the most realistic network topologies. The network size and the number of variables is difficult to estimate but the evaluation shows that our approach scales well even though no proof can be given so far. All experiments were repeated 10 times and the figures show the average of those 10 repetitions with their standard deviation. Each time a new belief network was created and variables were assigned randomly to nodes.

5.5.1 Network Topologies

We briefly describe some properties of the network topologies we used for our evaluation. The networks were visualized with the Pajek tool [Bat01] using the 2D Fruchterman Reingold layout for random networks and the Kamada-Kawai layout for the others. Additionally, we show the node degree distribution by sorting nodes according to their node degree and plotting their degree in log-log scale.

Random Networks

We constructed random networks by adding for each node degree/2 edges to other nodes with equal probability to reach the desired average node degree. Figure 5.3 shows a network of 1024 nodes with an average node degree of 4, nodes have between 2 and 10 edges. The degree distribution indicates that most of the nodes have a degree around the average.

Binary Trees

The second used topology is a binary tree with each node having exactly two children excluding leaf nodes. Each node has exactly one parent excluding the root of the tree. Therefore, the node degree varies between 1 and 3 with an average around 2. Figure 5.4 shows a binary tree with 1023 nodes. The degree distribution shows the leave nodes (half of the nodes) at the bottom with 1 edge, the root with 2 edges in the middle and the intermediate nodes with 3 edges at the top.

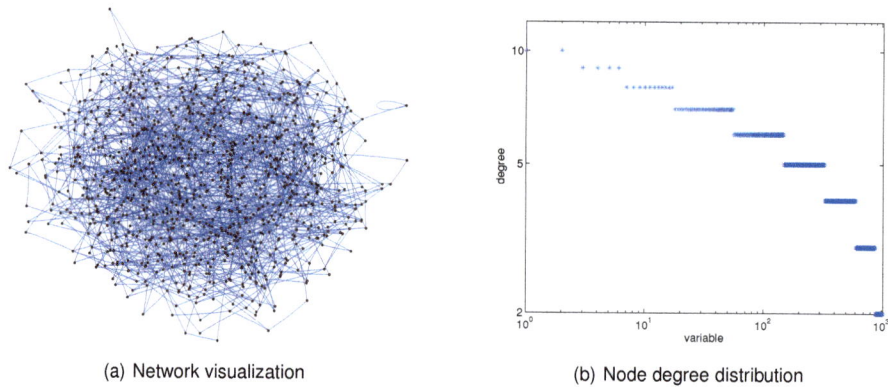

(a) Network visualization (b) Node degree distribution

Figure 5.3: A random network: 1024 nodes with average node degree 4

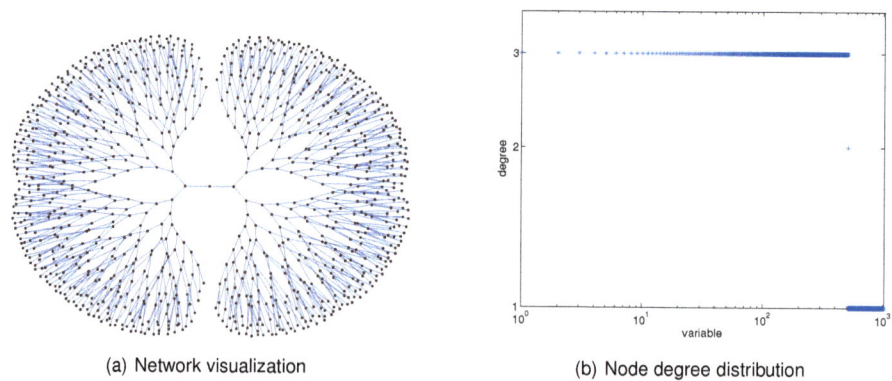

(a) Network visualization (b) Node degree distribution

Figure 5.4: A binary tree: 1023 nodes

Scale-Free Networks

The last used network topology is a scale-free network with the property that the number of links k originating from a given node exhibits a power law distribution $\mathbb{P}(k) \sim k^{-gamma}$. The network is constructed by progressively adding nodes to an existing network and introducing links to existing nodes with preferential attachment so that the probability of linking to a given node i is proportional to the number of existing links k_i that that node has, i.e.,

$$\mathbb{P}(linking\ to\ node\ i) \sim \frac{k_i}{\sum_j k_j}$$

Scale-free networks occur in many areas of science and engineering, e.g., including the topology of web pages (where the nodes are individual web pages and the links are hyperlinks), and are therefore a good model for our scenario. Figure 5.5 presents a scale-free network on the left side with highly connected nodes in the center and loosely connected nodes at the periphery. The node degree varies between 1 and 62 with an average around 4. The node degree distribution follows a power-law distribution.

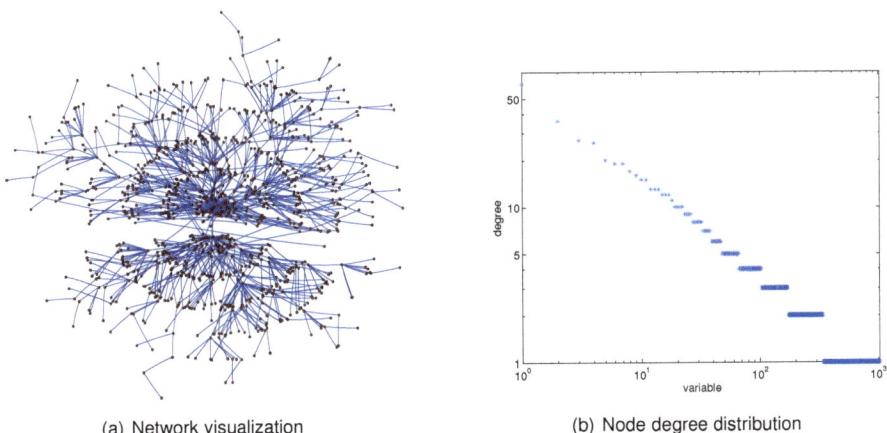

(a) Network visualization (b) Node degree distribution

Figure 5.5: A scale-free network: 1024 nodes with average node degree 4.

5.5.2 Message Reduction

The most interesting evaluation criterion is of course the message reduction achieved by redistributing the variables close to each other in the P-Grid network. Figures 5.7 – 5.9 present the results obtained for the three network topologies. The plots show the achieved message reduction after each iteration of the spring relaxation algorithm by relating the number of required messages to run one iteration of the belief propagation algorithm. At the beginning, 100% of the messages are required, while after each iteration of the spring relaxation algorithm, less messages are required. The message reduction is given with the standard deviation of 10 repeated simulations for each setup. Each run required different numbers of iterations to terminate the relaxation algorithm, therefore the figures show up to 20 iterations, the maximum number of iterations. Most runs finished after around 10 iterations and only a few reached the maximum number of executed iterations. Figure 5.6 shows the distribution of iterations for 100 runs of the relaxation algorithm for 1024 variables in a scale-free network and 128 P-Grid nodes. The figure shows that the algorithm terminated a few times already after 4 iterations and only a few required up to 16 iterations. Almost 90 percent, i.e., 90 runs out of 100 performed, were finished after 10 iterations.

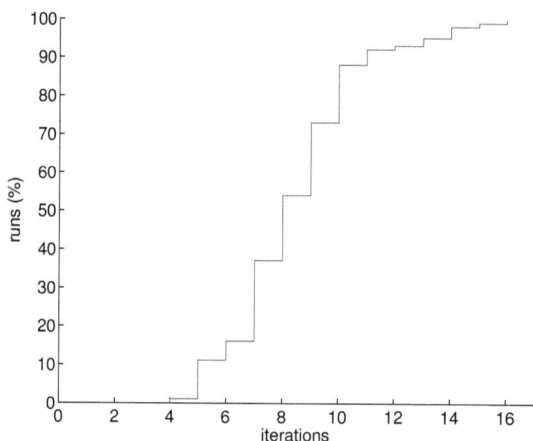

Figure 5.6: Distribution of required iterations of 100 runs for a scale-free network of 1024 variables on 128 P-Grid nodes.

Figure 5.7 shows that the algorithm does not perform well for any evaluated random network as expected. The random correlations of variables in these networks makes it difficult for the spring relaxation algorithm to cluster variables close to each other to reduce the message effort. The figures show that the message reduction increases with larger P-Grid networks but the achieved message reduction does not exceed 25% as achieved for 512 P-Grid nodes. As random networks are not considered as the most realistic model for our use case, this result is tolerable in our opinion. Random networks also require more iterations than other network topologies before the relaxation algorithm terminates, i.e., for 256 nodes, the algorithm even reached the maximum number of iterations (20). The average number of required iterations was between 10 and 15, slightly increasing with the number of P-Grid nodes.

5.5. Evaluation

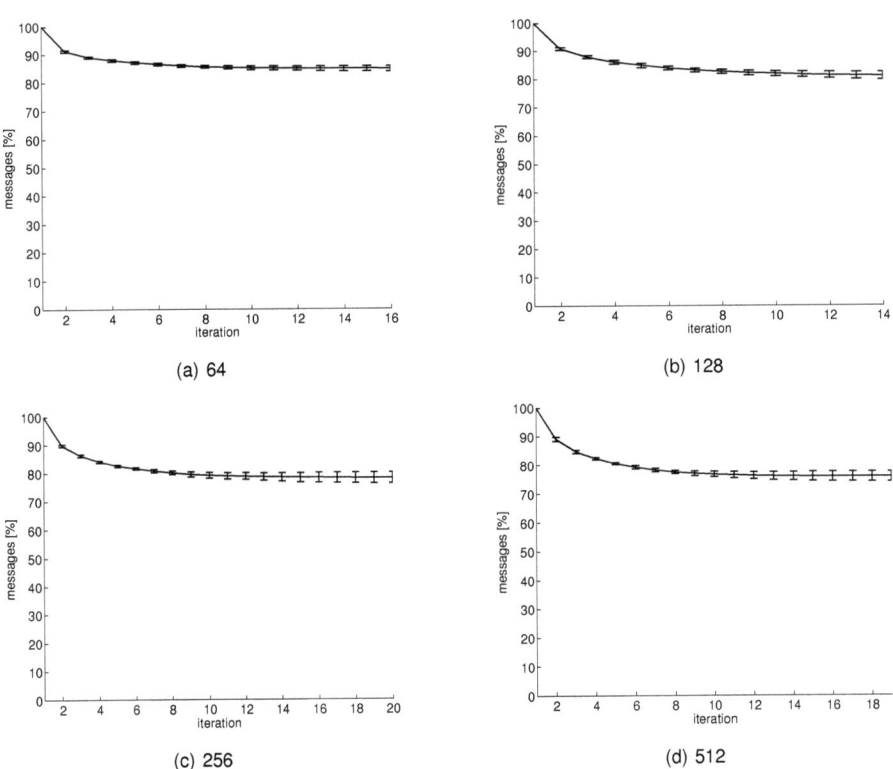

Figure 5.7: Message reduction for random networks with different numbers of P-Grid nodes and 2048 variables.

For binary trees, see Figure 5.8, the relaxation algorithm is able to reduce the number of required messages to around 35% of the initially required number before running the relaxation algorithm. The obtained results seem to be independent of the number of nodes in the P-Grid network. Binary-tree based networks also require less iterations of the relaxation algorithm. The average was for all networks around 10 and none of the 40 runs reached the maximum number of iterations of 20.

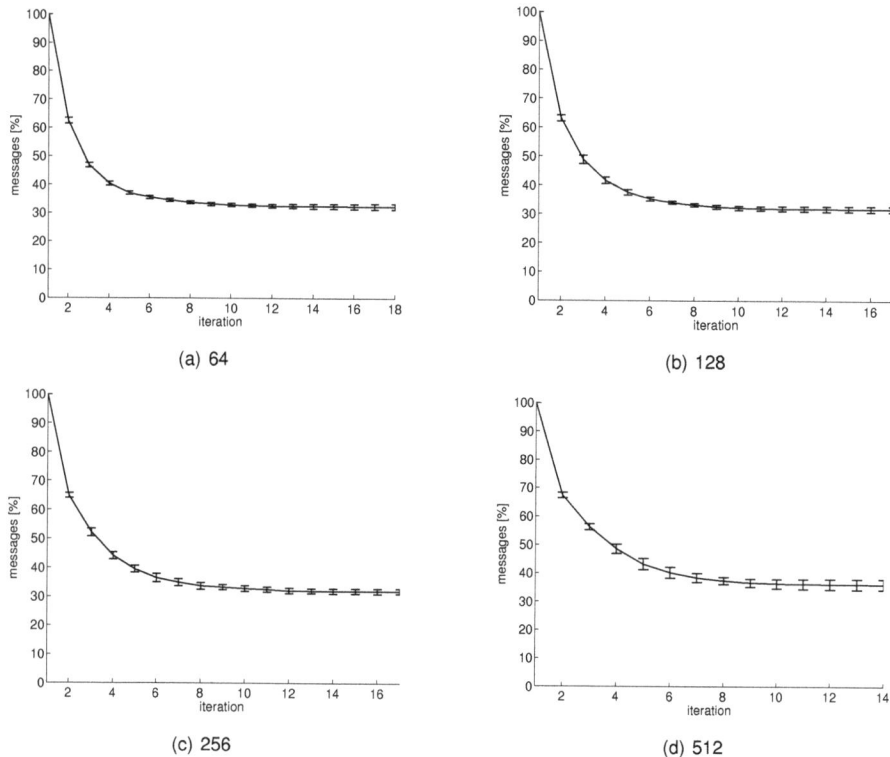

Figure 5.8: Message reduction for binary tree-based networks with different numbers of P-Grid nodes and 2048 variables.

Finally, we observe similar results for the scale-networks as shown in Figure 5.9. The relaxation algorithm is able to reduce the message cost by up to 75% for the smallest P-Grid network of 64 nodes still up to 55% for the largest P-Grid network of 512 nodes. The average number of required iterations is compared to the other two network topologies also smaller, around 10 and even less for larger networks.

The standard deviation is small for all network topologies and network sizes which is an indicator that the algorithm scales well. In all experiments, the algorithm was iterated up 20

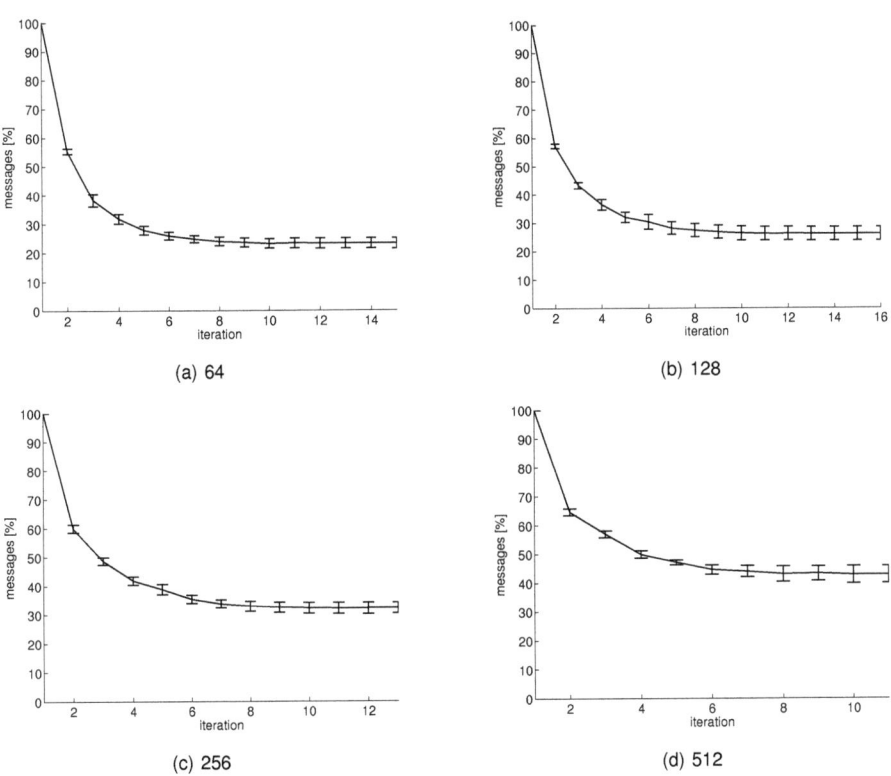

Figure 5.9: Message reduction for scale-free networks with different numbers of P-Grid nodes and 2048 variables.

times but the main reduction is achieved already in the first 10 iterations. Again, this seems to be independent of the number of nodes and number of variables in the networks.

5.5.3 Load Balancing

Apart from the reduction of required messages for the message-passing algorithm, it is important that the storage load of variables is balanced among the participating nodes. The storage load further corresponds to the message load during distributed inference as all variables are accessed exactly once per reasoning iteration. Figures 5.10 – 5.12 present the corresponding results obtained again for random networks, binary trees and scale-free networks. All figures show the average variable load which remains constant over all iterations as the number of variables and nodes does not change. The standard deviation indicates the load balance in the system. Additionally, the maximum load of nodes is given by the dotted line.

Whereas the relaxation algorithm did not perform well for random networks to reduce the number of required messages, it was more successful to balance the load among the nodes, as shown in Figure 5.10. The standard deviation is decreasing for all network sizes as well as the maximum number of variables per node (dotted line). For small networks, where the average variable load is higher compared to larger networks, the maximum load was even less than the maximum load of twice the average load nodes are willing to accept. This limit was more dominant for larger networks.

Similar results were obtained for the binary tree-based networks (see Figure 5.11).

Figure 5.12 shows that scale-free networks cause a slight increase of unbalance and at least one node reaches the maximum tolerable variable load independent of the network size. This is due to the fact that 1 or 2 nodes usually have very high degrees and therefore "attract" a lot of other variables causing the high load at the P-Grid node maintaining such highly-connected variables.

5.5.4 Reduction Effort

The accomplished message reduction for distributed inference achieved by the relaxation algorithms comes with the cost of moving around variables in the P-Grid network requiring one direct message between two peers for each movement. In the following, we will present the number of variables moved at each iteration for P-Grid networks of different size and 2048 variables in the Bayesian network.

Figure 5.13 shows the number of variables moved per iteration of the spring relaxation algorithm for random networks. Most of the variables are moved in the first iterations and more variables have to be moved in larger P-Grid networks as nodes store less variables on average. The variance increase at the end can be explained by the fact that some out of

5.5. Evaluation

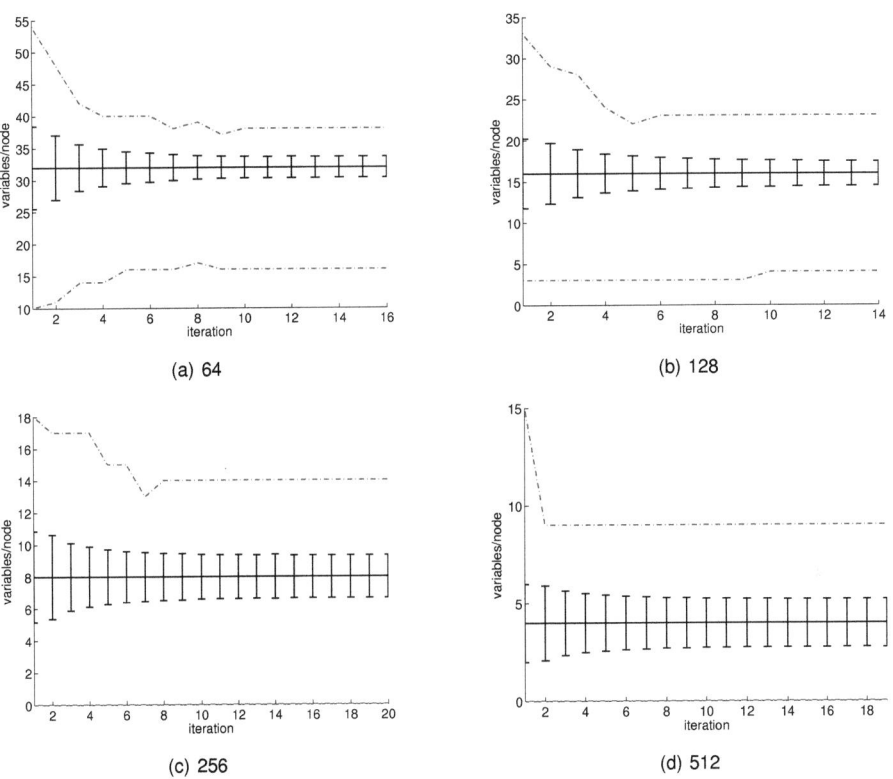

Figure 5.10: Variables per node for random networks with different numbers of P-Grid nodes and 2048 variables.

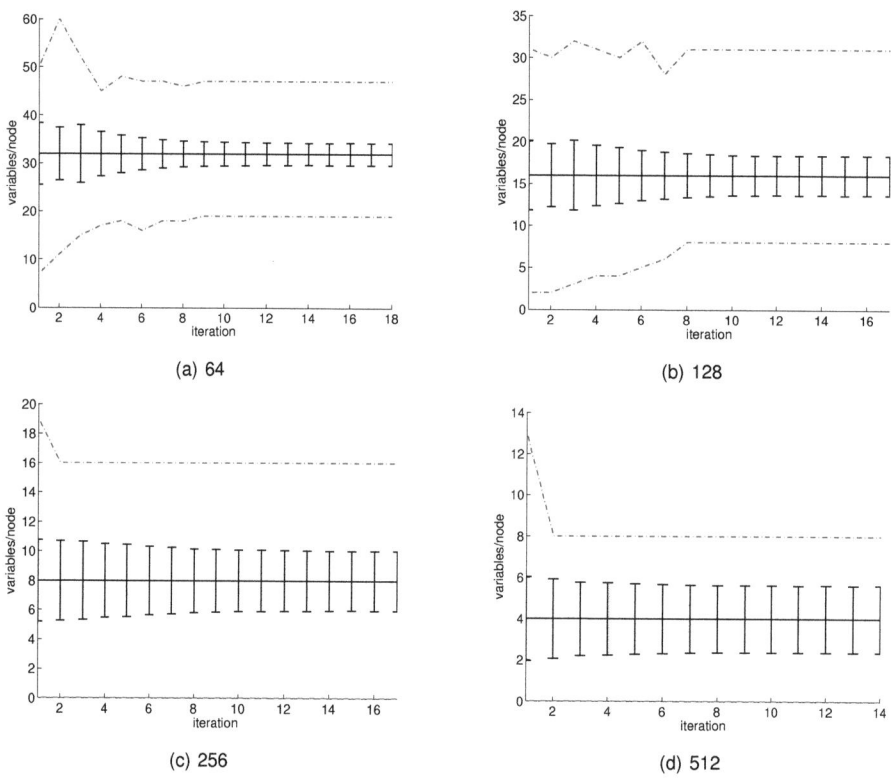

Figure 5.11: Variables per node for binary tree-based networks with different numbers of P-Grid nodes and 2048 variables.

5.5. Evaluation

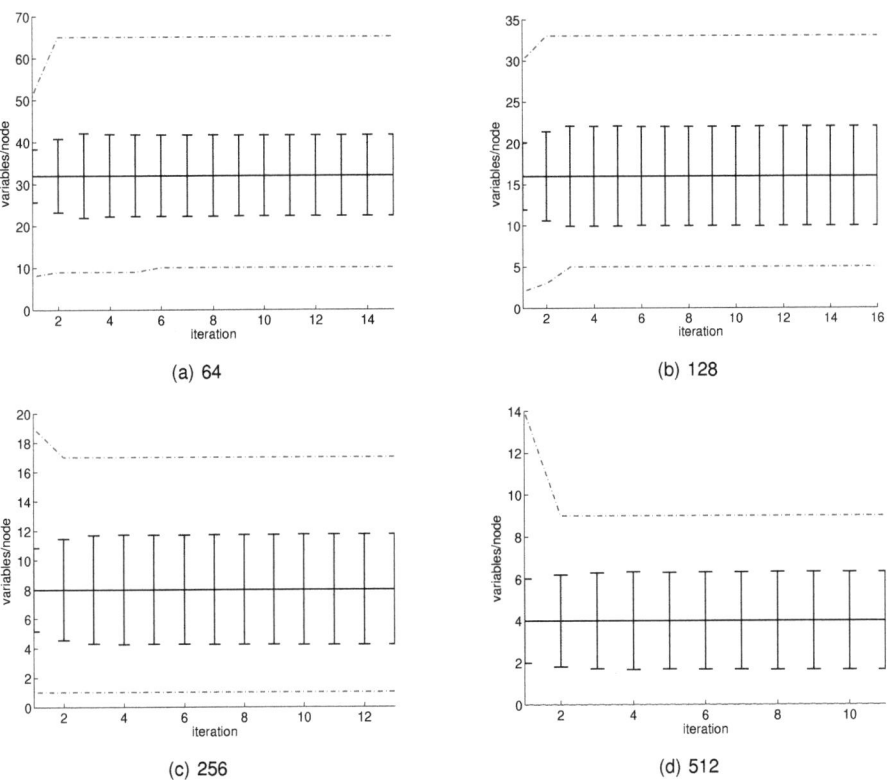

Figure 5.12: Variables per node for scale-free networks with different numbers of P-Grid nodes and 2048 variables.

the 10 runs already terminated and therefore did not move any variables at those iterations anymore. In the end, around 65% of the variables remained at the original node for the 64 node network and around 37% for the P-Grid network with 512 nodes.

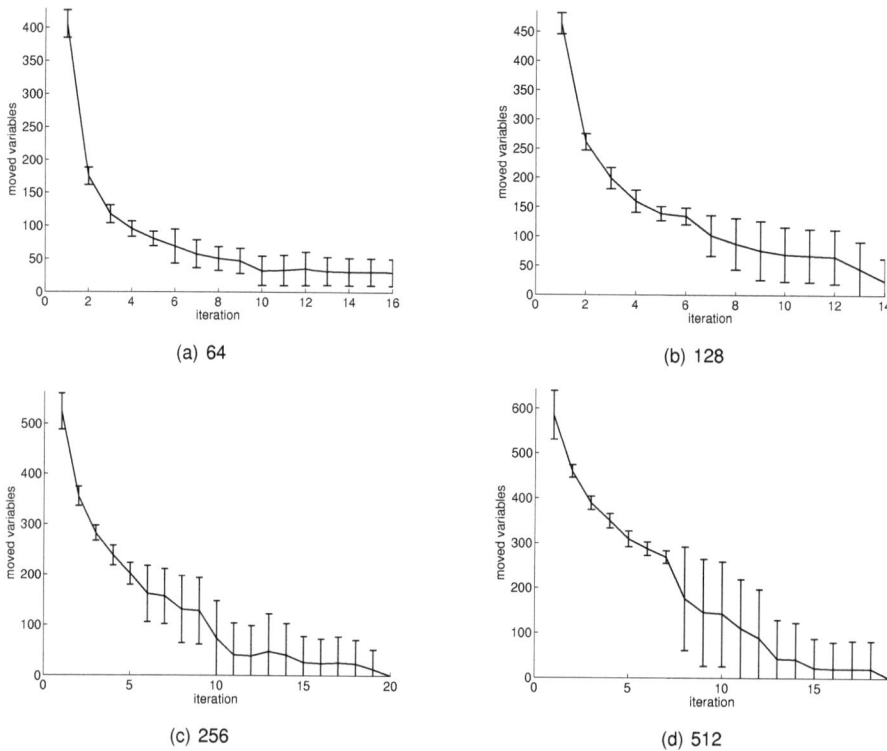

Figure 5.13: Variables moved per iteration for random networks with different numbers of P-Grid nodes and 2048 variables.

More variables are moved if they form a binary tree-based Bayesian network as seen in Figure 5.14). More than twice as many variables are already moved at the first iteration compared to the random networks though the number of moved variables decreases faster. The size of the P-Grid network has less influence as the overall number of variables moved is more or less equal for all network sizes. This is also reflected by the fact that the difference of variables remaining at their originators is smaller, from around 30% for the smallest network to around 26% for the largest evaluated network.

Similar numbers are observed for random networks as shown in Figure 5.15. The number of moved variables is similar to the tree-based networks as well as the fast decrease per iteration. In contradiction to the other two network topologies, only 22% of the variables

5.5. Evaluation

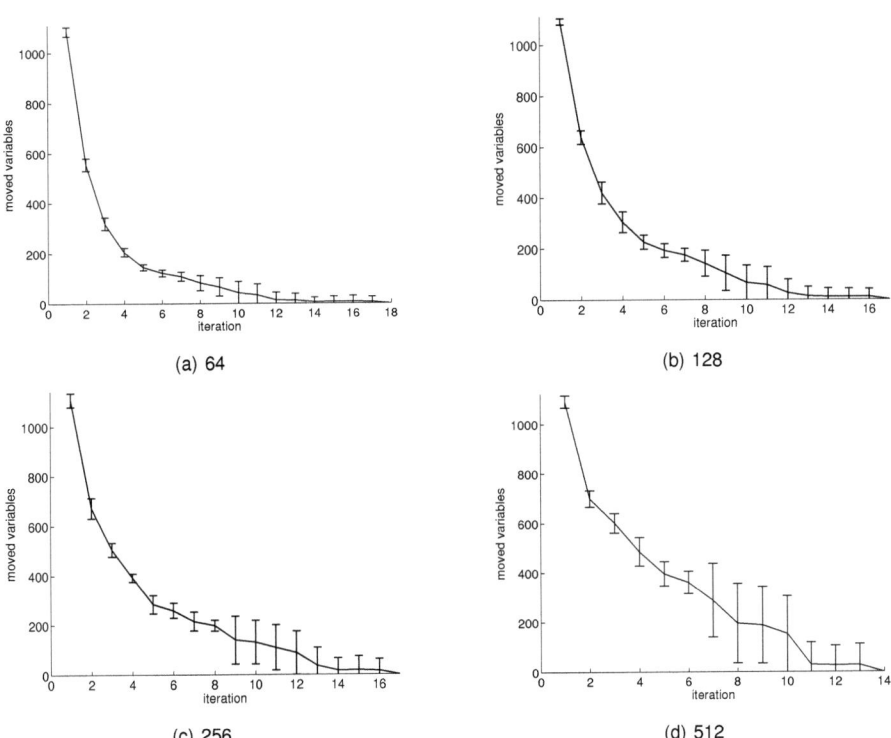

Figure 5.14: Variables moved per iteration for binary tree-based networks with different numbers of P-Grid nodes and 2048 variables.

remained at the orginating peer for the P-Grid network with 64 nodes and around 33% variables in largest network of 512 nodes. This result proves once more that the relaxation algorithm is able to cluster variables close to each other better if the ratio between variables in the Bayesian network and number of P-Grid nodes is larger, i.e., on average more variables are mainted per P-Grid node.

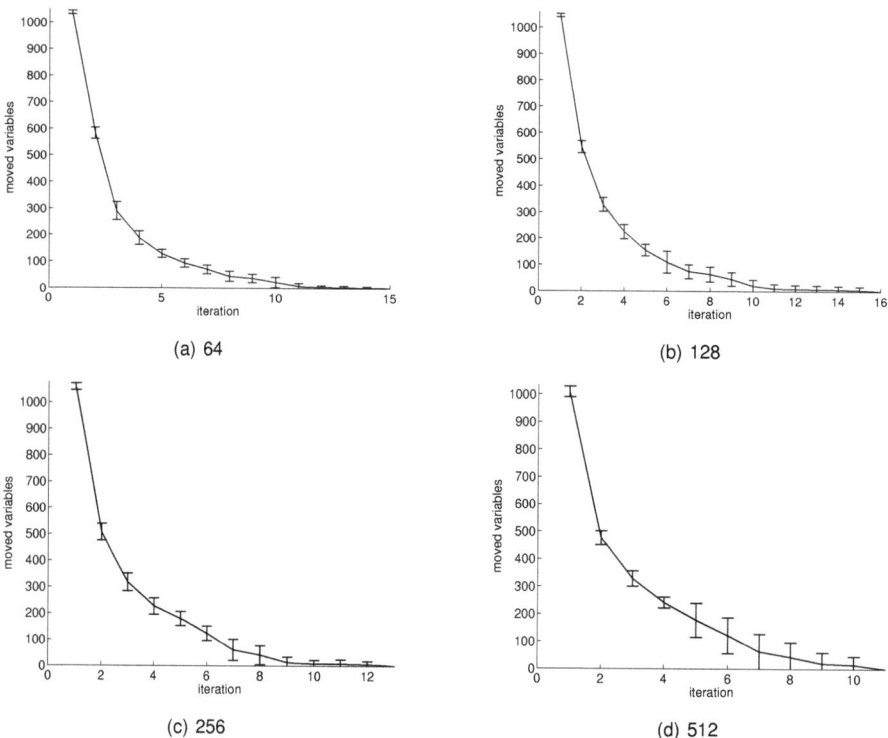

Figure 5.15: Variables moved per iteration for scale-free networks with different numbers of P-Grid nodes and 2048 variables.

5.5.5 Discussion

The results obtained from the Matlab evaluations look very promising. The relaxation algorithm is able to move correlated variables close to each other to reduce the message cost for distributed inference down to 30% of the original cost for some network topologies. Binary tree-based and scale-free network based Bayesian networks enable the largest message reductions by moving most of the variables away from their original nodes. Most of them are moved in the first iterations and the required communication effort will pay-off soon if the Bayesian network remains unchanged and a lot of inferences are performed. The performed evaluation also shows that the presented relaxation algorithm terminates already after a few iterations and only in few cases had to be stopped by the set maximum iteration limit of 20.

5.6 Related Work

Generalized Belief Propagation [YFW00] reduces the number of messages by clustering correlated variables together and sending only one message between those clusters. This approach has three drawbacks: (i) the message sizes increase exponentially ($number\ of\ states^{nodes\ in\ the\ cluster}$) because the exchanged messages now contain the joint probabilities of all nodes and states in the cluster; (ii) the complexity of processing the messages and beliefs at nodes also increases considerable with increasing number of nodes in a cluster; (iii) it is not obvious for us how clusters are formed in a distributed way without central coordination and knowledge which is essential in peer-to-peer systems. Though Generalized Belief Propagation provides more accurate beliefs than Pearl's belief propagation, it is currently not applicable for large-scale networks.

Reference [PGM05] presents an inference architecture for sensor networks based on message-passing on a junction tree. For this approach, a distributed algorithm is first used to form a spanning tree of nodes which is used later to construct the junction tree for inference. Junction trees group variables into cliques and their size determines the computation costs at nodes whereas the separator size between cliques determines the communication costs. The approach was evaluated with 54 sensor motes in a local experiment showing spanning tree optimizations and the communication costs of the junction tree. Inference on junction trees is exact and always results in the exact marginals at the cost of requiring building a tree with larger messages and higher computation costs. Belief propagation only provides approximate inference on lower overheads.

Spring relaxation is used in various domains and we will only present two examples for peer-to-peer systems. Vivaldi [DCKM04] is a decentralized network coordinate system using a spring-mass model to position nodes in a virtual coordinate system according to their latencies. Nodes run the distributed spring relaxation algorithm as soon as a new latency measurement was performed to reduce the distance error between nodes. An application of Vivaldi is described in [PSW+04] to optimize the path in stream-based overlay networks. Services are placed on nodes close to each other in the virtual latency space.

5.7 Conclusions

This chapter has shown a clustering approach for probabilistically correlated data items in a Bayesian network used for distributed inference. We used the data correlations given by the Bayesian network to reorganize the index of the structured overlay of P-Grid. Variables were moved close to their correlated variables and if possible even on the same peer. The consequence of this step for distributed inference is that less messages have to be sent in the network to perform the reasoning step. The presented evaluation has shown that, depending on the topology of the Bayesian network, a reduction of more than 50% can be achieved by our relaxation algorithm.

Chapter 6

Multi-Term Queries

A common practice in current information systems is the use of multiple keywords to search for information, as currently very successfully demonstrated by web search engines. The idea behind it is that information, such as web pages on the Internet, are indexed by distinctive keywords which are used later to resolve user queries consisting of one or multiple keywords. The simplicity and user-friendliness of this approach is responsible for its success as users do not have to struggle with complex query languages. But this simplicity on the user side leads to several challenging problems the field of information retrieval deals with. These problems have recently also gained popularity in the P2P community in the context of P2P web search engines.

The P2P community has tried to adopt approaches from information retrieval to build distributed information systems and P2P web search engines. The basic infrastructure of one of these systems will be presented later in this chapter. We will not focus on the indexing part, i.e., how distinctive keywords are extracted from documents, and rather focus on how a structured overlay network can be (re-)organized to efficiently resolve multi-term queries on the indexed information. Multi-term queries require to search for multiple keywords and return the intersection of the multiple result sets, i.e., all documents containing all given keywords. In structured overlay networks we have the problem that the multiple keywords are usually not maintained by the same peer requiring to gather all documents matching all keywords at one peer first before an intersection of the result set can be returned, if a complete answer including all matching answers is desired.

This chapter first presents an overview of how such intersections can be currently processed in distributed systems using a distributed index. We will then reuse our relaxation algorithm from Chapter 5 to reorganize the distributed index to more efficiently process multi-term queries on a single overlay index. An evaluation of the optimized algorithm with a real-life data set is given at the end of this chapter.

6.1 Motivation

A structured overlay network maintains a distributed index stored at peers in the network holding information about their shared data. The distributed index thereby holds references to the actually shared data remaining at providing peers. Whereas this approach works well for single-key lookups, multi-term queries require to intersect multiple result sets before a final result can be returned. The distribution of the index offers several ways of how such an intersection can be implemented.

Local Join A local join executes two independent queries and joins both received result sets at the end locally at the query initiator. This approach is basically supported by any structured overlay as it only requires local post-processing of queries already supported by the system. Another advantage is that the index itself does not require to store any additional information than the index term, i.e., if documents are indexed then each keyword is indexed only with a reference to the document containing the index term, ignoring all the other distinguishing terms. Although this approach is simple and easy to realize, the main drawback is the overhead induced by the multiple independent queries. For example, a query with two keywords leads to two independent queries to be resolved for each of the keywords. The two result sets will contain documents matching the corresponding query term and have to be transmitted to the requesting peer. The local join builds the intersection of these result sets and returns all documents present in both result sets. In case all documents contain only one of the keywords and not the other, the final result set will be empty. The two transfered intermediate result sets could have therefore be avoided. Figure 6.1 illustrates query resolution for two keywords involving two responding peers and local merging of received result sets.

To reduce communication costs for local joins, distributed top-k queries [MTW05, ZTZ07] can be used, i.e., find and return only the k best matching objects for a given query. Top-k queries rely on ranking operations to rank documents locally and globally, leading to additional overhead.

Sequential Join A query plan [PM02, ZS05] can be used to resolve multiple keywords of a query sequentially by forwarding the query and their intermediate results along all peers responsible for the keywords. The query plan should start at the most selective keyword to minimize the traffic of query resolution as only matching items are forwarded with the query to the peer responsible for the second keyword. The advantage of this approach is that the query initiator only receives one final response containing all items matching all keyword criteria. Further, the number of items matching the first resolved keyword bounds the size of sets transfered as following peers can only eliminate candidate results. The drawback of this approach is that a query and its intermediate results have to travel between multiple

6.1. Motivation

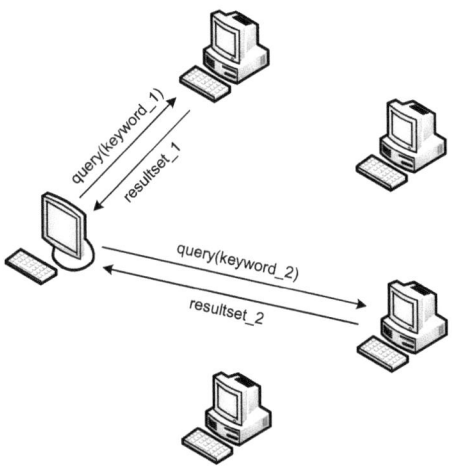

Figure 6.1: Query resolution for two keyword terms using local join

peers before a result is returned to the initiator. This causes a long delay for the query initiator as no results are returned before the last keyword was resolved. If the order in which keywords are resolved is not chosen wisely, i.e., the most selective keywords first, then this approach can further cause a high network overhead if intermediate results are relatively large compared to the final set. Finally, a P2P system would have to support query plan resolution which is not trivial to implement. Figure 6.2 illustrates query resolution for two keywords by a query plan passing along the received query with intermediate results till all query terms are resolved. The resulting answer set is returned to the query originator by the peer responsible for the last resolved query term.

Remote Join The problem of resolving multi-term queries was already studied for distributed database systems using approaches for data fragmentation as introduced in Section 2.2. Data is distributed on multiple physical devices connected by a network similar to the setup of P2P systems, though distributed databases are usually under central control. Nevertheless, a common approach is to look at queries issued against the database to identify relationships amongst data sets and cluster strongly correlated data fragments on the same physical machine. Therefore, all keywords of a multi-term query may be answered by a single machine enabling the remote join of results. A remote join is only possible if all necessary data is stored at one single peer, i.e., one peer is responsible for the queried attributes. This means for a multi-term query that the peer is responsible for all keywords of the query and can return result sets for each of them. Therefore, the peer is also able to perform the join directly before returning multiple records. From a distributed system's point

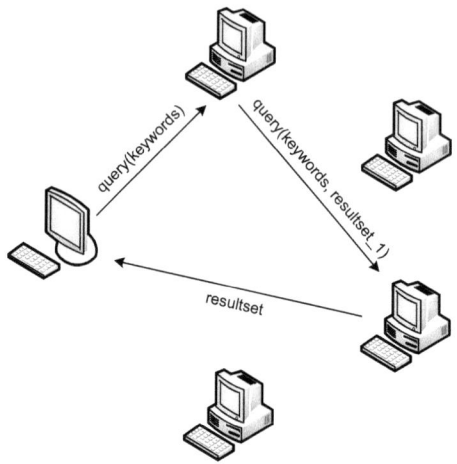

Figure 6.2: Query resolution for two keyword terms using a query plan

of view, a remote join is the optimal solution for multi-term queries as communication costs are minimal. As the answering peer has already all the necessary data to perform the join locally, e.g., in its own database, the resulting data set transmitted back to the query initiator will be the final set. No additional message respectively data has to be transmitted and therefore no bandwidth is wasted. Figure 6.3 illustrates query resolution for two keywords by a remote join at the peer responsible for both keywords resulting in only one final result set.

6.2 Related Work

The resolution of multi-term queries in structured overlay networks is currently mainly studied in the context of P2P web search engines, i.e., P2P full-text search.

[SA06] introduces the idea of query-driven indexing of multi-term queries using a Distributed Cache Table (DCT). DCT populates the storage space provided by participating peers with result sets (caches) for carefully chosen queries and uses this data to answer further queries. Each cache stores a list of document digests, containing an unique document identifier and a list of terms extracted from the document, and hence can be used to resolve any query if its result set is contained in the list. Peers maintain those caches which are frequently used to answer queries and consume little space. The reasoning behind the cache size restriction is related to limited storage and traffic consumption and refers to the approach that indexes discriminative term sets (queries in their case) associated with result sets of constrained size [PLR+06]. DCT performs an adaptive selection of queries to

6.2. Related Work

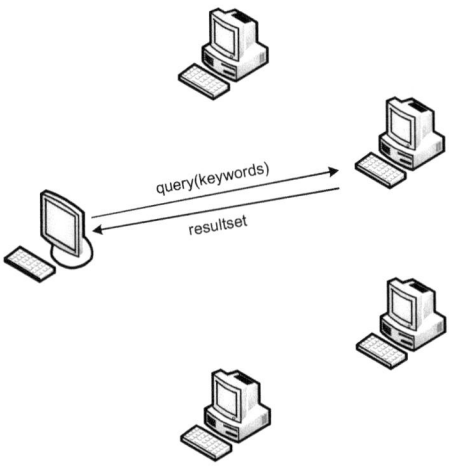

Figure 6.3: Query resolution for two keyword terms using remote join

cache, based on the monitored query statistics taking into account limited storage capacity with the goal of minimizing the number of cache-misses. In particular, each peer runs a greedy algorithm leading to a global quasi-optimal cache selection. Therefore, DCT adopts a *query-adaptive indexing strategy*.

A DCT can be built on top of any structured overlay as it relies on the single term index offered by all these systems. The goal of DCT is to add an additional cache for frequently queried multi-term queries so that these queries can be directly answered from the cache and do not have to be composed by separate single term queries (by a local join at the initiating peer). The implementation of the query-driven indexing is complex and requires the knowledge about query statistics to decide which multi-term queries have to be cached. DCT tries to optimize the utilization of the available cache size in the system which means maximizing the number of queries which can be answered by the cache directly. Details about how query terms are selected for caching can be found in [SA06] and in follow up publications like [SLP+07a, SLP+07b] where this approach is used in a distributed web retrieval setup. Caches for multi-term queries are maintained by peers of the P2P system and the overlay has to store locations of caches and update these regularly. It therefore builds a meta-index defining the position of a cache for a multi-term query, to which such a query is forwarded to be answered.

As a caching technique is used, the paper focuses on query hit rates and resulting query traffic reductions. The results show that a high rate of cache hits is able to considerable reduce the required traffic for query resolution. The main drawback of this approach though is that caches can be out-of-date and need to be refreshed regularly. Further, caches require additional storage space (even if "unused" space is used) which has to be provided by peers. [SLP+07a] further shows that caches are likely not to hold all relevant hits for a query if the query frequency of a term couple is below the threshold. Our approach does not rely on caches and therefore always has all hits available for a query, if desired. In our case, the query frequency threshold only has an influence on traffic effort and not on result quality (*recall*).

[BMT+06, MBN+06] addresses a similar problem of result quality in terms of *recall*, i.e., the fraction of relevant documents returned by a query. Their two-step approach uses a DHT to maintain lists of peers holding documents containing terms. Each entry contains the IP address of the peer together with statistics to calculate IR-style measures for a term to identify the most promising peers to submit a query. Term correlations are learned from query logs and propagated among peers mostly in a piggy-backed manner. This information is used by peers to publish not only statistical information for single terms in their documents, but further for highly correlated term combinations. These statistics can then be used during query resolution to identify prominent peers for (subsets of) multiple terms to reduce the number of contacted peers, respectively, to increase the relative recall. The two-step approach presented in [BMT+06, MBN+06] is different from our one-step approach as we resolve queries directly on a distributed index whereas they use a distributed index, and identified term correlations, to select candidate peers for local query resolution.

6.3 Query-Driven Clustering

The main drawback of the approach presented in [SA06] is its requirement to maintain caches for popular multi-term queries. We propose a slightly different solution for the same problem relying on methods presented in [SA06]. Based on the fragmentation techniques used in distributed databases, we propose to relocate index items based on their probability to occur together in multi-term queries. In distributed database systems, query executions are analyzed to identify data segments processed frequently together. While this can be done by a central component in distributed databases, P2P networks require a distributed solution for this problem. DCT proposes a solution that is applicable for any structured overlay. We will use it in the following. The query statistics allow us to build a probabilistic network of frequently queried terms. The edges between the nodes, i.e., query terms, of the probabilistic network represent correlations amongst query terms induced by multi-term queries. The strength of the probabilistic correlation, i.e., the strength of the edge, depends on how often the two terms are queried jointly. The probabilistic network therefore represents the most queried keywords and their strongest correlations with other keywords, as derived from the query statistics.

Instead of building a cache for frequently queried terms, we intend to move and cluster

6.3. Query-Driven Clustering

index items directly in the structured overlay network so that queries can be answered by peers directly. The advantage we see compared to the DCT approach is that entries in the cache can be out of date and need to be updated frequently. Our approach does not require any active maintenance for index entries and requires only a similar meta-index as DCT to lookup relocated index entries. The remaining question is how and where index items are clustered so that as many multi-term queries as possible can be answered by a single peer, i.e., if the peer is responsible for all terms of a query, or at least by as less peers as possible.

6.3.1 Architecture

Our approach is based on the distributed inference approach on top of structured overlay networks and their spring relaxation algorithm to cluster correlated data, as presented in Chapter 5. We adjust the inference architecture and the relaxation algorithm in the following ways to meet our new requirements to support multi-term queries:

Indexing We use P-Grid to index shared documents. Each term is indexed separately and can be found through P-Grid's single-key lookup mechanism. Therefore single-term queries are handled as usual by P-Grid. Additionally, index entries are allowed to move around in P-Grid and can be maintained by a different peer, i.e., a peer currently not responsible for the hash value of a term. In case index entries for a term have been relocated, a reference to this new partition/peer is maintained at the originally responsible peer. Query resolution for relocated terms therefore requires one more hop. For very frequently queried terms, we can envision a caching mechanism to avoid this one extra hop if desired.

Monitoring To identify frequently queried terms, we have to monitor and maintain keyword statistics for each query term. The statistics provide information about how often a query term was queried (recently) and how often other query terms were queried (recently) jointly. These statistics can be maintained at peers responsible for keywords and exchanged amongst them to calculate the probability that two query terms occur jointly in a query. This probability can then be used as correlation strength in a probabilistic network, similar to the Bayesian networks used in Chapter 5. A vertex represents a unique query term whereas an edge represents a correlation between two query terms. The correlation strength is calculated in the following way:

$$corr(t_i, t_j) = \frac{f(t_{ij})}{f(t_i) + f(t_j) - f(t_{ij})}$$

with $f(t_i)$ and $f(t_j)$ representing the term frequencies of term t_i and t_j, and $f(t_{i,j})$ the frequency of joint occurrences of term t_i and t_j in queries. The joint access frequency $f(t_{i,j})$

can be monitored at peers responsible for t_i and t_j as a multi-term query always holds all keywords of a query.

Relaxation The spring relaxation algorithm presented in Section 5.4 dealt with variables and their correlations of equal strength, i.e., each correlation was equally important to relax. In our case, correlations amongst query terms are associated with a probability, i.e., how likely two query terms occur together. Therefore, some correlations are more "important" to relax than others as a stronger correlation means that this correlation occurs more frequent. Favoring strong correlations during the relaxation leads to overall lower lookup costs as they have a larger influence on the overall number of messages and data exchanged in the system. The relaxation algorithm was therefore adopted to move variables, i.e., terms, with stronger correlations first by ordering uni-directional and multi-directional variables according to their correlation strength.

6.4 Evaluation

We evaluated our optimized relaxation algorithm with a Java simulator and network topologies derived from a real-world data set. We used the Wikipedia[1] document collection from the end of 2004 with more than 3 million articles and a collection of more than 4 million queries. We filtered out several queries and query terms, such as common stop words, as they are not interesting for our evaluation (e.g., stop words occur too often to be indexed). The remaining queries and query terms were used to obtain the most frequently queried keywords together with their frequently jointly accessed query terms. We are only interested in this subset of query terms as their frequent repetition allows us to optimize their access. As these terms occur frequently, they also have a high influence on the overall access costs compared to infrequent query terms. For example, [Wie83] has shown that the most active 20% of user queries account for 80% of the total data access.

We first analyzed the query log from Wikipedia to identify all keywords and their correlations. Keywords are correlated if they occur together in a query. We extracted all correlated terms as binary relations. These relations are further associated with their corresponding query frequency, i.e., how often a relation occurred within the query log. Figure 6.4 shows the frequency distribution of 87232 terms we found in the query log, and the frequency distribution of the corresponding 803222 term relations. The figure shows that the distributions resemble a power-law distribution with a few terms/relations occurring very often while most of the them occur rarely.

The here observed distributions further confirm our assumptions made in Chapter 5, that scale-free networks following a power-law distribution are a very good model for our

---

[1] http://wikipedia.com/

6.4. Evaluation

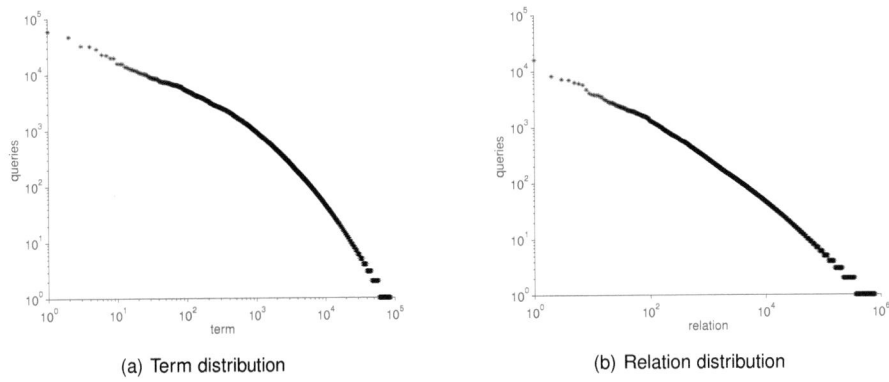

(a) Term distribution (b) Relation distribution

Figure 6.4: Distribution of term and relation frequencies (log-log scale)

evaluation of distributed inference.

6.4.1 Probabilistic Networks

Our evaluation focuses on the most frequently queried terms respectively query relations. We extracted the most frequently queried term relations. We chose the most 1024, 2048, and 4096 queried terms to build a probabilistic network. Each term is represented by a node in the probabilistic network, and each edge stands for one of the most queried term relations. The strength of an edge is defined by the strength of a relation, i.e., the query frequency as defined in the previous section. Figure 6.5 shows the probabilistic networks for the 1024 respectively 2048 most queried terms.

6.4.2 Term Posting Lists

To evaluate the lookup costs for our top-k queried terms and relations, we associated each term with its corresponding posting list. A posting list is a list of references to documents returned by a query. In our case the posting lists of a term contained references to Wikipedia articles in which the term occurred. Common terms have longer posting lists as they occur in more documents than distinctive keywords. For example, stop words are characterized by very long posting lists as they occur in almost all indexed documents, and are therefore ignored during indexing. We assume that users are interested in a complete answer set for queries, i.e., all documents matching the query. This requires to return all entries in a posting list. A lookup for a common term with a long posting list is therefore more expensive in terms of network traffic than a lookup for a term with a short posting list. The same holds of course for multi-term queries returning the intersection of all term posting lists involved in

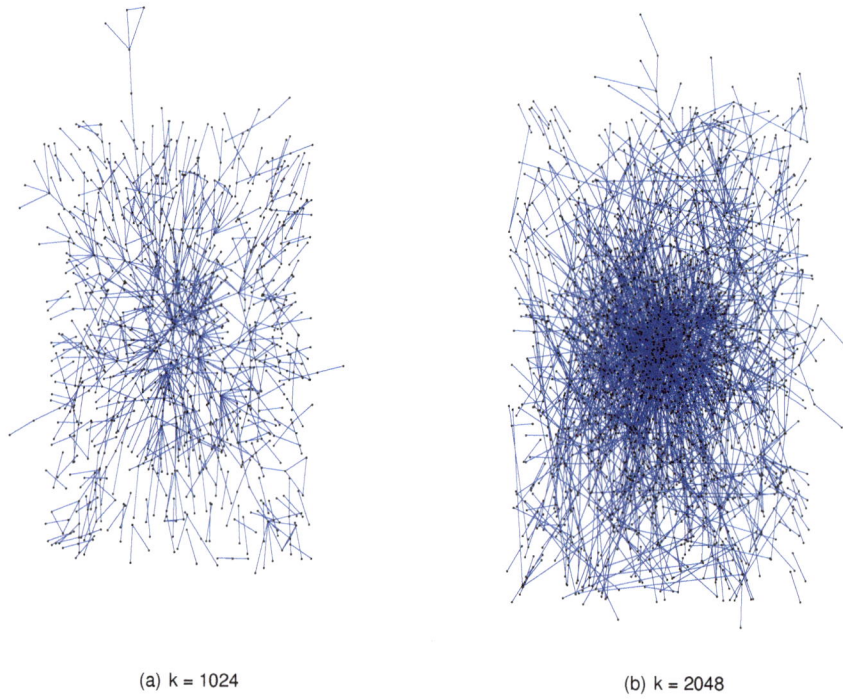

(a) k = 1024   (b) k = 2048

Figure 6.5: Probabilistic network of term relations for the top-k queried terms

6.4. Evaluation

the query.

Figure 6.6 shows the distribution of posting list sizes for all terms occurring in the Wikipedia query log. The figure follows again approximately a power-law distribution with a few terms occurring in many documents whereas most terms occur only in a few documents.

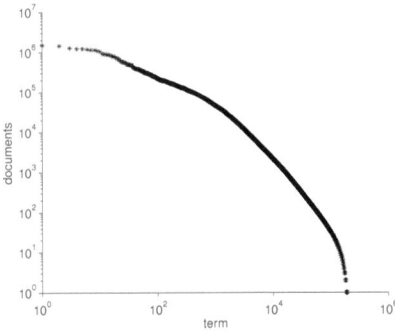

Figure 6.6: Distribution of term posting list sizes

6.4.3 Lookup Costs

The most important metric in our evaluation is the lookup cost reduction. We therefore count the number of references to documents transmitted over the network, based on the posting lists of terms. For example, the cost of a multi-term query with two keywords stored at two different peers is the sum of the posting list sizes of the two terms. The cost of the same query with the two keywords stored at the same peer is however the size of the intersection of the two posting lists. We are therefore only interested in multi-term queries with multiple keywords of our probabilistic network. The lookup costs of single-term queries always correspond to the posting list size of the queried term. Furthermore, infrequent terms, which are not considered in our probabilistic network, are not evaluated as their lookup costs are not reduced by the relaxation algorithm. The number of remaining queries, i.e., queries for the top-k queried keywords, used during our simulation depends on the size of the probabilistic network and increases with the number of considered terms as follows:

terms	queries
1024	22690
2048	48219
4096	89325

We store the probabilistic network for the top 1024, 2048, and 4096 queried term pairs in P-Grid networks of size 16, 32, 64, 128, 256, and 512 nodes. The average number of terms per node varies according to $|terms|/|nodes|$. Our optimized spring relaxation algorithm tries to cluster correlated terms on the same P-Grid node within 10 iterations. We set this limit as we did not observe any further improvements with more iterations during our experiments. In fact, most of the relations were already relaxed after one or two iterations of our algorithm. We ran 10 independent simulations for all setup combinations (varying number of terms and varying P-Grid network sizes) and present the averages and standard deviations of them in the following.

Figure 6.7 presents the achieved lookup cost reduction. The figures show the average lookup costs (and standard deviations) at the end of our relaxation algorithm for all sizes of probabilistic and P-Grid networks. The costs are the sum of all posting list sizes required to transmit to resolve all considered queries. Our baseline cost (100%) is the cost of query resolution before relaxation. As terms are assigned to P-Grid nodes randomly before relaxation, some related nodes already happen to be stored at the same node. This means that our baseline cost is already by up to 20% lower than the maximal lookup cost, i.e., no related terms are stored at the same node. The difference between maximal cost and initial cost is higher for higher ratios of terms per nodes, i.e., the two costs are almost the same, e.g., for 1024 terms stored on 512 nodes. We further provide the minimal lookup costs of a centralized solution, i.e., all terms are stored at one peer and only the intersection of all posting lists of queried terms are transfered. The minimal lookup costs can only be achieved if all term relations are relaxed, i.e., all multi-term queries can be processed by a remote join. The percentage of relaxed relations is also given in Figure 6.7. The figures show two trends:

(i) the relaxation and therewith the lookup cost reduction decreases if the ratio of terms per node decreases, i.e., the average load of nodes. This is explainable by the fact that a smaller ratio gives a P-Grid node less opportunities to move terms around and relax the system as it is only responsible for a few terms. Further, nodes cannot store more than $2 \cdot average\ load$ terms and therefore not store all related terms on one node. Note that the average load is relatively small in our experiments due to memory limitations. We expect that the ratio is higher in a real-world setup as real nodes are able to store more terms than nodes during our simulation.

(ii) the relaxation algorithm seems to perform better for term pairs with higher query frequency as considered in smaller probabilistic networks. The average lookup cost reduction is higher for smaller network sizes, independent of the P-Grid network size and terms per node ratio. This is explainable by the fact, that term pairs with higher query frequency have a higher impact on the lookup cost. Secondly, larger networks have more weaker correlations, which are more difficult to relax, and in total still have a considerable influence on the overall lookup costs. Figure 6.8 shows the absolute numbers for our relaxation algorithm in terms of

6.4. Evaluation

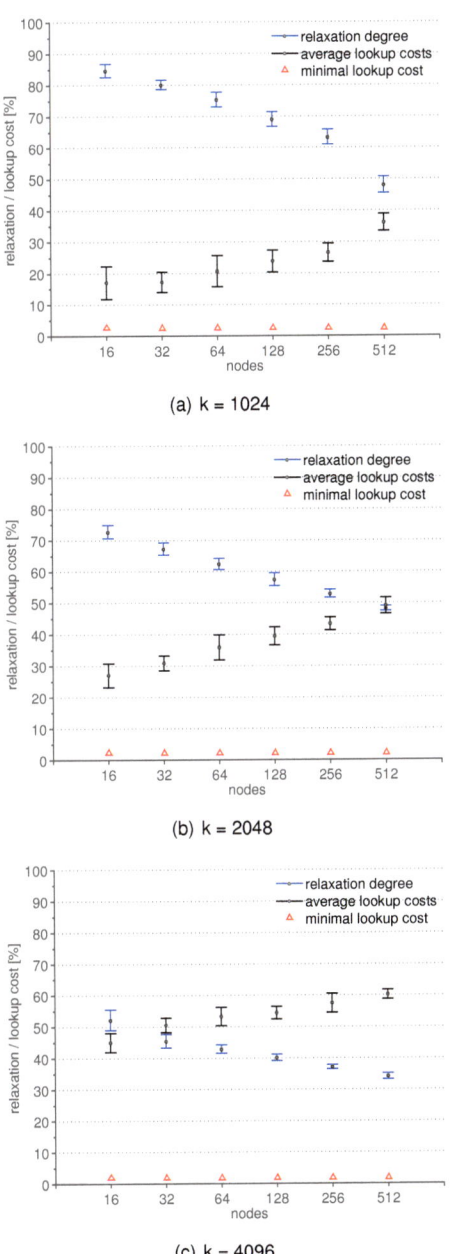

Figure 6.7: Lookup cost reduction and relaxation for the top-k queried terms

posting list transmitted for query resolution. The maximum number refers to the case when all related terms are stored at different peers, what is the case for P-Grid networks with 512 nodes before relaxation. The initial setup (after terms are assigned to P-Grid nodes) reduces the lookup cost for smaller P-Grid networks, e.g., for 16 P-Grid nodes. The figure shows that the cost after relaxation (relaxed) is smaller than the initial costs for all term network sizes and the P-Grid network of 16 and 512 nodes. Finally, the absolute cost reduction remains constant with growing probabilistic term network size, although the relative cost reduction as shown in Figure 6.7 decreases with growing network sizes.

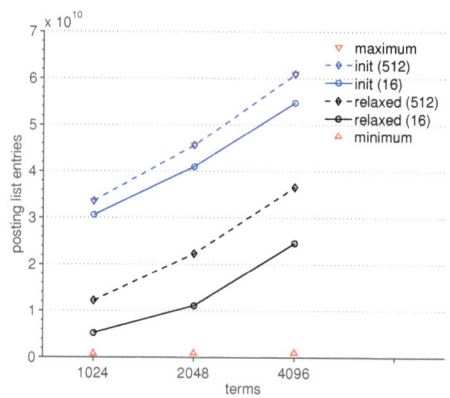

Figure 6.8: Posting list entries transfered for query resolution

6.4.4 Relaxation Effort

An interesting metric for our simulation is of course the invested effort to relax our probabilistic network and achieve lookup cost reductions. The relaxation costs comprise the cost of our relaxation algorithm to relocate terms, and the cost to relocate the posting lists of terms, if they were relocated, at the end of relaxation. The relaxation algorithm only requires small messages changing references in the P-Grid index and is therefore negligible compared to the relocation of large posting lists. The total number of posting lists and the number of relocated ones depends on the number of terms in the probabilistic network. Table 6.1 shows the total posting list size, i.e., the sum of all posting lists of terms, and the number of relocated ones at the end of the relaxation algorithm. If we compare these numbers with the absolute lookup costs presented in Figure 6.8, we can conclude that the relaxation effort is a magnitude smaller than the cost reduction by our relaxation algorithm, and therefore tolerable.

6.4. Evaluation

terms	total posting list size	mean relocated size
1024	$2.29 \cdot 10^9$	$1.63 \cdot 10^9$
2048	$3.96 \cdot 10^9$	$3.42 \cdot 10^9$
4096	$7.60 \cdot 10^9$	$6.98 \cdot 10^9$

Table 6.1: Number of relocated posting list entries

6.4.5 Load Balancing

Finally, we have to evaluate the impact of our relaxation algorithm on load balancing in the P-Grid network. We first look at variations of the term load from the aspired average load per node. Figure 6.9 shows the variations from the average load (value 0) for all simulated settings. The figures indicate reasonable load balancing as indicated by the standard deviation from the average load and the minimum respectively maximum load found at the end of relaxation. For smaller terms-per-nodes ratios, the maximum load reaches the set upper limit of $2 \cdot average\ load$, whereas the lower limit (a node does not store any terms) is never reached.

There are several other load metrics of interest for distributed systems. Our relaxation algorithm is able to deal with any kind of load, e.g., query load balancing, and can relocate terms accordingly. An important aspect not mentioned so far is the fact that terms do not have the same storage load impact on nodes, i.e., terms with long posting lists require to store more document references than terms with short posting lists. Unfortunately it is so far not possible for us to achieve good load balancing for posting lists. The reasons are that the distribution of posting list sizes as shown in Figure 6.6 follows a power-law distribution, i.e., some terms have very long posting lists. The largest posting lists are by magnitudes longer than the average load of nodes, and the load of nodes storing these long posting lists cannot be balanced as posting lists cannot be split up and divided among several nodes, i.e., posting lists belong to terms which are currently maintained by one peer only. Posting list load balancing can only be considered if the average load reaches the level of the longest posting lists or if posting lists can be split up on several nodes. Both requirements are currently not fulfilled in our simulations.

6.4.6 Discussion

The presented results indicate that multi-term queries can benefit from query-driven clustering through our spring relaxation algorithm. The clustering of correlated query terms reduces the cost of query resolution for these terms. The results are based on the assumption that these term correlations were gathered by monitoring user queries and kept up-to-date. Our results indicate that our approach works best for the most frequently queried term pairs, rep-

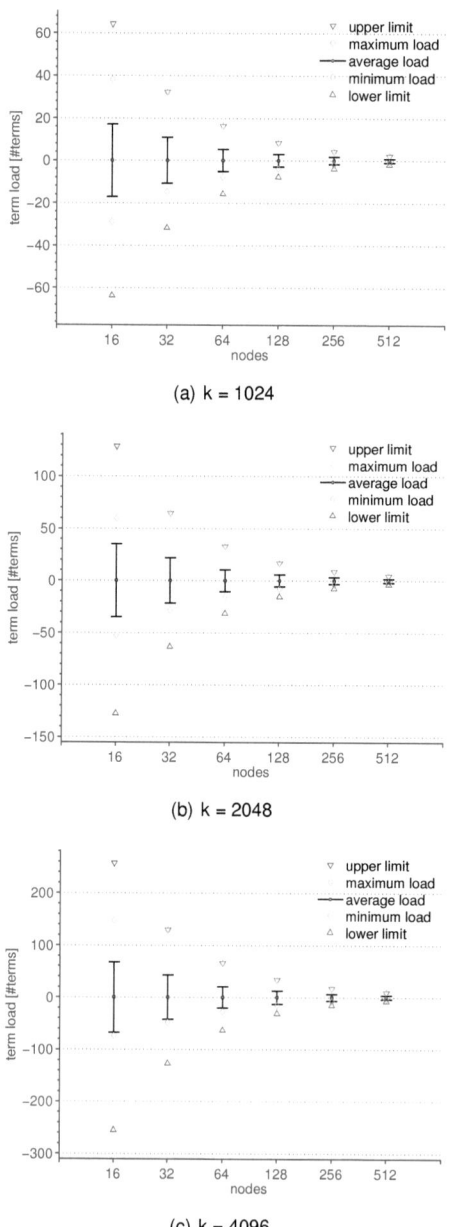

Figure 6.9: Variations of term load compared to the average load for the top-k queried terms

resented by small probabilistic networks, however, the absolute cost reduction is good for all evaluated networks sizes. Our relaxation algorithm works better if nodes store more terms, i.e., if the average number of terms per node is higher, as nodes have more opportunities to move terms around and thereby relax term relations. We envision that in a real-world setting this ratio will be even higher leading to even better results than presented here.

The cost for relaxing the term network is thereby smaller than the gain we were able to achieve. Our evaluation shows that relaxation pays off quickly, e.g., after less than 1 month for the used Wikipedia query logs.

Our simulation further considered load balancing, especially the number of terms stored by node. However, our relaxation algorithm is able to consider other types of load, e.g., query load and posting list load. Our experiments show that we are able to balance the number of terms stored at P-Grid nodes. The more interesting posting list load was not considered as the average load was not high enough to balance the power-law distributed sizes of posting lists.

6.5 Conclusions

This chapter has shown how multi-term queries in structured overlay network can benefit from term clustering. Highly correlated terms occurring frequently together in multi-term queries can be identified and clustered at one node to enable a remote join, i.e., returning only the intersection of their result set instead of the two result sets separately. Enabling remote joins therefore reduces the size of transmitted result sets and network overhead.

We used a probabilistic network to model term correlations, i.e., jointly queried terms. The probabilistic network is stored in a P-Grid network and relaxed by our spring relaxation algorithm. However, this approach is applicable to any other structured overlay network including DHTs using uniform hashing.

Part III

From Theory to Practice

In theory, there is no difference between theory and practice. But, in practice, there is.
Jan L.A. van de Snepscheut.

Chapter 7

Architecture

As any theory is only as good as its practical implementation and evaluation, one of the main goals of this thesis was to also implement and evaluate the designed algorithms. The theoretical efficiency of our approaches was proven in the previous chapters and evaluation results of our implementation were presented showing the applicability and performance in practice. For this purpose we implemented our algorithms in a standalone Java application used for testing and dissemination of our system.

P-Grid is currently one of the very few systems implemented and tested in a real deployable Java application whereas most other systems were only simulated. Some systems even only exist in theory and were never implemented in any form. We consider the practical proof of theory as the most important one and also as the most difficult one to achieve.

We therefore developed a modular Java application consisting of the basic components required to build a P2P system and extensions implementing some of the approaches presented in this thesis. P-Grid can run as standalone application providing basic information sharing functionality or it can be used as library by other applications to provide tailored services according to user and application requirements.

This chapter presents the modular architecture and interfaces designed in the implementation of P-Grid. The architecture currently consists of two main modules, a routing layer providing elementary routing functionalities and an indexing layer to build the structured overlay network and the distributed index infrastructure. Both layers have a well defined Java API. We will present them together with a simple usage example in the next implementation chapter.

7.1 Overview

The software architecture of P-Grid describes the main structure of the system, its main components and the relationships and interactions between them. Together with interface descriptions of externally visible components, an architecture description facilitates the understanding and usability of the described software for application developers and users as it provides a high-level overview of the design and its core components.

P-Grid's architecture consists of two main components, the routing layer and the indexing layer. The routing layer provides the basic concepts of P2P systems common to all P2P systems, including unstructured overlays such as Gnutella. It enables applications to route respectively send messages to other peers in the overlay network. The indexing layer on top relies on the routing services of the routing layer, and its corresponding interface, to provide indexing functionalities as common to structured overlay networks. The indexing layer enables to index the locally shared data and to distribute the generated index items to corresponding peers for maintenance. Unstructured overlays do not maintain a distributed index and their offered functionality is entirely covered by the routing layer.

The idea behind this separation of functionality is to make the basic routing layer interchangeable by other P2P routing structures as those introduced in Chapter 2. The routing layer only provides functionalities common to all P2P systems and its interface is not tailored towards P-Grid's specific properties but rather kept generic. The routing layer not only provides a well-defined interface for P-Grid but also defines a generic interface for developing P2P systems. This allows application developers implementing against this interface to interchange the underlying routing layer at any time. Applications using the indexing interface are additionally able to make their data available and searchable in the distributed index of structured overlay networks. The indexing interface therefore represents specific structured overlay functionality not supported by all P2P systems, e.g., Gnutella. Data can be shared in an application-specific way through so-called type handlers enabling applications to influence the way data is indexed.

Figure 7.1 presents P-Grid's architecture and its two layered structure. The routing layer is built on top of the TCP/IP layer offering simple communication and messaging services among Internet hosts. TCP/IP provides delivery guarantees UDP cannot offer and is more suitable for large message sizes requiring data streaming. Both P-Grid layers provide an API for applications respectively they are used internally. We will now in the following describe both layers and their components in more details.

7.2 Routing Layer and API

The routing layer provides an abstraction of the P2P network adding P2P routing functionality on top of the standard TCP/IP network layer. Whereas the network layer deals with streams and message packets sent between Internet nodes, the routing layer adds the concept of peers identified by a unique identifier independent of their current IP address. Additionally, in structured overlay networks peers are responsible for a partition of the key space and can therefore also be identified with a key or key range they are responsible for. The key or

7.2. Routing Layer and API

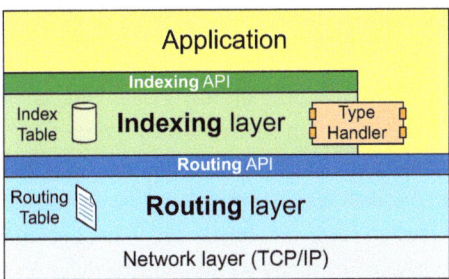

Figure 7.1: P-Grid's layered architecture

key range is not used by unstructured overlays as they are only responsible for their local data. The core service offered by the routing layer is the sending and routing of messages between peers using different routing strategies. To perform this operation, the routing layer maintains a routing table with peers of interest. The set of peers required to route within the network depends on the structure of the P2P network. For example, Gnutella only requires a set of random peers to route messages whereas P-Grid requires peers with certain positions in the network, i.e., peers with increasing distance in the key space. The routing table can further maintain replica peers responsible for the same partition of the key space.

As already mentioned before, the routing layer is kept generic so that it covers most of the currently existing P2P networks and their routing strategies. The idea behind it was that applications developing against the routing interface can interchange the underlying routing strategy, i.e., overlay network, at any time. Depending on application needs, certain routing topologies have advantages compared to others. Although each P2P system has its strengths and weaknesses, their core components and services are still the same and can therefore be unified in a common interface. We further hope that other P2P system developers make use of our routing interface and provide according interfaces in their system as well.

7.2.1 Routing Layer Components

The routing interface consists of some basic concepts such as peers and messages which we will introduce now briefly. These concepts are common for most P2P systems and provide a minimum set of components and services required to build a P2P system. The core components of a P2P system are the following:

GUID represents a global unique identifier used by peers, messages, queries, etc. to identify themselves uniquely in the network. They are created locally and their global uniqueness is guaranteed by combining the local IP address with the time of creation and a random seed.

Key defines the partition of a structured overlay a peer is responsible for or the partition an index entry will fall into. In P-Grid, a key is a binary string, e.g., '00101010', defining the partition a peer is responsible for, i.e., a peer's path. For each index item a binary key is generated defining which partition respectively which peer will store and maintain this index entry. A key is further used to route messages and index entries in the P2P network. It is compared to the local key or key range a peer is responsible for to decide if a message reached its destination peer or has to be further forwarded.

KeyRange consists of two keys as defined above, representing a lower and upper bound of a range of keys. Key ranges are used by peers to define the area they are responsible for and by messages to define the partitions they are supposed to reach, for example in a range query. Key ranges are only used by order-preserving overlay networks.

KeySet is a set of keys as defined above. A set of keys can be used to route messages to multiple destination keys not spanning over a key range.

Message is used to transmit any application specific data between two peers, either directly by opening a direct connection to another peer if its address is known, or by routing the information through the P2P network given a destination key. A message is uniquely identified in the network by a GUID.

Peer represents a peer participating in the P2P network. A peer can be identified by its global unique identifier GUID and by its current IP address and port. Be aware that the GUID remains the same even if a peer changes its IP address, e.g., if it gets assigned a new dynamic IP address by its provider for following logins. Additionally, a peer of a structured overlay is responsible for a key respectively key range.

7.2.2 Routing Layer Services

The core services of the routing layer are sending and routing messages as offered by the routing interface described next. All offered services can be classified in the following categories:

Local services are services dealing with the local state of a peer. Peers in a P2P system have to maintain certain information locally to keep the system alive including their position in the network and their routing table. Local services provide access to them or initialize them.

Join/leave operations are required by P2P systems to enable peers to join and leave the system at any time. Whereas a join operation is mandatory, some P2P systems do not necessarily require a leave operation informing peers of a network about the forthcoming departure of the local peer.

Routing service is the main service offered by P2P systems and implements the delivery of a message towards a destination key or keys. Unlike direct communication as described later, routing does not require to know the destination IP address of a peer and rather routes a message in the P2P network according to its destination key until a peer responsible for the key is reached. P2P systems are able to offer various routing strategies. The simplest one is the routing towards one single destination key. In our interface we further include the possibility to route messages to a key range defined by a lower and upper bound. A message with a destination KeyRange is routed to at least one peer of each partition spanning the key range. Similarly, a message can be routed to a set of keys implementing multicast routing in P2P systems. Finally, as data is usually replicated on several peers, the interface offers the possibility to route a message to all replicas of a peer.

Lookup service enables applications to discover a peer responsible for a given key. This is similar to the routing service though it does not deliver information through a message to a destination key but rather enables applications to communicate directly with peers of interest once they are discovered by the lookup service.

Direct messaging finally enables applications to directly communicate with other peers of the network if their current IP address is known. This service does not rely on the routing service as a destination peer's address must be know a priori. The advantage of direct communication with a peer is to avoid possibly expensive multi-hop routing. Therefore it is sometimes better to perform a lookup operation to discover a peer of interest and afterwards directly communicate with this peer to avoid routing overhead. Unstructured overlays such as Gnutalla only use direct messaging as peers are not responsible for a key range as required by the above described routing services.

7.3 Indexing Layer and API

The indexing layer on top uses functionalities provided by the routing layer to build the distributed index of structured overlay networks. This feature is separated from the routing layer as a distributed index is not supported by all P2P systems, especially unstructured ones, and therefore only useful for structured overlay networks. However, the indexing layer provides the concept of queries which was not included in the routing layer as queries can be seen as a special type of messages.

The main purpose of the indexing layer is to index the locally shared data and distribute the generated index items to corresponding peers for maintenance. It therefore uses local tools such as the TypeHandler, further discussed in Section 7.3.3, to extract and index information of shared data. Depending on the generated key for an index item and the key range the local peer is currently responsible for, the newly created index item is either entered into the local index table or routed via the routing interface to a remote peer. The index table collects all index entries the local peer is responsible for and is used during query resolution to find matching items.

7.3.1 Indexing Layer Components

The indexing layer uses all components of the routing layer and further introduces the following components.

IndexItem represents the index information extracted from shared data and distributed in the network to resolve queries. An index item contains at least a `Peer` element representing the sharing peer plus the indexed information. A `Key` element determines the partition it is maintained in. Each index item can further be identified by a unique identifier `GUID` and is associated with a `Type` we will explain shortly. Finally, index items can carry any data attached by the TypeHandler depending on application needs. We will further discuss this feature in Section 7.3.3.

Query is a specialization of the generic `Message` element of the routing interface to formalize a query of one or multiple keywords, respectively a lower and higher bound of a range query. Each query can be identified by its `GUID` and is again associated with a `Type`. Similar to an index item, a query contains a key or key range representing the hash value of the query strings or the lower and higher bound of a range query.

Type specifies the type of index information or query and is introduced by a TypeHandler. Index items and queries are associated with a type as different information requires different ways of how index information is extracted and how a query is locally matched against index items. This logic is provided by TypeHandlers responsible for an introduced type.

7.3.2 Indexing Layer Services

The core index services rely on services provided by the routing layer and include data manipulation operations and query processing.

Data manipulation is the process of inserting, modifying or deleting data in the distributed index. An insert adds a so far not present index item into the system to make it available for searches. An update of an index item results in the alternation of the index information for a given index item and a deletion removes an index item completely from the distributed index. As all these operations are executed in a distributed setting involving multiple peers and replicas, only best-effort guarantees can be given for these operations and longer manipulation delays are possible.

Search enables applications to find shared data of all participating peers in the network. A search involves the creation of one or multiple queries, routing the query messages to the responsible peer, respectively multiple peers responsible for the query, and finding all matching index items in the index table of the resolving peers. As a result, a query returns all matching items to a keyword or multiple keywords.

7.3.3 Data Type Handlers

Applications sharing data through the distributed index might wish to tailor the way data is indexed and queries are processed at responsible peers, enabling applications to bring in application-specific knowledge about the data. Different types of data, e.g., files, RDF tuples, Bayesian variables, etc., require different parts of the data to be indexed and searched during a query. P-Grid allows applications to define their own data types and corresponding type handlers. A data type is defined by a string choosen by applications to classify data of this type, e.g., "text/file" for simple file-sharing. A data type string should be unique in a P-Grid network to avoid conflicts, otherwise an application has to create a dedicated P-Grid network.

A data type handler builds the link between an application and the indexing layer respectively P-Grid. It enables an application to directly influence P-Grid's behavior of how data is indexed and queried. In a nutshell, by introducing a data type and providing a corresponding type handler, an application becomes responsible to create index items for new shared data and to resolve queries for its data type. These two functions are strongly related as the indexing part determines with which keywords data can be found and query handling reverses this step by matching queries against index items.

7.4 Interaction Diagrams

This section provides simple interaction diagrams to illustrate how the two layers interact with each other and how they can be used by applications to perform core services. We will present two use cases, the insertion and indexing of new data and the issue and resolution of a query.

7.4.1 Data Insertion

Figure 7.2 shows the sequence diagram for data insertion. At the beginning applications are required to register their own data type handler for their application-specific data. Defining a system wide unique data type and providing a corresponding data type handler to the indexing layer enables applications later to tailor the indexing of data they are willing to share with other peers. In Figure 7.2 data inserted by the application is therefore indexed by the application provided type handler and returned to the indexing layer for further processing. The indexing step extracts the relevant information from the shared data and generates binary keys for each extracted keyword. The data type handler is only responsible for the data extraction whereas the indexing layer provides the mapping between text strings and binary strings. Depending on the key for an extracted keyword, a data item is either stored in the local index table maintained by the indexing layer or distributed to a responsible peer. The data distribution is executed by the routing layer by routing the corresponding information to a peer of the local routing table closest to the target destination. This procedure is repeated at the remote peer, the next routing hop, till the destination peer is reached and the index information is added to the index table.

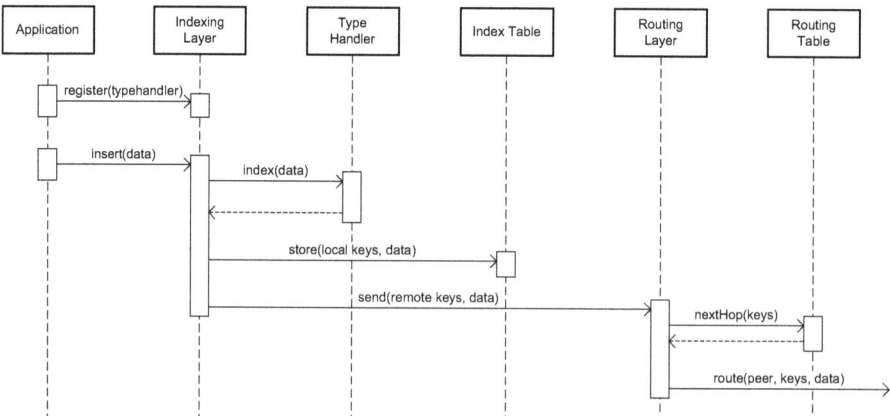

Figure 7.2: Data insertion sequence diagram

7.4.2 Query Resolution

Indexed and distributed data can now be searched by any application running on any peer in the network. Figure 7.3 shows how an application looking for a keyword uses the indexing layer to issue a query. The query containing the keyword is expanded by the type handler responsible for the given query type. The indexing layer requests from the registered data type handler for the query type a binary key generated out of the query. The type handler is, as in the data insertion use case, only responsible for extracting the significant information out of the query (e.g., keyword) to generate the binary key using indexing layer functionality. The key enhanced query is now routed to the responsible peer by the routing layer if the local peer is not already responsible for the query key. The routing layer uses the local routing table to determine the next hop peer the query will be forwarded to.

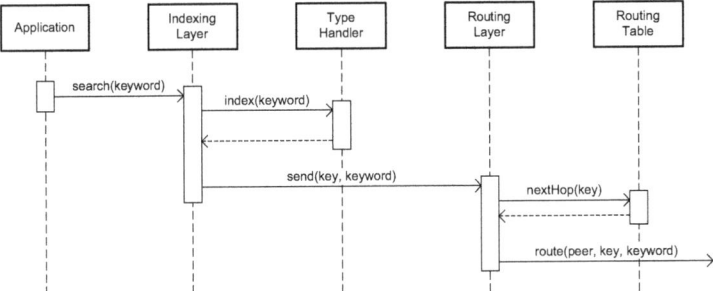

Figure 7.3: Query resolution sequence diagram (local side)

A query usually traverses over a couple of peers till it is routed to its final destination, a peer responsible for the routing key generated out of the query keyword. Figure 7.4 shows how an incoming query is processed at a query-responsible peer. The routing layer first checks if the local peer is really responsible for the routed message, in our case a remote query containing a query keyword. Assuming the current peer is responsible for the query, it hands over the query to the corresponding type handler for this query type. The type handler provided by the application for this data type is now responsible to match index information in the index table against the keyword using application-specific knowledge already used before for indexing and query key generation. The index table provides an interface assisting the type handler in finding matching items keeping the implementation efforts for data type handlers minimal. All matching items are finally returned back to the routing layer replying to the query request with a query response message sent back directly to the requesting peer already waiting for the response.

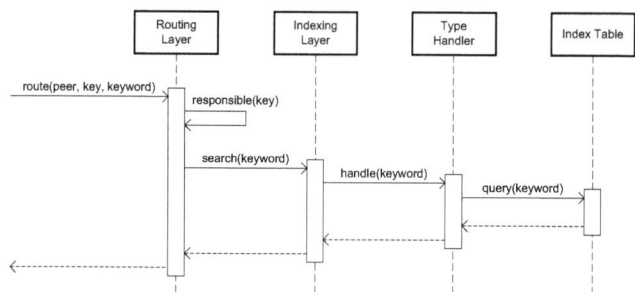

Figure 7.4: Query resolution sequence diagram (remote side)

7.5 Conclusions

This chapter presented the architectural design of the P-Grid implementation. The P-Grid architecture currently consists of two layers, the routing and the indexing layer. The separation enables applications to interexchange different routing strategies in the routing layer. The indexing layer is independent of the P2P network topology and offers indexing functionalities as known from structured overlay networks.

P-Grid offers a set of interfaces to help application developers in building their applications on top of P-Grid. The routing and indexing layer provide a well-defined API and can be used by applications directly. P-Grid further offers a so-called data type handler to tailor data indexing towards application specific needs. The next chapter will present the implementation of the architecture presented in this chapter in P-Grid's Java application.

Chapter 8

Implementation

The architectural design presented a high-level view of the implementation and introduced the basic concepts of P-Grid's Java-based implementation. This chapter provides more details about each package of the implementation and how each architectural component is realized in the code. Throughout the work in this thesis both theory and practice were considered and developed hand in hand. The result is a running and well-tested application which can be used as standalone application or as library by other applications.

The open and extensible architecture design of P-Grid enables applications to use all functionalities through well-defined interfaces and to tailor P-Grid using application-specific knowledge where necessary. We will therefore present in this chapter more details about the internal structure of the P-Grid code and how P-Grid can be used by other applications. The package descriptions should help developers willing to extend or modify code to quickly identify the area they have to look into whereas further details about the two interfaces (routing and index) will help application developers on top of P-Grid to get started. We will further provide a short code example of how P-Grid can be used by applications to share information in a structured overlay network.

At the end of this chapter, we will present an evaluation of P-Grid's bootstrapping approach and a small facet of the implementation tackling the problem of query load balancing. We were facing and investigating this problem during our implementation. The approach is briefly presented and evaluated on PlanetLab showing its impact on query resolution latencies.

8.1 Overview

The P-Grid system is currently implemented in several packages as shown in Figure 8.1. The root package pgrid comprises all general classes such as Constants, GUID (Global Unique IDentifier), Host, Properties, Statistics, and Type used by many other packages. The pgrid.core package implements all basic algorithms, e.g., the construction and query algorithms presented in Chapter 3, and will be further discussed in Section 8.2. The pgrid.interfaces package provides the interfaces for the routing and indexing layer introduced in the architectural design in Chapter 7. Both interfaces will be presented in more details in Section 8.3. The pgrid.network package is responsible for all aspects of network communication between two P-Grid peers as further shown in Section 8.4. Finally, the package pgrid.util provides useful tools and functions for all other packages such as unique identifier generation and logging.

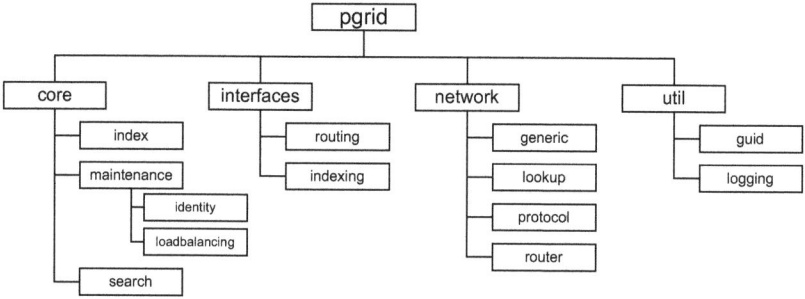

Figure 8.1: P-Grid's package structure

8.2 Core Package

The core package implements the core functionalities of P-Grid and therefore contains all implementations of P-Grid's algorithms for data indexing, load-balancing and searching. The package itself is further divided into three sub-packages. The pgrid.core.index package maintains the local index table and reliably stores them in a database back-end. The pgrid.core.maintenance package deals with all challenges related to the maintenance of the P-Grid network and the maintenance of the overlay network. Finally, all lookup operations are handled by the pgrid.core.search package.

8.2.1 Index Sub-Package

A P2P system may share millions of files and millions of peers and therefore needs an efficient local database back-end to maintain the local index information. This functionality is provided by the index sub-package of the core package. The main classes in this package are the IndexManager and IndexTable. The IndexManager provides all necessary interfaces to manipulate the local database back-end represented by the IndexTable. Among the functionalities offered by these classes are insert and delete operations required to implement

8.2. Core Package

the data manipulations offered by the indexing layer of P-Grid. Further the `IndexTable` enables data type handlers provided by applications to retrieve locally maintained index items given various selection criteria to resolve queries.

All offered functions are executed directly on a database back-end running in the same Java virtual machine as P-Grid itself. We currently use the embedded version of the H2 Database Engine [H2], a free SQL database. The advantage of an embedded database is its better performance compared to a client-server setup. It is further easier to deploy P-Grid with an embedded database as it can be shipped as library and does not require to be installed and maintained separately as a database server, further requiring a running daemon in the background.

For higher numbers of index items per peer a database back-end might become a bottleneck as massive insert and delete operations cause long execution delays due to re-indexing of stored data for efficient query resolution. Under these circumstances other solutions might perform better and require the replacement of our default back-end by either another database or different approaches. The `IndexManager` and `IndexTable` make this step transparent for P-Grid as these two classes provide a generic interface and are not related to H2 or any other SQL database.

8.2.2 Maintenance Sub-Package

P-Grid is a structured overlay network requiring to build and maintain a distributed data structure organizing peers in a virtual trie and assigning peers to partitions for making them responsible for index items. The implementation of these algorithms can be found in the `pgrid.core.maintenance` package.

For applications interested in details about P-Grid's maintenance, the most interesting class is the `MaintenanceManager` class. It provides access to all phases of the life-time of a P-Grid network, from the initial bootstrap phase until permanent load balancing to maintaining operational and efficient.

In brief, a P-Grid network is constructed during a so-called *bootstrap* phase in which peers join the network by contacting a bootstrap peer given by the application or the user. The `Bootstraper` class tries to contact a bootstrap peer until it successfully received addresses of peers already in the network for forthcoming interactions.

As next step P-Grid peers *replicate* their local index items at randomly selected peers in the network collected during the bootstrap phase. The `Replicator` initiates these requests locally and also processes incoming requests accordingly. The replication phase guarantees a certain level of fault-tolerance to overcome temporary failures of peers, peer departures, etc. during network construction.

Finally P-Grid's overlay structure is built by so called *exchanges*. An exchange is either initiated locally by the `ExchangeInitiator` or triggered by a remote request. In both cases, the `Exchanger` class prepares all required information for an exchange which will then be executed by the exchange algorithm implemented in the `ExchangeAlgorithm` class.

After the establishment of a well-structured and load-balanced overlay network acting as routing infrastructure for P-Grid, the `pgrid.core.maintenance.loadbalancing` package takes care of any changes in load balance, i.e., arising imbalances due to arriving or departing peers as well as data insertions and deletions. To enable re-joining peers to maintain their last identity in case they changed their IP address, as they might use a dynamic IP address provided by many Internet Service Providers (ISP) nowadays, the `pgrid.core.maintenance.identity` package guarantees that each peer can publish its new IP address in the P-Grid network itself. P-Grid therefore stores identifiers - IP address mappings of each peer and repairs local routing table entries on demand following various strategies as described in [ADH04].

8.2.3 Search Sub-Package

The previous two sub-packages `index` and `maintenance` provide the required infrastructure to efficiently resolve search requests and answer user queries. To that end, the `search` sub-package provides an `SearchManager` to issue new searches and to register for search results as soon as they are received by the local peer. Applications interested in search results have to implement the `SearchListener` interface presented in Section 8.3.2. The current implementation supports single and multiple keyword queries and range queries.

8.3 Interfaces Package

We have introduced in Chapter 7 the routing and indexing layer and their corresponding interfaces to access P-Grid's functionalities through a well-defined and stable interface. As we hope that these generic interface definitions are as well used by other P2P system developers, they are not part of the P-Grid package and defined in a separate package `p2p.*`.

P-Grid implements both the routing and the indexing interface defined in `p2p.routing` and `p2p.indexing` in its interfaces package `pgrid.interfaces`. We will now provide more details about the generic P2P interfaces and their implementation in P-Grid.

8.3.1 P-Grid's Routing Interface

The routing interface as defined in Section 7.2 offers basic P2P services such as join/leave and message routing. These services are considered common and necessary for all P2P systems and all other services can be built on top of them, such as the indexing layer for structured overlay networks.

8.3. Interfaces Package

The Java API is defined in `p2p.routing` containing all components as described in Section 7.2.1 to provide the services as described in Section 7.2.2. The Java interface for these services can be found in `p2p.routing.Routing` and is further presented in Listing 8.1.

```java
// Local services
public void init(Properties properties);
public Peer getLocalPeer();
public Peer[] getNeighbors();
public boolean isLocalPeerResponsible(Key key);
public void shutdown();

// Join/leave operations
public void join(Peer peer);
public void leave();

// Routing functions
public void route(Key key, Message message);
public void route(Key[] keys, Message[] message);
public void route(KeyRange range, Message message);
public void routeToReplicas(Message message);

// Lookup service
public Peer lookup(Key key, long timeout);

// Direct messaging
public void send(Peer peer, Message message);

// Listeners
public void addRoutingListener(RoutingListener listener);
public void removeRoutingListener(RoutingListener listener);
```

Listing 8.1: The routing interface

The **local services** deal with the local state of the peer running the P-Grid application and provide detailed information about:

- `getLocalPeer()` returns the local peer object with details about the local IP address, the listening port and current position of the peer in the P2P network, i.e., the key range the local peer is currently responsible for.

- `getNeighbors()` returns a list of all peers in the routing table used for routing and maintenance. The structure of routing tables varies between P2P network and can usually be rebuilt by the peers provided in the form of a list.

- `isLocalPeerResponsible(Key key)` verifies if the local peer is currently responsible for the given `key` depending on the current position of the local peer in the P2P network.

The local services further include an initialization method (`init(Properties properties)`) used to parameterize the local P2P instance for example by giving a listening port in the `properties` different from the default. If no properties are given, the P2P instance will be initialized with its defaults. If an application does no longer require the P2P instance, it should be properly closed by the `shutdown()` method.

The **join/leave operations** enable applications to

- `join(Peer peer)` join an existing network by contacting a known `peer` of the network, usually a so-called *bootstrap peer*.

- `leave()` leave a network, i.e., do not listen to any incoming connections and therefore not actively participate in the network anymore. The latest state is nevertheless stored locally for later joins enabling peers to continue at their latest position in the network.

The **routing function** of the routing interface is the main service offered and can be used to route a message to one or several peers depending on which function is used:

- `route(Key key, Message message)` represents the simplest routing operation and, as all other routing operations as well, routes a `message` to a peer currently responsible for the specified `key`.

- `route(Key[] keys, Message message)` routes a `message` to multiple destination `keys` in a bundle, i.e., the number of messages sent over the network is minimized by bundling messages into one as long as possible. As peers can be responsible for a key range, one peer can cover all destination `keys` making one message routed in the network sufficient.

- `route(KeyRange range, Message message)` is able to route a `message` to a given key range, i.e., the message will be received by all peers in the key range. The actual number of messages sent over the network is minimized as for multiple keys above.

- `routeToReplicas(Message message)` finally routes the given `message` to all replicas of the local peer. Unlike the other route operations where a message is only received by one peer per key (range), `routeToReplicas` routes the message to *all* peers responsible for a key (range), namely the key (range) the local peer is currently responsible for.

The **lookup service** is related to the routing operation as it routes a system-internal lookup message to a destination key to find a responsible peer. Therefore `lookup(Key key,` long timeout) returns the Peer responsible for the given key, otherwise null if no peer can be found before the timeout is reached.

Finally **direct messaging** enables applications to directly communicate with a peer of the P2P network without the overhead of routing a message over various peers to a destination peer. The function send(Peer, Message) opens a TCP/IP connection to the given Peer to deliver the Message directly. This method is interesting if larger data has to be transmitted between peers and if applications want to avoid the routing overhead as the destination peer can be identified beforehand by the lookup service.

P2P networks send messages between peers which requires a certain time depending on the network infrastructure, network and peer load, etc.. Therefore functions involving network communication cannot return results immediately but rather return results as soon as they are available. The routing interface allows applications to register a **Routing listener** for P-Grid which will invoke a newMessage(Message message, Peer origin) method every time a message is received. Applications thereby can react immediately on a received Message sent by a origin peer.

P-Grid's implementation of all these services plus some additional P-Grid specific services can be found in pgrid.interfaces.routing. PGridRouting. The generic routing services presented here cover most of the functionalities of P-Grid and are sufficient to build efficient P2P applications on top of P-Grid. Although some applications may not intend to interchange their underlying P2P system and can therefore benefit from P-Grid specific properties the generic routing interface cannot offer.

8.3.2 P-Grid's Indexing Interface

The indexing interface as defined in Section 7.3 offers indexing services on top of the aforementioned basic routing interface. Distributed indexing is offered by structured overlay networks only and therefore not common to all P2P systems. Nevertheless, all structured overlay networks such as P-Grid offer a basic set of functionalities to index shared data in a distributed index and to enable efficient lookups on the index.

The Java API is defined in p2p.indexing containing all components as described in Section 7.3.1 to provide the services as described in Section 7.3.2. The Java interface for these services can be found in p2p.indexing.Indexing and is further presented in Listing 8.2.

```
// Local operations
public Collection getLocalIndexEntries();
public void shutdown();

// Data manipulation
public void insert(Collection entries);
public void update(Collection entries);
```

```
public void delete(Collection entries);

// Search
public void search(Query query,
                   SearchListener listener);

// Listeners
public void addIndexListener(IndexListener listener,
                             Type type);
public void removeIndexListener(IndexListener listener,
                                Type type);
```

Listing 8.2: The indexing interface

The interface first offers again some **local operations**. The function `getLocalIndexEntries()` returns all currently maintained index entries at the local peer in a `Collection`. The `shutdown()` operation ensures that all local data items are stored persistently in the database back-end before the application quits.

The **data manipulation** operations enable applications to `insert`, `update` and `delete` data. All three functions take a collection of data entries as input. The `insert(Collection entries)` operation inserts all data items of the `entries` collection into the network distributing each data item to its corresponding peer currently responsible for the binary key of the data item. The `update(Collection entries)` assumes that the data items in the `entries` collection are already present in the network and updates them accordingly similarly as the insert method. Finally, the `delete(Collection entries)` operation deletes all `entries` provided as input. All three operations are executed with best-effort guarantees and best-effort consistency guarantees. Offline peers cannot be updated instantly as they are temporary not reachable by other peers. They have to be synchronized as soon as they rejoin the overlay network.

The **search** functionality is implemented by the `search(Query query, SearchListener listener)` function. The `query` thereby contains either a keyword or a keyword pair for range queries which will then by hashed by the data type handler and P-Grid into a binary key used to route the query to the destination peer. As query results are not immediately available, applications have to register as `SearchListener` to receive results as soon as they become available at the local peer. The search listener interface will be presented in further details in the next section.

Applications can also register a so-called `IndexListener` to observe locally added, removed and updated index items. The interface offers the functions

- `indexItemsAdded(Collection items)`
- `indexItemsRemoved(Collection items)`

- `indexItemsUpdated(Collection items)`

to inform applications about any modification on the local index table due to operations triggered by remote peers such as data modifications the local peer is responsible for or other applications operating on the same local index table.

Search Listener

The search listener interface is the only way for applications to receive search results and receive search status notifications. The interface provides the following functions and notifications:

- `newSearchResult(GUID guid, Collection results)` is invoked as soon as new search results for a query identified by the `guid` are received and available locally.

- `noResultsFound(GUID guid)` informs applications that a search with the identifier `guid` did not result in any matches.

- `searchFailed(GUID guid)` is invoked if a search failed, e.g., because the responsible peer could not be reached.

- `searchFinished(GUID guid)` represents the end of a search operations and is called if no further results are expected to be received respectively will be delivered to the application.

- `searchStarted(GUID guid, String message)` informs applications that a search has reached at least one peer responsible. This function is only useful for search operations involving multiple peers and longer processing delays.

The Type Handler

Applications willing to share application-specific and unique data are capable to define their own data type and provide a corresponding type handler to the indexing layer. A type handler enables applications to influence the way data is indexed and queried in P-Grid, using application-specific knowledge otherwise not used by P-Grid. A type handler is responsible for extracting the essential information from data used for the distributed index. A search can only succeed if the necessary information was indexed beforehand. Therefore these two operations are tightly coupled in structured overlay networks and should be performed by the application itself. Applications need to implement the following functions for a type handler:

- `IndexEntry createIndexEntry()` should return an empty `IndexEntry` with default values for the data type the type handler is responsible for.

- `IndexEntry createIndexEntry(Object data)` should return a new `IndexEntry` object for the given `data` object. All other values take the default value.

- `IndexEntry createIndexEntry(GUID guid, Key key, Peer host, Object data)` should return a new `IndexEntry` object with all values given. The `guid` defines the globally unique identifier of the index entry, the `key` is the binary string defining the partition the entry will be stored at, the `peer` object gives the peer sharing the index entry, and `data` represents the actual data indexed by this entry.

- `handleLocalSearch(Query query, SearchListener listener)` is invoked by the indexing layer when a `query` for the data type was received and should be processed by the type handler. The type handler should look into the local index table to find all matching items and return them to the given `SearchListener`.

- `Key generateKey(Object object)` should generate the binary string `Key` for the given data `object`. The data object can be any class known to the data type handler.

- `KeyRange generateKeyRange(Object lowerBound, Object higherBound)` should generate two keys for the `KeyRange` hashing the given `lowerBound` and `higherBound` of a range query.

Although it looks at the first glance difficult to implement all these functions for a type handler, P-Grid's routing layer and indexing layer offer great support to generate generic index entries and to map data in form of strings onto binary hash strings, the keys. The indexing layer and index table further have several functions allowing the type handler to easily browse, query and filter the local data set to find matching items.

8.4 Network Package

The network package is responsible for any network communication among P-Grid peers participating in the structured overlay network. The `pgrid.network` package contains several classes and sub-packages we will discuss later. A `ConnectionManager` handles all open connections to other peers and accepts incoming connection requests. Once a connection between two peers is established, the connection manager assists the `MessageManager` to send messages by providing the corresponding open connection. For the P-Grid protocol, only one open connection per peer is necessary and used. Incoming messages are also handled by the message manager once it was ensured that the local peer is responsible for it. The message is then pre-processed by the message manager before it is dispatched and forwarded to other classes of P-Grid outside the network package for further processing. Finally, the `pgrid.network` contains a stream reader and a stream writer together with a specific P-Grid message reader and writer.

8.4. Network Package

Network communication and message routing are the main functionality of a P2P system and the network package therefore further contains four sub-packages.

8.4.1 Generic Sub-Package

The GenericManager in the generic package is responsible for all generic messages received in P-Grid. A generic message offers applications the possibility to send application-specific data to other peers in a P-Grid network. Therefore generic messages are handled outside the P-Grid protocol engine as they are not used by P-Grid itself. A generic message can carry any type of data to a given destination peer or it can be routed to a destination address given a P-Grid binary key, respectively key range, using the routing strategies offered by P-Grid.

8.4.2 Lookup Sub-Package

The lookup package implements the lookup service offered by the routing interface as presented in Section 8.3.1. The lookup service is the only remote service which can be implemented directly in the network package as it does not require access to the local database. To remind, the lookup service returns a host responsible for a given binary key. A request is therefore routed to the destination address where the reached peer can respond directly with its local address.

The lookup package contains a LookupManager handling all locally issued lookup requests and returning received host address to the requester. The RemoteLookupHandler on the other hand handles all incoming lookup requests from other peers and responds with the local address to them.

8.4.3 Protocol Sub-Package

A P2P systems requires different messages to communicate with other peers and send data around the network. These messages are defined in the protocol sub-package of the network package. The P-Grid protocol currently consists of 25 messages ranging from simple greeting and bootstrap messages required by all peers over query and range query messages required to realize the routing and indexing services to P-Grid internal maintenance messages.

P-Grid messages are transmitted in a plain-text XML format or partially ZLIB-compressed to reduce message sizes and transmission times for larger messages. The use of XML makes it easier to debug and understand the communication between peers by adding little overhead in terms of message sizes and processing time. The ZLIB compression reduces the message sizes of large messages to a minimum, whereby the compression factor increases with increasing message sizes. A binary version of the protocol was also developed and will soon replace the XML version.

The protocol package contains a class for each message type available and used in P-Grid. A message class contains all the information a message will carry over the Internet, or does carry all the received information from a remote peer. The actual message stream is created by the message class itself using the information provided during initialization of the message, respectively, the message class can extract all the information from received data for further processing by P-Grid.

8.4.4 Router Sub-Package

A message created by the local peer or received by a remote peer has to be routed to a remote peer if a message has not reached its final destination yet. This decision is taken in the router sub-package by the `Router` class. A message can be sent to one or multiple remote peers depending on the given routing strategy of the message type. P-Grid currently supports the following routing strategies for messages:

- **Greedy**: is the standard prefix-resolving routing strategy of structured overlays routing a message closer and closer to its destination address. It is used for all single key lookups such as single keyword queries and host lookups.

- **Shower**: is used by a range query to reach all peers in a given key range. The shower routing strategy splits a message into several messages if necessary depending on the routing table structure of the local peer.

- **Topology**: is used to find the topological neighbors of a peer, e.g., for the min-max traversal algorithm to resolve range queries. The routing strategy takes a destination address together with a parameter to find the most-left or most-right peer in this area.

- **Broadcast**: sends a message to a random selection of peers in the local routing table similar to the routing strategy of unstructured networks using hop counts and a time-to-life (TTL) for messages.

- **Replica**: sends a message to all replicas known to the local host. A message thereby contains a list of hosts the message has already been sent to decrease redundancy and network overhead. It is used to broadcast a message within a replica group.

- **Random Walk**: sends a message to a random peer of the local fidget list until the time-to-life (TTL) is expired.

8.5 Util package

The util package provides useful helper classes used throughout the P-Grid code. Some classes such as the `Tokenizer` provide functionalities like splitting up a string into a string array given a separator, whereas others are only abstract classes implemented in the P-Grid package such as the abstract class `Properties` providing a framework to maintain properties for an application and in a file.

The util package further contains a sub-package `guid` providing classes to create globally unique identifier as required by P-Grid. The second sub-package `logging` provides some extensions to the default Java logger used in P-Grid to log events on the console and/or file.

All utility classes in this package are of course, as the rest of the code, disposable for reuse by developers for their developments and applications and can be downloaded from the P-Grid web site `http://www.p-grid.org/`.

8.6 Evaluation of P-Grid's Bootstrapping

Bootstrapping is one of the specific features of P-Grid not present in other overlays. Therefore, we evaluated the approach outlined in Section 3.4 particularly carefully using our P-Grid implementation. We used the PlanetLab infrastructure to obtain results from large-scale experiments under realistic networking conditions and to verify our theoretical predictions outlined in more details in [ADHS05]. Our experiments on PlanetLab ran on up to 300 nodes depending on the number of available nodes. Each node runs one instance of a P-Grid node. When interpreting the results presented in the following, it is important to consider that PlanetLab is shared by hundreds of research groups for experiments that are executed in parallel and thus mutually influence the performance considerably especially in respect to absolute latency.

Experimental setup We deployed the P-Grid software, i.e., the peers, on all available nodes at the times the experiments were conducted and assigned 10 keys from a real text collection (taken from the Alvis[1] information retrieval use case) to each peer. This relatively low number of keys was chosen to speed up experiments. [ADHS05] shows that sample size has little influence on load balancing. To validate our experiments, we also performed tests with larger numbers (up to 2000 keys per peer) and used different key distributions, including uniform random distribution and Pareto distribution.

The time-line of the experiments was as follows: In an initial phase starting at time t peers join the system by contacting a bootstrap peer (until $t + 30min$) and the peers form

---
[1] http://www.alvis.info/

an unstructured overlay network (from t until $t + 45min$) which is used afterward to mutually replicate their data a fixed number of times to increase availability (from $t + 45min$ until $t + 60min$). In this replication phase peers randomly choose 5 peers from the unstructured overlay network to replicate their data. Subsequently, from $t+60min$ to $t+300min$, the structured overlay network is constructed using the approach presented in Section 3.4. We were especially interested in evaluating the bandwidth consumption during this phase and verify whether the theoretically predicted load balancing properties of the algorithm are achieved under realistic networking conditions. Then we run queries on the constructed overlay network ($t + 300min$ to $t + 400min$) to analyze search performance. Each peer performed a single key lookup every 1–2 minutes. In the final phase ($t + 400min$ to $t + 500min$) network churn is simulated to evaluate the failure resilience of P-Grid. Each peer independently decides to go offline 1–5 minutes every 5–10 minutes which causes considerable churn the system has to compensate.

Experimental results We first verified that the system behavior matches the theoretical predictions and the simulations presented in [ADHS05]. The experiment was performed with 296 peers and compared to simulation results using the same number of peers and the same key set.

The quality of load balancing is evaluated as defined in [ADHS05] and is matching for simulations and experiments with an average of 0.38 for 10 simulations (the standard deviation is 0.05) respectively a value of 0.39 for the experiment. This indicates that the theoretically predicted load distribution properties are met quite accurately by the implementation even under realistic network conditions with slow connections and communication failures.

We now report some system measurements that we made to evaluate the performance of the overlay network, both during the construction phase, as well as its operational life both in a static situation (no change in peer population) as well as under churn (peers leave and join the network).

Figure 8.2 shows the number of peers in the overlay at a given time. We see how first peers join the network and the number of peers in the network increases to the maximal number. Then during the construction phase this number is stable (approximately 300 peers) while decreasing again in the final phase where we simulate network churn and a substantial dynamic fraction of peers becomes unavailable.

Figure 8.3 shows the aggregate bandwidth consumption of all peers (maintenance and queries) in Bytes/sec. During the construction phase the bandwidth consumption reaches a peak of 250 Bytes/sec per peer. The maintenance consumption decreases quickly down to less than 100 Bytes/sec and becomes negligible compared to the bandwidth consumed by queries.

Figure 8.4 shows the average query latency and its standard deviation. The absolute values are relatively high and essentially reflect the poor response time of PlanetLab nodes.

8.6. Evaluation of P-Grid's Bootstrapping

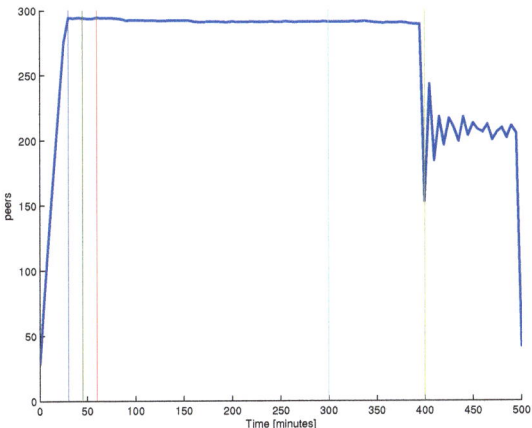

Figure 8.2: Number of participating peers

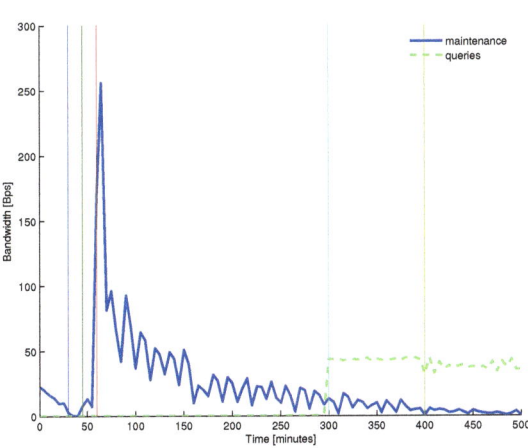

Figure 8.3: Aggregate bandwidth consumption

The response time is slightly higher with a larger deviation during the network churn because requested peers may be offline which has to be compensated.

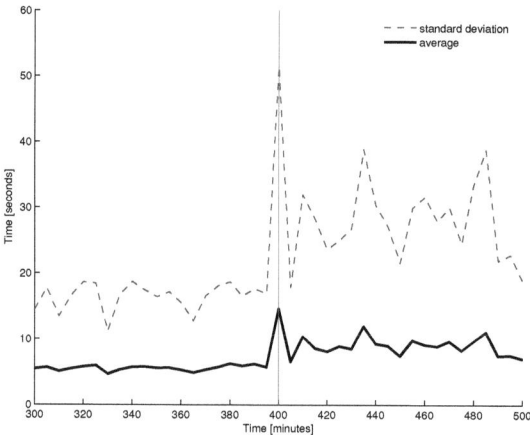

Figure 8.4: Query latency

We observed that the number of query hops per query is as low as theoretically expected, i.e, approximately half of the mean path length, even during churn. The average path length was slightly below 6 and the average number of query hops per query was approximately 3. Moreover after the construction phase has led to full evolution of the overlay network, all peers discovered all their replicas, and the system had an expected mean replication factor of 5, as intended, and success rate for queries was between 95% and 100% even during network churn. Queries were mainly unsuccessful because of network problems such as lost or corrupted messages.

8.7 Load-Aware Message Routing

During the implementation of P-Grid, we faced several problems concerning correctness, efficiency, robustness, expandability, etc. of our system. Some of these challenges originated from the heavily distributed, randomized and parallelized algorithms used by P-Grid. A source of problems, or better challenges, we did not foresee at the beginning is the used testbed for our testing and evaluations. Our aim was to develop an application tested and evaluated in a realistic network environment before deployed on the Internet. PlanetLab provides such an environment and recently became the state-of-the-art testbed for distributed systems.

The success of PlanetLab among researchers and developers soon lead to limited resources for users to test their systems as all resources are shared among users, i.e., users

8.7. Load-Aware Message Routing

cannot reserve resources and time slots for their tests. The consequences for applications were manyfold: (i) limited memory resources available forcing developers to reduce memory requirements of their application and to close possible memory leaks; (ii) limited CPU cycles available lead to long delays for local calculations and therefore further to unpredictable message response times; (iii) the high load on peers and their network connections caused higher message loss rates than in local area networks or the Internet.

The first challenge was mainly solved by the already presented well designed software architecture and local debugging to reduce memory consumption and to find memory leaks. The later two limitations have an influence on correctness, robustness and efficiency of one of P-Grid's core services, message routing. It was therefore important for us to find solutions for these problems as they can also occur on the Internet in a real-world deployment. For example, overloaded PlanetLab peers can be seen as slow peers on the Internet respectively peers with a slow Internet connection. High message loss rates can further occur on low bandwidth or wireless network links of the Internet.

This chapter will focus on optimizing message routing for query messages in a P-Grid network of PlanetLab peers with various loads. Message routing in a structured overlay network involves multiple intermediate peers (hops) till the destination peer is reached. In case of a query, the destination peer has to perform a lookup operation on the local index to return all matching entries to the query initiating peer. The query response time is defined at the initiating peer by the delay between sending out the query and receiving the query reply. The time can be improved, i.e., reduced, by avoiding overloaded, i.e., slow, peers during routing. This comprises peers involved in forwarding the query towards its destination and selecting the fastest peer in the destination partition, if multiple are available, to find matching entries. Please note that overloaded PlanetLab peers can represent slow Internet peers respectively peers with a slow Internet connection as in both cases their response time will be long considering realistic result set sizes. Overlay networks maintain for fault-tolerance multiple entries in their routing tables (data replication) and replicate index information (structural replication) to compensate node and network failures. Therefore, peers have multiple peers at hand to forward a query and to select the destination peer to process a query and reply matching entries.

8.7.1 Routing Strategies

Considering the diversity of peer response times and CPU loads of PlanetLab peers, we implemented five different next-hop selection strategies in the P-Grid application to evaluate their influence on query response times and query load distribution in a realistic environment. The five strategies are the following:

- *Random*: Queries are forwarded to a random peer of the corresponding routing table level.

- *Fixed*: The first time a query is forwarded to a certain level, a peer at this level is selected randomly and all subsequent queries are forwarded to the same peer. This is analogous to having no routing redundancy.

- *Least Frequently Used (LFU)*: Peers maintain a counter of sent messages for all peers in their routing table and queries are forwarded to the peer with the lowest counter per routing level. This strategy uses a local estimate of other peers load, and hence will not depend on other peers' honesty.

- *Currently Least Loaded (CLL)*: Queries are forwarded to the peer with the lowest reported query load at a level; peers piggy-back their query load in the last minute on acknowledgment messages.

- *Currently Fastest Response (CFR)*: Peers forward queries to the currently fastest responding peer at a level; peers therefore measure the time between sending a query to a peer and receiving the corresponding acknowledgment message. This strategy inherently takes care of congestion caused by either traffic within the overlay, or any extrinsic reasons. This strategy can also be seen as proximity-based routing as peers in the proximity tend to respond faster than peers further away.

8.7.2 Evaluation

These five routing strategies were evaluated on PlanetLab on up to 300 nodes, depending on the number of available nodes. Each PlanetLab node runs one instance of a P-Grid node, and possibly several other experiments by other users in parallel. Therefore PlanetLab nodes are subject of various loads depending on the simultaneously running experiments on the testbed. Although these external factors influence our experiments they also provide a realistic environment with slower and faster peers.

We deployed the P-Grid software, i.e., the peers, on all available nodes at the times the experiments were conducted and assigned 10 keys to each peer. This relatively low number of keys was chosen to speed up experiments. We waited 150 minutes till the P-Grid network was constructed, i.e., peers became responsible for key partitions and their routing tables contained the necessary references to other peers/partitions to resolve queries. The delay of 150 minutes is based on experience and depends mainly on the number of nodes participating in the experiment, the number of inserted data and the testbed environment. The constructed P-Grid network had the following characteristics: (i) on average, 5 peers were responsible for a partition, i.e., on average 5 peers could answer a query; (ii) peers maintain up to 10 routing entries per level, i.e., a query could be routed to up to 10 different peers. Please note that 10 is the maximum number of references per level and decreases for higher routing levels as it is further bound by the maximum number of peers available per

8.7. Load-Aware Message Routing

sub-tree/partition, i.e., on average 5 for the highest routing level according to the replication factor.

After this initial construction phase, each peer issued queries with intervals between 1 and 2 minutes. For the five different next-hop selection strategies, each strategy was used for 50 minutes. In the following we will discuss the influence of the different routing strategies on the required bandwidth, number of messages, query response time, and the load distribution for peers.

Bandwidth and Number of Messages First of all, we compare the required bandwidth and number of messages for query resolution for the 5 routing strategies. Figure 8.5 shows the average bandwidth consumption and number of messages per peer and minute for query and query replies for each strategy. Both, the bandwidth and number of messages, remains the same for all five strategies, i.e., all strategies perform equally. This was expected as the effort to resolve a query remains the same. This observation is further confirmed by the fact that the number of hops a query requires remains the same for all strategies.

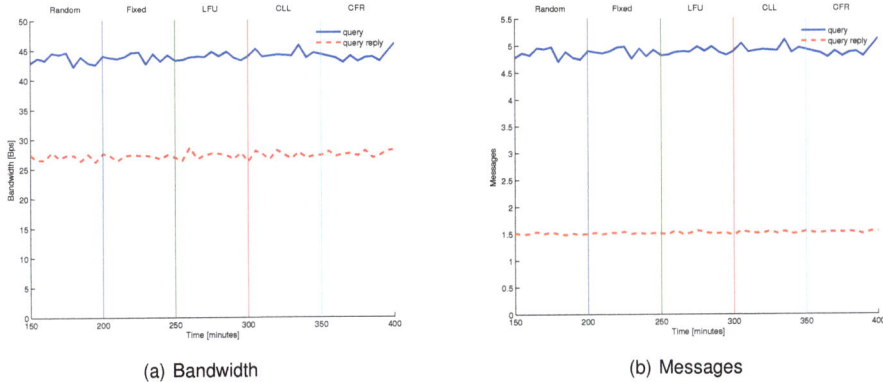

(a) Bandwidth   (b) Messages

Figure 8.5: Bandwidth and number of messages

Query Response Time and Success Next, we compare the query response time together with the query success rate for our five next-hop routing strategies. On the left hand side of Figure 8.6, we can see that the response time is the same for the strategies *Random*, *Fixed*, and *LFU* as expected. Those three strategies distribute the forwarding load for queries uniformly among all peers in the network, i.e., all peers forward on average the same number of queries leading to similar query response times.

The response time drastically increases for the *CLL* strategy. The reason is that slow peers which cannot process many queries are overloaded and therefore become even slower. The *CLL* strategy always prefers globally underloaded peers and does not take into account the heterogeneity of peers regarding their bandwidth connection and processing power. On the other hand, the *CFR* strategy always prefers peers which responded recently fast to query forwarding requests. Therefore, queries are not forwarded to slow peers anymore and the average query response time is lower than for the other strategies. We will show later that this improvements comes along with an increased imbalance for the query forwarding load.

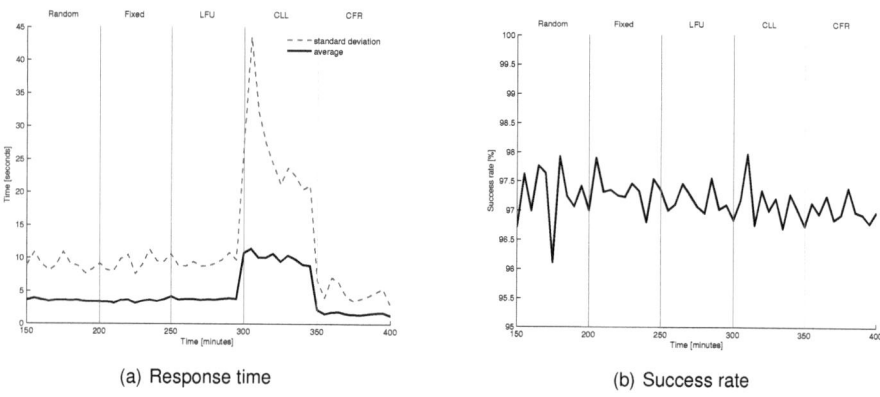

Figure 8.6: Query response time and query success rate

Figure 8.6 also shows that all strategies perform equally well in terms of success rates. Most queries reached a responsible peer being able to respond to a query initiator with the requested answers. The missing 3% of success rate are explainable by lost query reply messages as query initiators do not acknowledge their receipt to their senders. A lost query message can therefore not be detected and will not be retransmitted in case of an error.

Load Distribution Finally we look at the load distributions observed by peers to forward respectively answer queries. Figure 8.7 shows the CDF for both loads and for the five next-hop strategies. It is obvious that the strategy has an influence on the forwarding load and basically none on the resolution load. The *Random* and *LFU* perform almost equally as they locally balance the load among their references over time. The *Fixed* strategy already increases the imbalance as one peer is selected at the beginning and kept as forwarding reference over time. Therefore, some peers already have to handle almost twice as many queries compared to the *Random* and *LFU* strategy. The worst strategy in terms of load balancing is as expected *CFR*. As queries are only forwarded to fast responding peers, slow peers do not observe any query load anymore leading to a considerable imbalance of query forwarding load. The best load balancing strategy however is the *CLL* strategy. Again, as

8.7. Load-Aware Message Routing

expected as this strategy considers the observed query load at each peer and peers use the reported loads to select their next candidates.

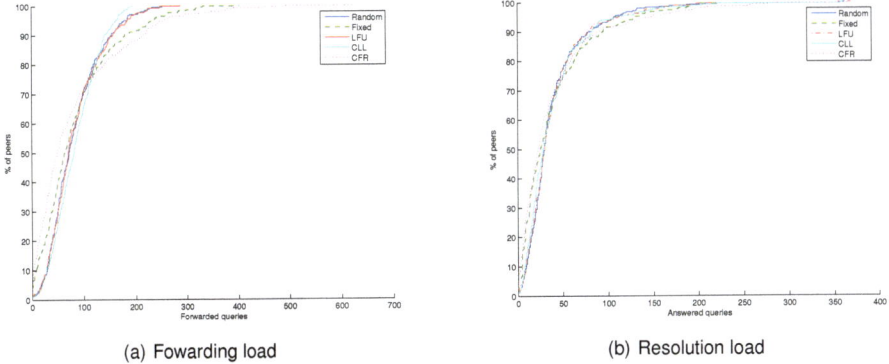

(a) Fowarding load

(b) Resolution load

Figure 8.7: Query load to forward and resolve queries

The load observed by peers to resolve queries is almost the same for all strategies as the routing strategy only has an influence at the last hop to choose the finally responsible peer to answer a query. [DSA07] studies a query load balancing approach for structured overlays considering a combination of caching and the existence of route redundancy. The paper shows that caching helps to reduce the answering load of peers as more peers become responsible for popular index entries. The paper further shows that route redundancy cannot balance the answering load as queries still have to be answered by a few responsible peers and only depends on the distribution of issued queries. The forwarding load on the other can very well be balanced by load-aware routing strategies using multiple routing entries in structured overlay networks present for fault-tolerance, as also shown by our evaluation.

Discussion P2P networks of peers with heterogenous resources and performance are common in the Internet and are therefore to consider by overlay networks. Our evaluation shows that routing strategies can improve routing performance in such environments considering only local or small piggy-backed information. The three randomized forwarding strategies *Random*, *Fixed*, and *LFU* have similar properties and represent current practice in overlay networks. The *CLL* and *CFR* strategies have the highest impact, as expected, as they consider the recent load and response delays observed by peers. Although *CFR* shows the worst query load balancing characteristics, we still consider it as the best strategy as it is the only one considering peer and link heterogeneity. Faster and better connected peers will receive more queries to forward and/or to respond to but they are also able to do so whereas the *CLL* strategy slows down the overall system by also selecting slow peers.

Our *CFR* routing strategy is further similar to proximity-based routing as studied in [HLWY06, CDHR03]. The idea of proximity routing is to select, among the set of possible next hops, the one that is closest in the physical network or one that represents a good compromise between progress in the key space and proximity. RTT, the round trip time of message packets, is often used as distance measure among hosts, resembling our response time measurements used for the *CFR* routing strategy.

8.8 Conclusions

This chapter presented more details about P-Grid's implementation of the architectural design presented in the previous chapter. We showed how the two-layered approach, their components and services were realized in the code. For each package, we presented the most relevant classes enabling application developers to easily use and extend our code if desired.

The advantages and challenges of implementing P-Grid in a deployable and testable application was outlined in the case study of load-aware message routing. Although, the implementation of such a distributed and complex system is challenging and time-intensive, the benefit of testing and evaluating the system in realistic environments is invaluable. Not only is an implementation the only proof that approaches work in reality, real-world tests also yield to new insights into the system which have to be considered in theory to fine-tune and improve approaches. Theory and practice are therefore inseparable for the development of structured overlays.

Chapter 9
UniStore

The implementation of P-Grid enabled us to build applications on top of it relying on a stable structured overlay network providing efficient single key lookups as well as more complex search predicates. Nowadays, many new applications, for example Wikis, social networks, and distributed recommender systems, require the efficient integration of decentralized and heterogeneous data sources at a large scale. In this chapter, we present our approach of a universal storage for RDF-like triple data based on P-Grid and the universal relation model as its key enabling technologies to achieve flexibility, robustness, and efficiency for large-scale distributed data storage and query processing.

We first outline the motivation for building a global-scale universal distributed storage (UniStore) to support new web applications and provide an overview of the corresponding challenges related to it. The architecture of UniStore is based on P-Grid, solving already some of the challenges such as scalability, robustness and availability. On top, a triple store deals with the problem of data organization following the idea of the universal relation model allowing schema-independent query formulations. We introduce our query language VQL, based on SPARQL, in the context of similarity queries. Similarity queries are an important feature together with schema mappings to support data heterogeneity on data and schema level. We support several similarity query operations such as similarity joins and ranking operations. Their evaluation on PlanetLab shows that our implementation on top of P-Grid meets our theoretical cost predictions.

This chapter represents work carried out in collaboration with Prof. Kai-Uwe Sattler and Marcel Karnstedt from TU Ilmenau, who originated the idea of UniStore and implemented the application. We contributed to the design of the application and algorithms presented in this chapter, and provide the underlying P2P infrastructure.

9.1 Motivation

An increasing number of applications on the Web are based on the idea of collecting and combining large public data sets and services. In such *public data management* scenarios, the information, its structure, and its semantics are controlled by a large number of participants and integration and data management functionalities come into existence through the collaborative efforts of the users, i.e., the system's public. Examples of such applications are Wikipedia, social networks such as friend-of-a-friend networks, or recommender systems.

Despite being distributed or decentralized in respect to data from a conceptual point of view, the supporting infrastructures of these systems are still inherently centralized, as in the original web approach web servers manage their data locally and only communication and hyper-linking introduce the aspect of decentralization (though the Web itself is decentralized). For example, in Wikipedia articles are edited in a decentralized way, but adding the information permanently to the (central) data collection is done under central control; in social networks, e.g., friend-of-a-friend networks, although inherently decentralized, users typically enter via centralized portals and data management is centralized at the portal. Though often centralization makes sense to maintain full control of the information management, the downsides are bottlenecks and single-point-of-failures, which have to be accounted for by expensive hardware and secondary Internet connections.

In this chapter, we argue for a decentralization of data management for novel web applications and search engines. This means that information sources are highly distributed, data is described according to heterogeneous schemas, no participant has a global view of all information, and data and service quality can only be guaranteed in a best effort way. Best effort may seem to be a severe limitation at first glance. However, many services we use on a daily basis follow this approach and still provide meaningful service, for example email, DNS, and P2P systems which do not provide any "transactional" service guarantees.

For such type of public information systems, the P2P approach offers an interesting alternative to existing information system architectures. On the infrastructure side, data is accessed directly at the source, i.e., always fresh, efficient indexing is available, and the systems scale well in terms of nodes and data mounts. Additionally, new systems can be deployed at very low costs as no specialized infrastructures are required as the resources of the participants are being used, high-quality data from the "edge" of the Internet, i.e., the annotated knowledge of the participants, can be made available very easily, and the systems are robust due to their decentralized architecture. On the data level, however, new research problems have to be addressed, the most prominent being: Data may exist in a large number of different schema organizations, it is unclear how trust-worthy the data is, and expressively of queries and possible guarantees (existence, completeness, etc.) are limited at the moment.

Despite these open questions, we argue that global-scale universal distributed storages have a number of important advantages that outweigh the problems and are a new type of Internet storage system. Our vision is to build a light-weight universal distributed storage for public data/metadata as an enabling backbone technology for storage, which exploits the gigantic storage and processing capacity of the available Internet nodes in the same way as the network layer exploits the worldwide communication devices for routing messages between nodes. In the following sections, we will present the challenges to be addressed and possible solutions.

9.2 Challenges

In contrast to systems such as OceanStore [KBC+00, REG+03], which aim at secure archival storage for a single data source, we aim at integrating data sources into a universal storage at an Internet scale. While some of the challenges may be similar, there exist several different aspects and others have to be taken into account differently because of disjoint requirements. We overview the key issues for a universal store in the following and classify the challenges along three questions:

1. How to structure and organize data in massively distributed settings?

2. How to query data and how to query efficiently?

3. What is necessary to build a robust and practical solution?

The first question deals with *data organization* and raises two challenges:

Genericity and flexibility Because we cannot assume that all users and applications agree to a common schema, a generic and extensible schema is required for structuring data. It should facilitate to add new elements without restructuring or conflicts. This should be accompanied by a schema-independent query language relieving the user of the burden to know relations, classes or element paths. A good choice would be a universal relation model [MUV84] or –as a new incarnation– an RDF-like triple-based model.

Dealing with heterogeneity In order to be able to combine data from different domains without forcing all providers to use the same schema, techniques for resolving heterogeneities both on schema level (different names or structures for the same concept) as well as on data level (different representations of the same real-world object) are required. Particularly in large systems, resolving conflicts should be left to the individual user but be supported by appropriate modeling concepts (e.g., correspondence relationships for schema elements) as well as by explicitly handling schema information as data.

The second question is related to *query processing* with the following challenges:

Expressiveness of queries Querying data in a large-scale distributed storage requires both classical DB-like queries allowing to restrict and combine data (selection, projection, join, set operations) as well as IR-style queries (e.g., keyword search over all attributes, similarity). In addition, a query language for this domain should support querying schema data (attributes, correspondences) as well and treat this as plain data.

Efficient query operators Distributed implementations of the query operators should come with worst-case guarantees (e.g., $O(\log n)$ for structured overlays) and exploit the features of the underlying infrastructure (e.g., for DHTs hash-based placement, topology-aware routing and multicasting). Furthermore, processing more complex queries, which typically result in several equivalent execution plans, should involve cost-based and adaptive query optimization considering the dynamicity of the whole network and the autonomy of the individual nodes.

Question (3) touches practicability of a large-scale distributed platform. Among others the main challenges are:

Scalability Certainly, an important property of a distributed system is scalability with respect to the number of nodes. For a structured overlay network this is inherently guaranteed for lookup operations. However, scalability has to be also addressed for more complex query operations as well as particularly for data import/update (e.g., bulk inserts/updates) and more generally maintenance operations.

Robustness and availability A distributed storage has to be robust and reliable, which basically means to be resilient against node and link failures. This has to be addressed by maintaining redundant links (as already provided by structured overlays), but also by replicas of data. Data replication raises several further issues, such as the required number of replicas in order to guarantee a degree of availability or the strategies used for update propagation in a decentralized environment. Moreover, the existence of replicas allows the system to choose among different nodes for retrieving data based on the current load of nodes, but requires distributed monitoring of load in a dynamic environment.

Privacy, trust, and fairness In structured overlay networks where data is not stored on a provider's site there exists a strong requirement to prevent malicious behavior of nodes (e.g., modifying locally stored data). Thus, privacy of the hosted data as well as trusting peers on the returned result of a query are important challenges. Secondly, a fair distribution of data and/or load has to be guaranteed in order to avoid negative affect of the overall performance.

9.3 Architecture

Structured P2P overlays are a good basis for a distributed universal storage because problems like scalability, robustness and fair balance of load and work are covered as described in the previous sections. Structured overlays offer logarithmic search complexity in the number of nodes and are based on hashing for data placement, which allows for realizing efficient query processing strategies. Additionally, they offer guarantees and limits needed for defining an appropriate cost model.

Figure 9.1 shows the architecture of the implemented system. Based on the P-Grid overlay layer, triple storage functionality is provided by a second layer, which is used by P-Grid's *StorageService* to store triple data and to process structured queries.

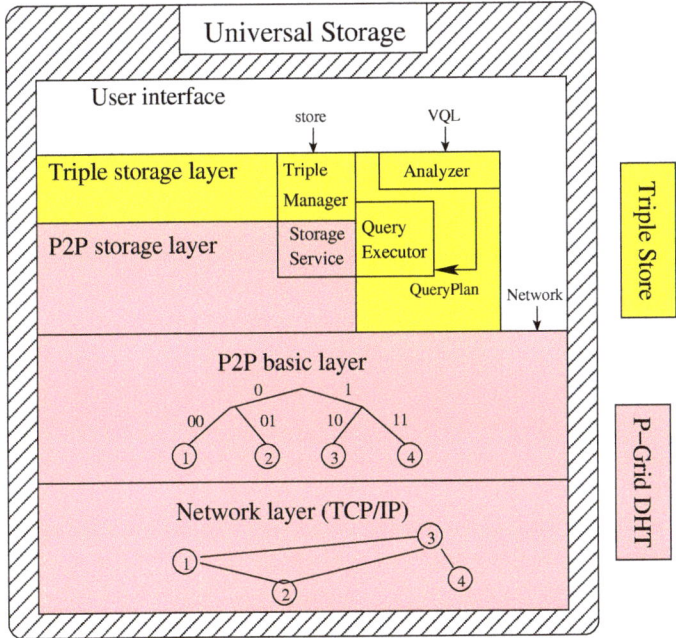

Figure 9.1: Distributed universal storage

9.3.1 Distributed Storage Layer

As mentioned earlier, we aim to provide a scalable distributed infrastructure for storing, retrieving and integrating structured meta-data like data for the Semantic Web. In this regard, a natural way of supporting these features, to some extent, is to exploit scalability, location transparency, logarithmic search complexity as well as guarantees offered by the P2P infrastructure. In the implementation, P-Grid is used as distributed storage layer because of its support for scalability as well as robustness as required by our infrastructure. It is also used for data management in general and index management in particular. We further rely on P-Grid's efficient support for exact key lookups and more complex search predicates such as substring search, range queries, similarity queries (see Section 9.4) and multi-term queries.

9.3.2 Triple Storage Layer

In order to face the challenges of data organization, we follow the idea of the universal relation model allowing schema-independent query formulation. However, because exploiting the features of a structured overlay for fast lookups requires to index all attributes, we store data vertically, similar to the idea of RDF. RDFPeers [CF04] exploits a similar data organization for RDF data as in our work, but does not address, for instance, similarity-based queries. If we assume relational data, each tuple $(OID, v_1, \ldots, v_n)$ of a given relation schema $R(A_1, \ldots, A_n)$ is stored in the form of n triples

$$(OID, A_1, v_1), \ldots, (OID, A_n, v_n)$$

where OID is a unique key, e.g., a URI, and the attribute names A_i may contain a namespace prefix ns which allows the user to distinguish different relations and avoid conflicts.

Figure 9.2 illustrates this for two example tuples representing papers at a workshop and conference. Each tuple contains three attributes: title, conference and year. The 18 resulting triples are distributed in the network of 8 peers (corresponding hash keys are sketched: e.g., `OID->t` means triple `t` was inserted according to `hash(OID)`). Additionally, we allow to store triples representing a simple kind of schema mappings in order to overcome schema heterogeneities.

The vertical storage supersedes the explicit representation of null values making the universal relation approach feasible even for heterogeneous data. Obviously, this data storage model is exactly the same layout as RDF – therefore RDF data can be stored seamlessly.

Note that, though we use an OID field, we do not assume unique and homogeneous identifiers for all objects – instead the OID is system generated allowing to group the triples for a logical tuple. Integration tasks, i.e., merging different tuples representing the same real-world object, are expected to be performed on top of this in a user/application-specific way as part of queries.

The hash-based approach of the underlying overlay system allows for inserting each triple multiple times into the structured overlay using different keys. This is analogous to indexing data in relational systems, as each entry and any combination of the triples' entries (e.g., "hot" attributes) may be chosen, and several kinds of indexes may be implemented (e.g., textual or spatial indexes). This can increase efficiency of query processing by far.

9.3. Architecture

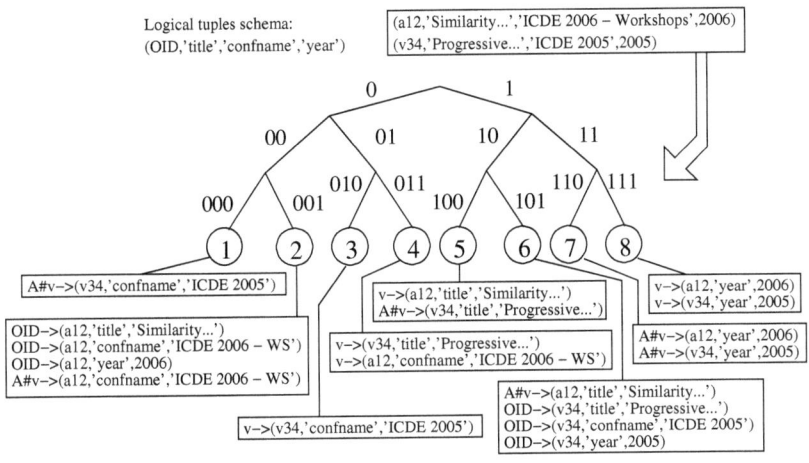

Figure 9.2: Example tuples stored in P-Grid

Moreover, by inserting full triples each time, we introduce a kind of replication on triple level, additionally to replication on peer level, which is essential in structured overlay systems.

By default, we index each triple on the OID, $A_i\#v_i$ (the concatenation of A_i and v_i), and v_i. This enables search based on the unique key, queries of the form $A_i\#v_i \geq v_j$, and using v_i as the key for queries on an arbitrary attribute. Like this, efficient reproduction of origin data, as well as access to parts of special interest, is ensured in each situation, as the elements of an origin tuple are stored

(i) clustered – good to achieve low bandwidth consumption and a small number of messages, and

(ii) well distributed – better suited for dynamic situations and load balancing.

By applying order-preserving hash functions similar values are stored at the same peer or neighboring peers, which decreases the efforts incurred in processing range queries, joins, or similarity operations.

9.3.3 Schema Mapping

On top of the data triple storage we additionally allow to store data representing a simple kind of schema mappings in order to overcome schema heterogeneities. In a universal relation model, mappings are simply correspondence links between attributes, whereas different kinds of correspondences can be represented (e.g., "semantically equivalent", "subsumes",

...). Figure 9.3 shows an example of a mapping situation. Two relations (i.e., a set of attributes that belong to each other) are sketched and two equivalence mappings between attributes are indicated. This can be enriched by other correspondences like subclass and also be extended to relations themselves, respectively concepts they represent.

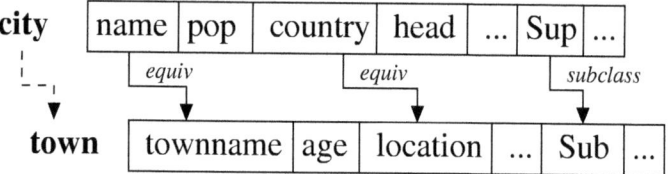

Figure 9.3: Attribute mapping

An equivalence mapping between the attributes A_1 and A_2 is represented by a triple

$$(A_1, \textit{map:equiv}, A_2)$$

where *map:equiv* describes the kind of correspondence and A_1 is the identifier of the source attribute. This additional metadata can be queried explicitly by the user – or even automatically by the system to retrieve relevant data without needing the user to interact. Moreover, we think of schema matchers to "crawl" the system (at regular intervals or initiated by the user) and find correspondences (semi-)automatically – thus, the user only needs to join the system, provide his (desired) data and/or schema, and may query remote data at once, without any further intervention and special knowledge. However, such schema matching approaches are beyond the scope of this thesis. Instead we refer to the respective work [RB01]. However, we envision methods as presented in [CMAF06] to (semi-)automatically infer on the correctness of schema mappings. The required architecture for efficient distributed inference is thereby already provided by P-Grid.

The introduced data organization helps to deal with some of the earlier mentioned challenges, because it provides a generic and flexible schema, which can even be extended by meta information to overcome the burden of data heterogeneity. By building the triple store on top of a structured overlay, we can exploit powerful features of these systems to create a robust, scalable and reliable distributed storage. However, problems like trust and privacy in such environments are treated by the P2P overlay and database research communities, but are far from being solved finally. From the view of data integration, the introduced model provides a wide range of capabilities to utilize integration techniques for dealing with data heterogeneities.

9.4 Similarity Queries

Similarity queries are a key requirement in distributed content management systems for two simple reasons: (1) users are unable to specify their information needs correctly and (2) large information amounts with possibly suboptimal data quality are queried. Data quality may be suboptimal due to spelling errors and typos and we cannot assume that all users will agree on exactly the same schema and value representations, i.e., naturally people will use different though often syntactically similar conceptualizations for the same data. Therefore, we argue that similarity-based query operations play a key role in dealing with heterogeneities by enabling to retrieve data (similarity lookup and filtering) as well as to combine data (similarity join and grouping) based on fuzzy matching conditions.

Based on our triple storage model we present and discuss strategies for efficient processing of similarity selections and joins in a structured overlay. We will show that there are several possible strategies exploiting structured overlay features to a different extent (i.e., key organization, routing, multi-casting) and thus the choice of the best operator implementation in a given situation (selectivity, data distribution, load) should be based on cost information allowing the system to estimate the computation and communication costs of query execution plans. Obviously, this cannot be done in the same way as in classical centralized database systems where all necessary statistical cost information are available. Hence, we present a cost model for similarity operations on structured data in a structured overlay network.

Basically our approach is generally applicable to any P2P system, be it structured, e.g., Chord, CAN, P-Grid, or unstructured, e.g., Gnutella. However, structured P2P systems have a couple of advantages, we can exploit in processing similarity queries: (1) Cost-aware processing requires the definition of accurate cost measures which in turn requires the knowledge about the complexity involved in the processing tasks, which cannot be provided for unstructured systems like Gnutella, but are available for structured systems. (2) Structured overlays offer very low overheads for locating data items, typically $O(log(n))$. As we insert and query large amounts of small data items in our approach, this is an important factor for minimizing costs. (3) Structured overlays offer better data-processing related guarantees, for example, for completeness, existence, etc., which are important properties for database-like processing of predicates.

9.4.1 The Query Language VQL

Users should be able to search for (1) data, (2) metadata, and (3) combinations of both by defining constraints on both the data and schema levels. Queries should encompass simple search conditions but also advanced operations on the distributed data such as joins or ranking should be supported. To enable the user to express these types of queries, we use the *VQL query language* which is based on SPARQL [PS06], a query language for RDF. As query formulation and the logical algebra used for representing query plans are not in the focus of this thesis, we will only informally introduce VQL and the logical algebra through some simple examples demonstrating its capabilities and the types of queries we discuss in the following sections.

Let us assume that each user in a P2P system has a movie database similar to IMDB (http://www.imdb.com/). For simplicity, without constraining generality, we assume that the following simple relations are used by the participants:

```
movies:  (title, year, type)
top100:  (movie, director)
actors:  (name, mtitle, rolename)
```

The basic construct of a query in VQL is a SELECT - WHERE block similar to SQL, but as we do not manage relations in a horizontal manner we do not have to provide a FROM clause. The WHERE clause is defined on triples (OID, A_i, v_i), selection is done using optional FILTER(expr) statements in the WHERE clause, and the functions *dist* and *edist* allow the user to express similarity in terms of distance (Euclidean or edit distance). Each term in a query starting with a question mark represents a variable and all expressions in the WHERE clause are implicitly combined conjunctively. Additional clauses such as ORDER BY, LIMIT and OFFSET are optional and have the same meaning as in SQL.

The following VQL statement defines a query for all directors who worked with actors named similar to "Billy Bill" in the years 2000 – 2004, including also the movie title and year in the result set, and ordered by the year the movie was produced. Additionally, we make the complicating assumption that the data provided by the users is erroneous and thus also the join operation on the movie titles, required to produce the final result uses similarity-based string matching.

```
SELECT ?d,?t,?y
WHERE { (?o1,name,?n) FILTER (edist(?n,Billy Bill)<3)
        (?o1,mtitle,?t) (?o2,movie,?s)
        FILTER (edist(?t,?s)<2)
        (?o3,title,?u) FILTER (edist(?t,?u)<2)
        (?o3,year,?y) FILTER (dist(?y,2002)<3)
        (?o2,director,?d) }
ORDER BY ?y DESC
```

A powerful advantage of the vertical storage model we use is the possibility to express similarity on the schema level in addition to similarity on the data level, which simplifies homogenization tasks. The following example joins data from movies with corresponding data from actors, by applying similarity first on the schema level (only edist(title,mtitle)=1

9.4. Similarity Queries

can satisfy the filter condition on schema level in line 3) and then on instance (data) level (the actual movie titles). Moreover, to keep the final result size small, we only select those 10 movies which where produced closest to 2005 (*top-N* query).

```
SELECT ?v1,?v2,?n,?r,?y
WHERE  { (?o1,?a1,?v1) (?o2,?a2,?v2)
         FILTER (edist(?a1,?a2)<2)
         FILTER (edist(?v1,?v2)<3)
         (?o1,rolename,?r) (?o1,name,?n)
         (?o2,year,?y) }
ORDER BY dist(?y,2005) LIMIT 10
```

The logical algebra used to represent the resulting operator plans is closely related to the relational algebra, but extended by some special operators.

9.4.2 Similarity Measures and Processing

The typical distance measure for numerical values is the Euclidean distance which can be mapped to range queries in the overlay network. Range queries have received quite some attention recently and several structural overlays can handle them already. We will not discuss range queries in further details here. We nevertheless rely on P-Grid's ability to process such range queries efficiently. For similarity measures on string values the situation is different as they cannot be mapped to range queries. This is especially true for the popular *Levenshtein distance* or edit distance [Lev66]. Without constraining the general applicability of our approach, we will focus on the processing of single string similarity predicates based on the edit distance $edist(s_1, s_2)$, though our approach works for any distance measure $d(x, y) \rightarrow \Re$.

In its simplest form the edit distance of two strings s_1 and s_2 is the number of operations (insertion, deletion or substitution of characters) needed to transform s_1 into s_2. For instance, the edit distance d of "edna" and "eden" is 2. Several approaches exist to efficiently process similarity measures based on the edit distance. We base our work on that of Navarro et al. [NBY98] and Gravano et al. [GIJ+01] who suggest the evaluation of the edit distance using substrings of fixed length q, so-called *q-grams*. We briefly discuss the main results of these works which we exploit in our approach. The main observation is that if we pick any $d+1$ non-overlapping q-grams extracted from string s_1, at least one of the q-grams must be fully contained in the comparison string s_2 (the two matching q-grams *correspond* to each other) [NBY98] if their edit distance is $edist(s_1, s_2) = d$.

As a consequence, we extend the original storage scheme highlighted before as follows: Rather than indexing only whole strings, we additionally split them into q-grams and index those (both on the instance and on schema levels), i.e., for a triple $t = (OID, A_i, v_i)$ we store the following in P-Grid:

$[h(oid), (OID, t)],$
$[h(A_i \# qg_1(v_i)), (OID, t)], \ldots, [h(A_i \# qg_n(v_i)), (OID, t)],$
$[h(qg_1(v_i)), (OID, t)], \ldots, [h(qg_n(v_i)), (OID, t)],$
$[h(qg_1(A_i)), (OID, t)], \ldots, [h(qg_n(A_i)), (OID, t)]$

($h()$ denotes the hash function of P-Grid to generate the key under which the triple is stored, and $qg_i(s)$ denotes the ith q-gram of s). This storage scheme involves a non-negligible overhead (depending on the actual choice of indexed attributes), but decreases query processing costs considerably, as we will show in the following sections.

As an example, consider a tuple t: $\{123, edna\}$ with schema s: $\{id, name\}$. In the original scheme the following data items would be stored in the structured overlay (we assume that the triple's OID is 1):

$[h(1), (1,\texttt{id},123)], [h(\texttt{id}\#123), (1,\texttt{id},123)], [h(123), (1,\texttt{id},123)],$
$[h(1), (1,\texttt{name},\texttt{edna})], [h(\texttt{name}\#\texttt{edna}), (1,\texttt{name},\texttt{edna})],$
$[h(\texttt{edna}), (1,\texttt{name},\texttt{edna})]$

Extending this by a 3-gram index on instance level of attribute name produces the following additional data items to be stored:

$[h(\texttt{name}\#\texttt{edn}), (1,\texttt{name},\texttt{edna})], [h(\texttt{name}\#\texttt{dna}), (1,\texttt{name},\texttt{edna})],$
$[h(\texttt{edn}), (1,\texttt{name},\texttt{edna})], [h(\texttt{dna}), (1,\texttt{name},\texttt{edna})]$

Additionally, indexing on schema level results in the following additional data items to be stored:

$[h(\texttt{nam}), (1,\texttt{name},\texttt{edna})], [h(\texttt{ame}), (1,\texttt{name},\texttt{edna})]$

9.5 Physical Operators

Having discussed the basic conceptual approach for similarity queries, we will now describe the implementation of similarity operators available in our query engine. As already mentioned, we distinguish between queries on instance level, on schema level, and queries combining both levels. We will only describe the processing of queries on instance level as the handling of queries on schema level differs only in the selection of part of the triples which is processed. We start with similarity selections as the basis for advanced operators and then present similarity joins and ranking operators as examples for advanced operators. In the following we will only deal with string similarity as numerical similarity measures can simply be mapped on range queries and additionally, string data will be the dominating data type in most systems (not only on schema, but also on instance level).

In principle, we could process string similarity queries by only utilizing the functionality already provided by P-Grid. By issuing key lookups, we can locate the data concerned by similarity predicates, e.g., by prefix searches on the attribute names. However, this would be very expensive as instance level queries can result in involving the whole overlay if popular attributes are distributed among all peers, e.g., as in Chord. If this is combined with similarity measures on the schema level the situation would be even worse as we have to look at even more data using this simplistic approach. Additionally, only a fraction of the queried peers will actually contribute to the final result. We will denote this simple strategy as *term-based processing* which will serve as a baseline for comparison to show the gain we can achieve through our *q-gram-based processing* strategy. This strategy exploits additional indexes based on q-grams as described above and incurs additional messages for querying these indexes, but saves a lot of bandwidth and message costs for processing the queries in most cases.

To be able to compare the costs of these two alternatives we will define a cost model in Section 9.6. However, it is not the focus of this thesis to redefine optimization and planning tasks already known from relational and distributed database systems. Rather we target the costs incurred by the actual gathering of data distributed among the peers of the overlay network which is required to be able to process similarity queries.

9.5.1 Similarity Selection

The most fundamental operation we have to support in processing similarity queries is *similarity selection*, which means that all data corresponding to a similarity predicate is located and returned to the peer having initiated the query. With term-based processing, we contact *each* peer responsible for a part of the data to be queried as shown in Algorithm 9.6 for basic similarity predicates such as $edist(A_i \# v_j, s) < d$, where A_i is a given attribute name, p is the peer executing the query, $h()$ is the hashing function used by the overlay, s is the search string, and d is a positive integer denoting the edit distance.

Algorithm 9.6 Term-based similarity selection $TSel(p, A_i, s, d)$
1: $T = SimRetrieve(p, h(A_i), s, d)$;
2: $R = \emptyset$;
3: **for all** $t \in T$ **do**
4: $\quad R = R \cup Retrieve(p, h(\xi(t, 1)), \xi(t, 1))$
5: **end for**

Assuming that $Retrieve(p, k, s)$ is the normal query forwarding and search function of an overlay, $SimRetrieve$ extends it with similarity search functionality, i.e., the normal routing is not touched but each peer receives the search string s to be used for similarity matching plus the required similarity d for local evaluation. We also assume that $Retrieve$ can do both exact and prefix (path) queries, for example, as in P-Grid. Thus a query for $h(A_i)$ would be successful although we actually indexed $A_i\#v_i$ as already described. This is just a shortcut to exploit existing overlay functionality and to be more efficient in query processing. For systems not offering prefix search, triples (OID, A_i, v_i) would be indexed with A_i as the key. However, in the following we implicitly assume that prefix search is supported by $Retrieve$ and thus also by $SimRetrieve$, without constraining the general applicability of the algorithms. As we are dealing not only with triples but with tuples, line 4 uses the OID to retrieve all parts of a tuple and reconstruct it (this is equivalent to $Retrieve(p, key(\xi(t,1)), \xi(t,1)))$, where $\xi(t,i)$ simply means to take the ith field of a tuple t, which in our storage model is the OID for $i=1$). The result of this operation is then collected in R. If we would only work with triples, e.g., RDF, or are not interested in all attributes of a tuple, this step would not be necessary.

The q-gram based variant of similarity selection is shown in Algorithm 9.7.

Algorithm 9.7 Q-gram-based similarity selection: $QSel(p, A_i, s, d)$
1: determine $d+1$ q-grams Q from s;
2: $R = \emptyset$;
3: **for all** $q \in Q$ **do**
4: $\quad T = SimRetrieve(p, h(A_i\#q), s, d)$;
5: $\quad$ **for all** $t \in T$ **do**
6: $\quad\quad R = R \cup Retrieve(p, h(\xi(t,1)), \xi(t,1))$
7: $\quad$ **end for**
8: **end for**

The main difference to the term-based variant is that $SimRetrieve$ is called in a loop, once for each q-gram. Then, we again reconstruct the tuples (line 6) by querying for all found OIDs. Both similarity selection algorithms allow an improvement and parallelization if the whole tuple should be reconstructed, as done at line 4 in Algorithm 9.6 and at line 6 in Algorithm 9.7. Instead of returning first temporary results at line 1 respectively line 4 by $SimRetrieve$ to a query initiating peer and then materializing all tuples sequentially, peers responsible for a $SimRetrieve$ can materialize a tuple before it is returned to an initiator. The query is thereby forwarded to peers responsible for the corresponding $OIDs$ which then reply directly to the initiating peer. We call this method *DelSel* and the impact of this variant depends on the current network state and data distribution, and is covered by our cost model which we present in Section 9.6.

9.5.2 Similarity Join

A similarity join is one of the most important similarity operators as it is a powerful tool to overcome heterogeneity at the schema level, which allows the system to deal with semantic inconsistencies, i.e., supports schema integration, and at the data level to address inconsistencies or inaccuracies in the data to be processed. The following discussions are based on the definition of similarity string joins given in [Coh00]: Given two input sets of tuples r and s with schemas $\hat{r} : (X_1 \ldots X_k)$ and $\hat{s} : (Y_1 \ldots Y_l)$ a similarity join produces the cross product of all tuples and returns those tuples t with schema $\hat{t} := (X_1 \ldots X_k Y_1 \ldots Y_l)$ for which a similarity predicate $p : edist(X_i, Y_j) < c, \; i \leq k \wedge j \leq l \wedge c$ is constant, is true.

Such joins are also conceivable only on schema level, but we expect joins comprising both levels to occur much more frequently. This corresponds to similarity predicates like $edist(\hat{A}_i, \hat{B}_j) < c_1 \wedge edist(A_i, B_j) < c_2$. In the following we discuss similarity joins on the instance level as the same algorithms can be applied on the schema level and a combination of the two levels then is straight-forward. To process such a join, three basic approaches exist:

1. Process the left and the right side separately and evaluate the join on the data gathered locally. The disadvantage of this strategy is that a lot of data may be transferred unnecessarily which will not contribute to the result.

2. Process the left side first, i.e., *materialize* data for the left side (w.l.o.g. we expect the left side to be materialized) and apply a nested loop approach for querying similar data from the right side.

3. Include both selections into the join processing: a peer responsible for object(s) from the left side delegates the query to one peer responsible for the right side, similar to the standard approach of *mutant query plans* [PM02].

Term-based processing implies to gather all data needed at the query initiator and process everything locally. This corresponds to the first variant above and involves the execution of two (similarity) selections, which again can be varied in the actual way of processing.

Assuming that the left input set is materialized completely, we can use the approach of processing string similarity based on q-grams in order to find matching candidate tuples from the right side, before completely fetching all of the corresponding strings (variant 2 above). An intuitive implementation is based on a (block) nested loop access, which means that each materialized tuple from the left side is used as input for a corresponding similarity selection on the right side (not single tuples, but actually block(s) of them, respectively). Algorithm 9.8 illustrates this approach.

To get a more complete view, we also included the left-side selection (here exemplary by calling *Retrieve* in line 1), though this is a separate operator. The actual join tuples are

Algorithm 9.8 Nested Loop Similarity Join: $NLJoin(p, A_i, B_j, d)$
1: $L = Retrieve(p, h(A_i), A_i)$;
2: $R = \emptyset$;
3: **for all** $t \in L$ **do**
4:    $R = R \cup \{Retrieve(p, h(\xi(t', 1)), \xi(t', 1)) : t' \in QSel(p, B_j, \xi(t, 3), d)\}$;
5: **end for**

built in line 4: Each tuple from the left side is joined with all similar tuples from the right side (located by calling $QSel$). The final result is collected in R. The somehow "centralized" character of this method allows for minimizing the repeated querying of duplicate strings and q-grams. This can be achieved by merging the single queries into multiple blocks (or only one single block). This eliminates the disadvantage of variant 1, but still puts the join processing load on a single node.

An interesting alternative for distributed environments as P2P systems is to include both materializing operations into the join operator, rather than only the left one (variant 3 above). In this case, peers responsible for parts of the left side delegate directly to right side peers: $DelJoin(p, Retrieve(p, key(A_i), A_i), B_j, d)$. $DelJoin$ calls $Retrieve$ as introduced before, but responsible peers do not return results directly. Rather, they forward similarity selections to the peers responsible for the right side. These peers reply to the initiating peer directly if any tuples are actually joined according to $edist(A_i, B_j) < d$. This variant may be extended to a block-based processing at each involved peer, similar to Algorithm 9.8. The advantage of this method is, that we do not include any waiting states in the processing. The disadvantage is that less opportunities exist to eliminate repeated querying of identical strings and q-grams, as outlined for Algorithm 9.8.

9.5.3 Ranking Operators

In large-scale environments, like, for example, Google, where only best-effort solutions are applicable, ranking queries are a necessary query type. As an example, we discuss top-N similarity queries. Top-N queries are always based on a certain ranking function. We describe the implementation of a nearest neighbor ranking (NN), though other rankings are supported, but rather unsuitable for string processing.

For the term-based variant we simply query for the attributes needed and determine the top-N strings locally at the initiating peer. The q-gram-based version relies on the predetermination of an interval to query. This interval is determined such, that it potentially comprises all N needed tuples. If not, this interval is successively extended until at least N objects are available locally. Algorithm 9.9 illustrates the method.

First each peer determines the number of local data elements for attribute A. Based on this number the peer calculates a data density which approximates the number of values from A that are stored at a single peer. If the data is distributed uniformly among peers, this

Algorithm 9.9 Top-N Query: $TopN(p, A, s, N)$
1: $c = |\{d \in \delta(p) : h(d) \supseteq h(A)\}|$;
2: {determine the size r of the local range of A;}
3: $range = N/\frac{c}{r} = N \cdot \frac{r}{c}$;
4: $d = DetIntv(range, s, 0)$;
5: $R = \emptyset$;
6: **repeat**
7: $\quad R = R \cup QSel(p, A, s, d)$;
8: $\quad range = N/\frac{|R|}{2 \cdot d} = N \cdot \frac{2 \cdot d}{|R|}$;
9: $\quad d = DetIntv(range, s, d)$;
10: **until** $|R| \geq N$
11: $R = Limit(Sort(R, A), N)$;

density is a good first choice for determining an according query interval. The interval can adapted by calculating a new data density based on values already retrieved.

9.6 Similarity Operator Costs

The crucial part about optimizing query plans is to obtain the required data in the distributed system, i.e., how to access the corresponding peers in the structured overlay in an optimal way without unnecessary (re-)transmissions. If data is available locally, cost estimation for operators is identical to the relational case. The main possible alternatives for obtaining data are (1) to collect all data and process operators locally and (2) to use the indexes defined in the underlying overlay as access structures in a way that minimizes data transmission and query costs. In this section we discuss the problem of cost estimation for the introduced physical operators in order to be able to compare the different variants and enable a P2P system to choose the optimal query plan.

In a distributed environment the main costs measured are the number of messages m and the number of hops h needed to process a query. Low bandwidth consumption and short query answer times may also be of interest, but are very hard (if not impossible) to predict. Fortunately, the number of query hops is usually directly related to the query response time. In the following we provide estimates for m and h for each of the introduced operators for processing a single similarity lookup in the overlay system. Usually, a logarithmic limit in the number of peers N for m and h is guaranteed. In the following we will refer to this limit as m_l for the number of messages a lookup results in, and as h_l for the number of hops, respectively. We will only consider query messages, possible additional system and reply messages are not considered in our estimates.

We provide knowledge about string and q-gram selectivities by managing local indexes on each peer for approximating the data distribution. One approach for this is using tries as in [SGS04]. In the following we expect all needed values to be available at each peer, although in a real-world environment some of these values will have to be approximated.

operator op	m_{op}	h_{op}
$Fetch(A_i)$	$m_l + r_{A_i} - 1$	$h_l + r_{A_i} - 1$
$TSel(p, A_i, s, d)$	$m_{Fetch(A_i)}$	$h_{Fetch(A_i)}$
$QSel(p, A_i, s, d)$	$(d+1) \cdot m_l$	h_l
$DelSel(p, A_i, s, d)$	$(d+1) \cdot m_l$	h_l
$TJoin(p, A_i, B_j, d)$	$m_{LeftSel(A_i)} + m_{Fetch(B_j)}$	$max(h_{LeftSel(A_i)}, h_{Fetch(B_j)})$
$NLJoin(p, A_i, B_j, d)$	$m_{LeftSel(A_i)} + c_{left} \cdot m_{QSel(p,B_j,s_{A_i},d)}$	$h_{LeftSel(A_i)} + h_{QSel(p,B_j,s_{A_i},d)}$
$DelJoin(p, A_i, B_j, d)$	$m_{LeftSel(A_i)} + c_{left} \cdot m_{QSel(p,B_j,s_{A_i},d)}$	$h_{LeftSel(A_i)} + h_{QSel(p,B_j,s_{A_i},d)}$

Table 9.1: Costs for physical operators

Table 9.1 summarizes our cost estimations for all introduced similarity operators, ranking operators are not considered. The *Fetch* operation was not introduced separately so far, it provides the functionality of the first step in $TSel$ to fetch all values of a single attribute. This operation is processed in a sequential way: first, a query is sent to one peer responsible for a part of the queried attribute. This peer returns matching data and forwards the query, if there are other peers responsible for the attribute. This process is repeated until the last responsible peer is reached. We have to consider m_l messages to reach the first peer, and $r_{A_i} - 1$ messages to forward the query to other peers, if r_{A_i} represents the number of peers responsible for attribute A_i and key data is clustered according to A_i. Instead of fetching all data of an attribute, the q-gram-based similarity selection $QSel$ queries for $d + 1$ q-grams in parallel.

If c_{A_i} represents the number of unique values in A_i and sel_s the selectivity of the predicate $edist(A_i, s) \leq d$, we have to query for $c_{A_i} \cdot sel_s$ complete tuples in the final step of both selections, resulting in $c_A \cdot sel_s \cdot m_l$ messages. This is an additional constant factor for all implementations if the tuples are materialized at the end. The formulas in Table 9.1 do not include these costs for tuple materialization. Sub-queries for this operation can be processed in (quasi) parallel, which results in h_l hops.

The main impact on performance between $TSel$ and $QSel$ lies in r_{A_i}. A term-based selection gets more expensive if more peers are responsible for a part of the queried attribute. Furthermore, performance of $TSel$ strongly depends on the current network state, because of its sequential character. The $QSel$ similarity selection operator is particularly suited for dynamic environments as no temporary answers and no waiting states are required at the initiating peer. This is at the expense of more query messages, as several tuples will be queried multiple times for materialization (issued by different peers).

The costs for advanced operators are estimated on the basis of the costs of similarity selections. $LeftSel(A_i)$ symbolizes any suitable (similarity) selection on attribute A_i. The nested loop similarity join promises to be efficient if $LeftSel(A_i)$ refers to a selection that reduces the size c_{left} of the left input, e.g., a similarity selection $QSel(p, A_i, s_{A_i}, d_{A_i})$. In $TJoin$ the right input is always fetched completely. Another main difference should be the consumed bandwidth, as $TJoin$ completely fetches B_j and $NLJoin$ usually only a small fraction. Similar to $QSel$ and $DelSel$, the third join implementation $DelJoin$ differs in the number of answer messages and the economized waiting state at the query initiator.

9.7 Evaluation

We implemented our algorithms on top of the Java-based P-Grid overlay and performed experiments on PlanetLab. The aim of these experiments was to evaluate the bandwidth consumption and the number of messages as the key performance characteristics. Furthermore, we give a first proof of concept for the introduced cost model by comparing estimated costs to the real costs.

In the experiments we used a network of approximately 400 peers each running on a dedicated physical PlanetLab node. Each node inserted 10 strings of lengths between 8 and 45 characters, randomly chosen from a 4000 entry sample of movie titles from the IMDB database with a skewed heavy-tail key distribution as shown in Figure 9.4 (log-log scale). The figure only shows keys which were inserted more than once and highlights a power-law like key distribution, as it is usual in structured overlay systems when working on string data. The figure provides a general view on the actual data distribution and thus, gives directions for selectivity estimation on strings (and q-grams, in particular), which is used in the introduced cost model. With all q-grams and replication (average replication factor: 5) each peer was responsible for approximately 900 index entries. The constructed P-Grid tree had a height of 8.

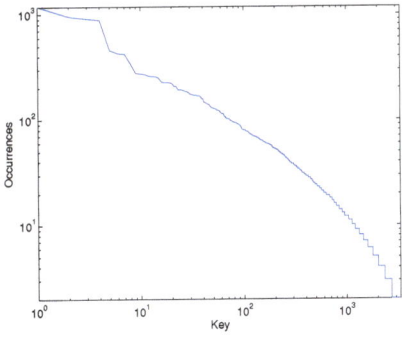

Figure 9.4: Key distribution (log-log scale)

We implemented all of the introduced physical operators. In Section 9.6 we already discussed possible problems of several processing strategies in dynamic environments. The term-based operators can result in involving a main part of the peers in the overlay system into the processing of a single similarity selection. As a consequence we encounter a huge amount of messages and heavy load, which results in poor answer times and can even bring peers to crash. Moreover, the sequential character of the strategy results in poor performance in general, and processing of a query may not be finished at all, as crashed peers can interrupt a corresponding sequence of queried peers completely. We experienced these symptoms in the real-world environment of PlanetLab and could not achieve useful results with the described experimental setup. Thus, we can only provide cost estimations for these operators, but which reflect the bad performance of this approach. For the future it could be necessary to improve this strategy by applying parallelized routing techniques and extended usage of acknowledgment messages in order to overcome the performance problems.

To evaluate other operators we used similarity queries which affected data from all partitions of the data set. A set of 5 randomly chosen strings was queried in distance 3 using the q-gram based similarity selections. We extended the query mix by 5 similarity string joins. The left input of these joins was provided by a q-gram based selection in distance 1. We set the actual join distance for tuples from the right to 3. Each peer initiated a randomly generated query mix by starting a query every 5-8 minutes. All of the following figures show the average number of messages, average bandwidth consumption, respectively, measured per minute at each peer.

9.7.1 Experimental results

Figure 9.5 shows the measured and estimated number of messages for similarity string joins.

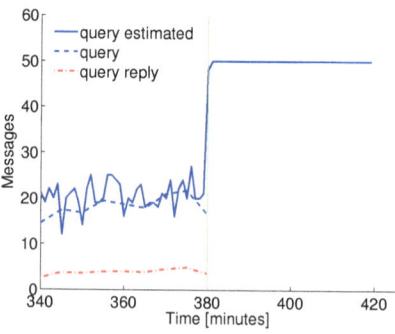

Figure 9.5: Real and estimated costs for $NLJoin$ (time 340-380) and $TJoin$ (time 380-420)

9.7. Evaluation

From time 340-380 (time 0-340 was used to bootstrap the P-Grid overlay system) we ran the $NLJoin$ operator and predicted corresponding costs. From time 380-420 the plot of estimated costs also shows the estimate for term-based similarity joins. As explained before, we did not achieve useful results with this operator in the described experimental setup. But, this is anticipated by the estimated costs as well. The performance of the nested loop join behaves as expected, i.e., as estimated. The small peaks signalize materialize operations of tuples contained in the final result. These subqueries result in several extra messages because object IDs are spread all over the system. As we want to determine the correct relations between costs of different physical implementations, rather than exact costs, these results are acceptable. The plot shows that we are able to achieve this. The small offset in the predicted costs – the burst starts at time 385, not at time 380 – is due to the implementation of the cost predictor. The point is not to predict the exact time of occuring messages, but rather the prediction of a correct amount of messages.

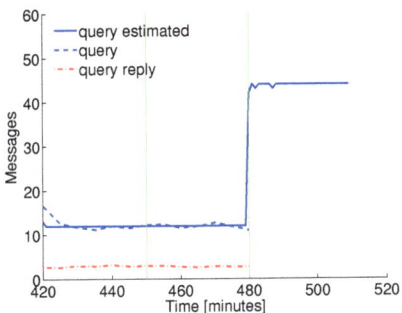

Figure 9.6: Real and estimated costs for $QSel$ (time 420-450), $DelSel$ (time 450-480) and $TSel$ (time 480-510)

Figure 9.6 presents analog results for similarity selections. Time 420-450 corresponds to the execution of $QSel$, time 450-480 to $DelSel$, and time 480-520 to the term-based selection $TSel$ (again, only predicted costs are plotted). The estimated costs are constant as we only involve the processing of actual queries into the calculation (no query replies). This is reflected by the real costs, small fluctuations are due to the following materialize operations. Again, the burst in the plot of estimated costs reflects the bad performance of the term-based similarity selection. As estimated, the costs of $QSel$ and $DelSel$ are almost identical. Similar to the experiments on joins, the plots show the correctness of our cost model and that the bad performance of the implemented term-based selection is predictable a-priori.

Finally, we illustrate the bandwidth consumption of both query types in Figure 9.7. This figure shows that, despite the storage overhead we experienced, the consumed bandwidth is within acceptable limits. The tested selection types show little difference between bandwidth used for queries and bandwidth used for query replies. The plots also show the higher bandwidth consumption of join queries in contrast to selections. This goes conform with our expectations, because the join operators combine selection operators with additional queries.

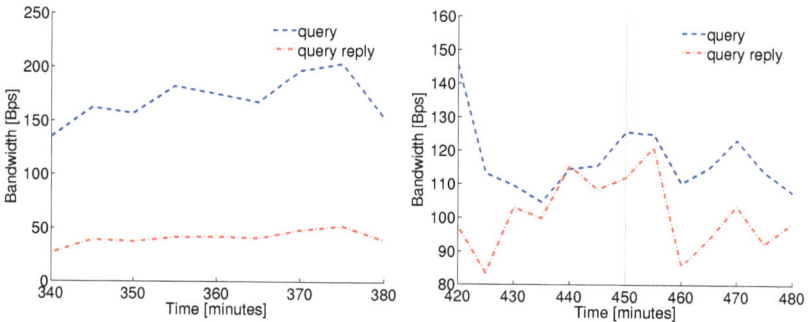

Figure 9.7: Bandwidth consumption for similarity join (left) and similarity selections (right)

As a consequence, we experience that the q-gram based algorithms are an important extension to known overlay systems in order to process similarity queries efficiently. In contrast to traditional implementations this approach scales up to high numbers of peers and is applicable to dynamic environments with skewed data distributions. The costs of these operators can be estimated in an easy fashion, allowing optimizers to speed up processing and lower network load. Such estimates are based on small information, but are quite accurate, which is reflected by the correct relations of estimated costs for analog operators implemented differently.

9.8 Related Work

There is a number of related approaches aiming to support complex structured queries and data heterogeneity on top of structured overlay networks in peer data management systems (PDMS). Most of these systems have either a focus on implementing classical relational algebra operators and particularly joins on top of a structured P2P system such as PIER [HHH+02, HHL+03], or on supporting data integration and schema heterogeneity such as GridVine [ACMHP04, CMAA07].

OceanStore [KBC+00, REG+03] is not a peer data management system per definition, nevertheless we will introduce it briefly here for the sake of completeness. OceanStore is a global persistent data store designed to scale to billions of users. It provides a consistent, highly-available, and durable storage utility atop an infrastructure comprised of untrusted

9.8. Related Work

servers. Any computer can join the infrastructure to contribute local storage and using already shared resources. Shared resources are accessed through a distributed file system in which users can store data objects, analog to files in a classical file system. OceanStore caches data promiscuously to increase data availability and system performance, i.e., local replicas provide faster access to data. Promiscuous caching requires redundancy and cryptographic techniques to protect the data from the servers upon which it resides. OceanStore further employs a Byzantine-fault tolerant commit protocol to provide strong consistency across replicas, which can be weakened by applications for higher performance and availability.

UniStore shares only a few similarities with OceanStore, amongst them are data distribution and replication, data location transparency and system robustness. Other than that mentioned these two systems have different aims and provide different functionalities.

PIER [HHH+02, HHL+03] is an Internet-scale query engine built on top of the distributed hash table Bamboo [RGRK04]. It was the first general-purpose relational query processor targeted at a P2P architecture of thousands or millions of participating nodes on the Internet and supports massively distributed, database-style dataflows for snapshot and continuous queries. PIER stores data in the DHT in tuple form and every tuple in PIER is self-describing, containing its table name, column names, and column types. Data is accessed through 14 logical operators and 26 physical operators (some logical operators have multiple implementations). Most of the operators are similar to those in a DBMS, such as selection, projection, tee, union, join, group-by, and duplicate elimination. These operators are executed in a distributed fashion by query plans using the UFL dataflow language, i.e., UFL currently stands for Unnamed Flow Language. PIER currently has three kinds of indexes to locate peers responsible for query operators: a true-predicate index, an equality-predicate index, and a range-predicate index. The true-predicate index allows a query that ranges over all the data to find all the data. Equality predicates support operations that need to find a specific value of a partitioning key and can be routed to the relevant node using the DHT. For range search, PIER uses a Prefix Hash Tree (PHT) [RRHS04].

PIER aims at distribution and scalability challenges as our approach but does not consider the problem of heterogeneity. On the contrary they assume that agreement on a global schema is feasible and desirable. Both systems implement a tuple based data management schema enabling self-describing data and therefore schema mappings. Both systems also share a similar approach of distributed query processing using query plans holding query operators, executing on several indexes provided by a structured overlay.

GridVine [ACMHP04, CMAA07] is a peer data management infrastructure addressing both scalability and semantic heterogeneity. Scalability is addressed by peers organized in a structured overlay network forming the physical layer in which data, schemas and schema mappings are stored. Semantic interoperability is achieved trough a purely decentralized and self-organized process of pair-wise schema mappings and query reformulation, forming a semantic mediation layer on top and independent of the physical layer. The semantic layer enables peers to share data in the overlay network according to local schemas interlinked by user-defined schema mappings. These schema mappings are then used for automatic query reformulation allowing queries to traverse a sequence of schemas at the mediation layer and retrieve all relevant results, irrespective of their schemas. GridVine offers a recursive and an iterative gossiping approach, i.e., query reformulation approach. In iterative gossiping, the peer issuing the original query is responsible for retrieving all mappings and reformulating all queries by itself iteratively. In recursive gossiping, the reformulation process is iteratively delegated to those peers receiving reformulated queries. Recursive gossiping performs systematically better because it distributes the reformulation load among peers.

GridVine shares most of the aims and features of our approach, e.g., both systems use the same underlying overlay network. The differences relate to the challenges expressiveness of queries and dealing with heterogeneity. GridVine implements triple pattern queries with support for conjunctive and disjunctive queries realized by distributed joins across the network. We support similarity-enriched SPARQL queries with in-network query execution realized by query plans executed in parallel. On the contrary we currently do not implement something similar to GridVine's verification of schema mappings [CMAF06] to identify incorrect schema translations though both are able to deal with data and schema heterogeneity to the same extend.

Piazza [HIM+04] is as well a peer data management system dealing with scalability and data heterogeneity. It uses a mapping language for mapping between sets of XML source nodes with different document structures (including those with XML serializations of RDF). The architecture, that uses the transitive closure of mappings to answer queries, is able to follow mappings in both forward and reverse directions can both remove and reconstruct XML document structure. Unlike GridVine Piazza uses central indexing and an extension to use an underlying DHT only seems to be planned for the future, a key requirement for Internet-scale systems.

RDFPeers [CF04] presents a scalable and distributed RDF triple repository for storing, indexing and querying individual RDF statements. RDFPeers self-organize into a multi-attribute addressable network (MAAN) which extends Chord to efficiently answer multi-attribute and range queries. The system's query processing capabilities are very similar to the ones of GridVine as it supports triple pattern queries, disjunctive and range queries and conjunctive multi-predicate queries using RDQL. In contrast to our approach and GridVine, query resolution is done locally and iteratively. Further, RDFPeers also does not address the problem of schema heterogeneity and is therefore not as generic and flexible as GridVine or us.

LSH forest [BCG05] uses a locality-sensitive hashing (LSH) function to index high-dimensional data for answering (approximate) similarity queries. The queries return the m points in the data set closest to the query according to a distance function. The system is based on P-Grid and stores documents in the overlay network using the LSH function. Therefore, similarity queries can be performed by first routing to the peer closest to the initial query and then returning documents similar to the query by using existing neighbor links in P-Grid. The paper does not provide an evaluation of required messages or bandwidth as provided by us.

EZSearch [Tra05] is based on the Zigzag hierarchy which clusters semantically close nodes in a multi-layer hierarchy and supports range queries and top-N queries. The evaluation of the system by a simulation shows that the system works well for both query types even for Zipf-like query distributions but it remains unclear how the system deals with skewed data distributions which require sophisticated load balancing mechanisms. Additionally, no experimental evaluation exists.

9.9 Conclusions

We presented UniStore, a global-scale universal distributed storage system targeted at new web applications for public data management. In this scenario data is collected through a large number of collaborative participants which are not obliged to use common schemas and terminologies. UniStore enables them to store and query heterogeneous data in a reliable and distributed fashion. We support heterogeneity on schema and data level by using a vertical triple-based storage model, similar to the universal relation model, and the support of schema mappings and similarity queries. Our evaluation shows that our query operators are efficiently implemented on top of P-Grid and meet our theoretical expectations.

UniStore is currently the only implemented system available offering both large-scale storage of heterogeneous data in triple form (equally RDF) and database-like query operations with completeness guarantees. UniStore can be downloaded from http://www.dbis.prakinf.tu-ilmenau.de/unistore.

Chapter 10
Conclusions

Since the beginning of the new millennium, the Internet has changed from a more-or-less passive information resource and email service provider, to a rapidly changing playground for a new generation of Internet users, willing to provide information to other internauts. Early P2P systems made file-sharing as easy as web browsing and emailing for all Internet users, boosting their popularity and user community. The increasing amount of shared data motivated research for more sophisticated P2P data management systems and led to the first PDMS. Their database-like query processing capabilities bring up new requirements for structured overlays, on which PDMS are based upon. Similar to local databases [AMMH07], PDMS can benefit from structured overlays tailored towards Web 2.0 applications and data structures. These new requirements were so far not tackled by the P2P community although their performance impact is considerable.

Throughout this thesis, we considered to improve correlated data access of applications like PDMS on top of structured overlays using a distributed index to access shared resources. In contrast to the classical use of structured overlays for resource sharing and discovery, PDMS require frequent joint data access exploiting and inducing data correlations amongst shared data. Most structured overlays optimized their distributed index for efficient single key lookups only, and a few are further suitable for efficient range scans, minimizing network access and the number of nodes involved during data access. Data correlations induced by joint data access beyond range queries are currently not considered by data/index partitioning approaches in structured P2P systems. As examples, we studied three relevant types of data correlations in the context of their use in PDMS. We presented our approach to efficiently process range queries in structured overlays exploiting the order relationship of data entries and the order-preserving hash function used by several overlays. Probabilistic data correlations can be used to model a wide spectrum of data correlations. We used two examples, distributed inference and multi-term queries and their induced correlations. We presented our approach of re-organizing the distributed index to cluster strongly correlated data entries at one node, or at least in the proximity, to improve processing performance.

The spring relaxation technique allowed us to "relax" correlations among data entries, following the P2P principle of no central control and local decisions by autonomous peers in pair-wise interactions. The evaluation of our approach has shown a considerable reduction of network access and a significant improvement in joint data access for our two studied problems of distributed inference and multi-term queries.

Although our approach was designed for the P-Grid overlay system, their applicability for other overlays with similar properties is discussed for each solution. We nevertheless presented implementation details about P-Grid and evaluations of core functionalities and extensions, such as range queries. P-Grid's open and extensible architecture enabled us to further implement a public data management systems called UniStore on top of it. One of UniStore's distinguishing features is its support for similarity queries to overcome schema and data heterogeneities. We presented UniStore's similarity query operators, an analysis of their processing costs and an evaluation on PlanetLab meeting the predicted costs. UniStore is, together with GridVine, the only implemented PDMS with support for database-like query operators and schema heterogeneity. P-Grid's underlying role as distributed data management layer is crucial for the performance and scalability of UniStore.

Directions for Future Research

This thesis provided first means for structured overlays to deal more efficiently with correlated data access. We believe that structured overlays will soon become the dominant type of P2P systems with more-and-more applications building and relying on them. PDMS are the best example as their success is almost not stoppable anymore. The Web 2.0 with its rich structured metadata requires already today such open and distributed information management systems to further evolve. P-Grid is currently part of several initiatives in this direction, amongst them in the Nepomuk project[1], with the ambition to build a distributed semantic desktop enabling users to share information from their desktop with friends and colleagues.

A next step for us is the implementation of our approach to cluster correlated data in P-Grid. We envision building a generic middleware on top of P-Grid dealing with any kind of probabilistic data correlations to build a meta-index on top of the distributed index of P-Grid. A first step has already been reported in [BMA07], implementing our approach for distributed inference in P-Grid. The first results achieved look as promising as our simulation results presented in this thesis. We are certain to achieve similar results for multi-term queries and other operations requiring joint data access, once our implementation efforts are finalized.

The example of UniStore has shown the capabilities of structured overlays for public data management systems. Research on PDMS still has to solve certain challenges, such

---
[1] http://nepomuk.semanticdesktop.org/

as security and trust, before they will be used by a larger set of applications and users. Nevertheless, we see PDMS as a very suitable application for structured overlays to finally bring them the success they were waiting for since their invention. Supporting and tailoring structured overlays towards the new requirements raised by PDMS will therefore certainly be an important field of research for the P2P community in the near future.

List of Frequently Used Symbols and Abbreviations

Greek Symbols

$\delta(p)$	The set of data keys peer p currently maintains.
$\pi(p)$	The path of peer p.
Π	The set of all paths, i.e., all partitions of P-Grid's key space.
$\rho(p, l)$	The references of peer p at level l.
$\sigma(p)$	The references of peer p to peers with the same path, i.e., the peer's replicas.

Abbreviations

DBMS	Database Management System
DDBS	Distributed Database System
DHT	Distributed Hash Table
GUID	Globally Unique Identifier
P2P	Peer-to-Peer
PDMS	Peer Data Management System
PHT	Prefix-Hash-Tree
SHA	Secure Hash Algorithm
TTL	Time-To-Live

Bibliography

[Abe01] Karl Aberer. P-Grid: A self-organizing access structure for p2p information systems. In *Proceedings of Sixth International Conference on Cooperative Information Systems (CoopIS)*, pages 179–194, 2001.

[Abe02a] Karl Aberer. Efficient search in unbalanced, randomized peer-to-peer search trees. Technical Report IC/2002/79, Ecole Polytechnique Fédérale de Lausanne (EPFL), 2002.

[Abe02b] Karl Aberer. Scalable data access in p2p systems using unbalanced search trees. In *Proceedings of the Fourth Workshop on Distributed Data and Structures (WDAS'2002)*, Paris, France, March 2002.

[ACK$^+$02] David P. Anderson, Jeff Cobb, Eric Korpela, Matt Lebofsky, and Dan Werthimer. SETI@home: an experiment in public-resource computing. *Commun. ACM*, 45(11):56–61, 2002.

[ACMHP04] Karl Aberer, Philippe Cudré-Mauroux, Manfred Hauswirth, and Tim Van Pelt. Gridvine: Building internet-scale semantic overlay networks. In *International Semantic Web Conference*, pages 107–121, 2004.

[ADH04] Karl Aberer, Anwitaman Datta, and Manfred Hauswirth. Efficient, self-contained handling of identity in peer-to-peer systems. *IEEE Transactions on Knowledge and Data Engineering*, 16(7):858–869, 2004.

[ADH05] Karl Aberer, Anwitaman Datta, and Manfred Hauswirth. Multifaceted simultaneous load balancing in dht-based p2p systems: A new game with old balls and bins. *Self-star Properties in Complex Information Systems*, 3460:373–391, 2005.

[ADHS05] Karl Aberer, Anwitaman Datta, Manfred Hauswirth, and Roman Schmidt. Indexing data-oriented overlay networks. In *Proceedings of the 31st International Conference on Very Large Databases (VLDB)*, August 2005.

[AKK+03] Marcelo Arenas, Vasiliki Kantere, Anastasios Kementsietsidis, Iluju Kiringa, Renée J. Miller, and John Mylopoulos. The Hyperion project: from data integration to data coordination. *SIGMOD Rec.*, 32(3):53–58, 2003.

[AKK04] James Aspnes, Jonathan Kirsch, and Arvind Krishnamurthy. Load balancing and locality in range-queriable data structures. In *Proceedings of the twenty-third annual ACM symposium on Principles of distributed computing (PODC '04)*, pages 115–124, New York, NY, USA, 2004. ACM Press.

[AMMH07] Daniel J. Abadi, Adam Marcus, Samuel R. Madden, and Kate Hollenbach. Scalable semantic web data management using vertical partitioning. In *VLDB '07: Proceedings of the 33rd international conference on Very large data bases*, pages 411–422. VLDB Endowment, 2007.

[AP03] Karl Aberer and Magdalena Punceva. Efficient search in structured peer-to-peer systems: Binary v.s. k-ary unbalanced tree structures. In *Proceedings of the International Workshop On Databases, Information Systems and Peer-to-Peer Computing (DBISP2P)*, Humboldt University, Berlin, Germany, September 7-8 2003. Collocated with VLDB 2003.

[AS03] James Aspnes and Gauri Shah. Skip graphs. In *Proceedings of the fourteenth annual ACM-SIAM symposium on Discrete algorithms (SODA '03)*, pages 384–393, Philadelphia, PA, USA, January 2003. Society for Industrial and Applied Mathematics.

[BAS04] Ashwin R. Bharambe, Mukesh Agrawal, and Srinivasan Seshan. Mercury: supporting scalable multi-attribute range queries. *SIGCOMM Computer Communication Review*, 34(4):353–366, 2004.

[Bat01] Vladimir Batagelj. Pajek - program for large networks analysis and visualization. Online, 2001. http://vlado.fmf.uni-lj.si/pub/networks/pajek/.

[BCG05] Mayank Bawa, Tyson Condie, and Prasanna Ganesan. LSH forest: self-tuning indexes for similarity search. In *Proceedings of the 14th international conference on World Wide Web (WWW '05)*, pages 651–660, New York, NY, USA, 2005. ACM Press.

[BGK+02] P. Bernstein, F. Giunchiglia, A. Kementsietsidis, J. Mylopoulos, L. Serafini, and I. Zaihrayeu. Data management for peer-to-peer computing: A vision. In *Proceedings of the Fifth International Workshop on the Web and Databases (WebDB '2002)*, 2002.

BIBLIOGRAPHY

[BGT93] Claude Berrou, Alain Glavieux, and Punya Thitimajshima. Near shannon limit error-correcting codes and decoding: Turbo codes. In *Proceedings of the IEEE International Communications Conference*, 1993.

[Bit] BitTorrent website. Online. http://www.bittorrent.org/.

[BKadH05] Marcin Bienkowski, Miroslaw Korzeniowski, and Friedhelm Meyer auf der Heide. Dynamic load balancing in distributed hash tables. In *Proceedings of the 4th International Workshop on Peer-To-Peer Systems (IPTPS'05)*, 2005.

[BKS01] Stephan Börzsönyi, Donald Kossmann, and Konrad Stocker. The skyline operator. In *Proceedings of the 17th International Conference on Data Engineering*, pages 421–430, Washington, DC, USA, 2001. IEEE Computer Society.

[BM72] Rudolf Bayer and Edward M. McCreight. Organization and maintenance of large ordered indices. *Acta Informatica 1*, 1:173–189, 1972.

[BMA07] Nicolas Bonvin, Grégoire Montavon, and Damien Auroux. Implementing Belief Propagation on P-Grid. Technical Report 2008-004, EPFL, Lausanne, Switzerland, January 2007.

[BMR04] Danny Bickson, Dahlia Malkhi, and David Rabinowitz. Efficient large scale content distribution. In *Proceedings of the Workshop on Distributed Data and Structures (WDAS)*, Lausanne, Switzerland, 2004.

[BMT+06] Matthias Bender, Sebastian Michel, Peter Triantafillou, Gerhard Weikum, and Christian Zimmer. P2p content search: Give the web back to the people. In *Proceedings of 5th International Workshop on Peer-to-Peer Systems (IPTPS 2006)*, Santa Barbara, USA, 2006.

[CCR+03] Brent Chun, David Culler, Timothy Roscoe, Andy Bavier, Larry Peterson, Mike Wawrzoniak, and Mic Bowman. Planetlab: an overlay testbed for broad-coverage services. *ACM SIGCOMM Computer Communication Review*, 33(3):3–12, July 2003.

[CDHR03] Miguel Castro, Peter Druschel, Y. Charlie Hu, and Antony I. T. Rowstron. Topology-aware routing in structured peer-to-peer overlay networks. In *Future Directions in Distributed Computing*, pages 103 – 107, 2003.

[CF04] Min Cai and Martin Frank. RDFPeers: a scalable distributed rdf repository based on a structured peer-to-peer network. In *Proceedings of the 13th international conference on World Wide Web (WWW '04)*, pages 650–657. ACM Press, 2004.

[CMAA07] Philippe Cudré-Mauroux, Suchit Agarwal, and Karl Aberer. GridVine: An infrastructure for peer information management. *IEEE Internet Computing*, 11(5):36–44, 2007.

[CMAF06] Philippe Cudré-Mauroux, Karl Aberer, and Andras Feher. Probabilistic message passing in peer data management systems. In *Proceedings of the 22nd International Conference on Data Engineering (ICDE'06)*, page 41, Washington, DC, USA, 2006. IEEE Computer Society.

[CNP82] S. Ceri, M. Negri, and G. Pelagatti. Horizontal data partitioning in database design. In *Proceedings of the 1982 ACM SIGMOD international conference on Management of data (SIGMOD '82)*, pages 128–136, New York, NY, USA, 1982. ACM Press.

[Coh00] William W. Cohen. Data integration using similarity joins and a word-based information representation language. *ACM Transactions on Information Systems*, 18(3):288–321, 2000.

[CSK04] R. Chen, Krishnamoorthy Sivakumar, and Hillol Kargupta. Collective mining of bayesian networks from distributed heterogeneous data. *Knowledge and Information Systems*, 6(2):164–187, 2004.

[CSWH00] Ian Clarke, Oskar Sandberg, Brandon Wiley, and Theodore W. Hong. Freenet: A distributed anonymous information storage and retrieval system. In *Proceedings of the International Workshop on Design Issues in Anonymity and Unobservability*, volume 2009/2001, page 46, Berkeley, CA, USA, July 2000.

[Dat91] C. J. Date. *An Introduction to Database Systems*. Addison-Wesley Longman Publishing Co., Inc., Boston, MA, USA, 1991.

[DCKM04] Frank Dabek, Russ Cox, Frans Kaashoek, and Robert Morris. Vivaldi: A decentralized network coordinate system. In *Proceedings of ACM SIGCOMM*, 2004.

[DHA03] Anwitaman Datta, Manfred Hauswirth, and Karl Aberer. Updates in highly unreliable, replicated peer-to-peer systems. In *Proceedings of the 23rd International Conference on Distributed Computing Systems (ICDCS '03)*, page 76, Washington, DC, USA, 2003. IEEE Computer Society.

[DSA07] Anwitaman Datta, Roman Schmidt, and Karl Aberer. Query-load balancing in structured overlays. In *Proceedings of the Seventh IEEE International Symposium on Cluster Computing and the Grid (CCGRID'07)*, Rio de Janeiro, Brazil, May 2007. ACM Press.

[eDo] eDonkey: Unofficial protocol specification. Online. `http://kent.dl.sourceforge.net/pdonkey/eDonkey-protocol-0.6.2.html`.

[Fas] FastTrack: known parts of the protocol. Online. `http://cvs.berlios.de/cgi-bin/viewcvs.cgi/gift-fasttrack/giFT-FastTrack/PROTOCOL?rev=HEAD\&content-type=text/vnd.viewcvs-markup`.

[GAE03] Abhishek Gupta, Divyakant Agrawal, and Amr El Abbadi. Approximate range selection queries in peer-to-peer systems. In *Proceedings of the First Biennial Conference on Innovative Data Systems Research (CIDR 2003)*, Asilomar, California, United States, January 2003.

[GBGM04] Prasanna Ganesan, Mayank Bawa, and Hector Garcia-Molina. Online balancing of range-partitioned data with applications to peer-to-peer systems. In *Proceedings of the 30st International Conference on Very Large Databases (VLDB)*, Toronto, Canada, September 2004.

[GHI+01] Steven Gribble, Alon Halevy, Zachary Ives, Maya Rodrig, and Dan Suciu. What can databases do for peer-to-peer? In *Proceedings of the Fourth International Workshop on the Web and Databases (WebDB '2001)*, 2001.

[GIJ+01] Luis Gravano, Panagiotis G. Ipeirotis, H. V. Jagadish, Nick Koudas, S. Muthukrishnan, and Divesh Srivastava. Approximate string joins in a database (almost) for free. In *Proceedings of the 27th International Conference on Very Large Data Bases (VLDB '01)*, pages 491–500, San Francisco, CA, USA, 2001. Morgan Kaufmann Publishers Inc.

[GKK+03] Phillip B. Gibbons, Brad Karp, Yan Ke, Suman Nath, and Srinivasan Seshan. Irisnet: an architecture for a worldwide sensor web. *IEEE Pervasive Computing*, 2(4):22–33, October–December 2003.

[Gnua] Gnutella development forum. Online. `http://groups.yahoo.com/group/the\_gdf`.

[Gnub] Gnutella: Protocol version 0.6. Online. `http://rfc-gnutella.sourceforge.net/src/rfc-0_6-draft.html`.

[GS05] P. Brighten Godfrey and Ion Stoica. Heterogeneity and load balance in distributed hash tables. *Procceedings of the 24th Annual Joint Conference of the IEEE Computer and Communications Societies (INFOCOM'05)*, 1:596–606 vol. 1, March 2005.

[H2] H2 database engine. Online. `http://www.h2database.com/`.

[Hec95] David Heckerman. A tutorial on learning with bayesian networks. Technical Report MSR-TR-95-06, Microsoft Research, Redmond, USA, 1995.

[HHH+02] Matthew Harren, Joseph M. Hellerstein, Ryan Huebsch, Boon Thau Loo, Scott Shenker, and Ion Stoica. Complex queries in dht-based peer-to-peer networks. In *Revised Papers from the First International Workshop on Peer-to-Peer Systems (IPTPS '01)*, pages 242–259, London, UK, 2002. Springer-Verlag.

[HHL+03] Ryan Huebsch, Joseph M. Hellerstein, Nick Lanham, Boon Thau Loo, Scott Shenker, and Ion Stoica. Querying the internet with pier. In *Proceedings of 19th International Conference on Very Large Databases (VLDB '03)*, pages 321–332, Berlin, Germany, 2003.

[HIM+04] Alon Y. Halevy, Zachary G. Ives, Jayant Madhavan, Peter Mork, Dan Suciu, and Igor Tatarinov. The piazza peer data management system. *IEEE Transactions on Knowledge and Data Engineering*, 16(7):787–798, 2004.

[HJS+03] Nicholas J. A. Harvey, Michael B. Jones, Stefan Saroiu, Marvin Theimer, and Alec Wolman. Skipnet: A scalable overlay network with practical locality properties. In *Proceedings of the Fourth USENIX Symposium on Internet Technologies and Systems (USITS '03)*, Seattle, WA, March 2003.

[HK07] Manfred Hauswirth and Mark Kornfilt. Efficient processing of rare queries in gnutella using a hybrid infrastructure. In *Proceedings of the 5th International Workshop on Databases, Information Systems and Peer-to-Peer Computing*, Vienna, Austria, September 2007.

[HLWY06] Feng Hong, Minglu Li, Minyou Wu, and Jiadi Yu. Pchord: Improvement on chord to achieve better routing efficiency by exploiting proximity. *IEICE - Trans. Inf. Syst.*, E89-D(2):546–554, 2006.

[HSPM06] Y. Thomas Hou, Yi Shi, Jianping Pan, and Scott F. Midkiff. Maximizing the lifetime of wireless sensor networks through optimal single-session flow routing. *IEEE Transactions on Mobile Computing*, 5(9):1255–1266, 2006.

[HTT] Http - hypertext transfer protocol. Online. http://www.w3.org/Protocols/.

[IJWFMW04] Alexander T. Ihler, III John W. Fisher, Randolph L. Moses, and Alan S. Willsky. Nonparametric belief propagation for self-calibration in sensor networks. In *Proceedings of the Third international symposium on Information processing in sensor networks*, pages 225–233, New York, NY, USA, 2004. ACM Press.

[KaZ] KaZaA website. Online. http://www.kazaa.com/.

[KBC+00] John Kubiatowicz, David Bindel, Yan Chen, Steven Czerwinski, Patrick Eaton, Dennis Geels, Ramakrishna Gummadi, Sean Rhea, Hakim Weatherspoon, Chris Wells, and Ben Zhao. Oceanstore: an architecture for global-scale persistent storage. *SIGARCH Computer Architecture News*, 28(5):190–201, 2000.

[Kle99] Jon Kleinberg. The small-world phenomenon: An algorithmic perspective. Technical Report 99-1776, Cornell Computer Science, October 1999.

[KLL+97] David Karger, Eric Lehman, Tom Leighton, Rina Panigrahy, Matthew Levine, and Daniel Lewin. Consistent hashing and random trees: distributed caching protocols for relieving hot spots on the world wide web. In *Proceedings of the twenty-ninth annual ACM symposium on Theory of computing (STOC '97)*, pages 654–663, New York, NY, USA, 1997. ACM Press.

[KMS07] Marcel Karnstedt, Jessica Müller, and Kai-Uwe Sattler. Cost-aware skyline queries in structured overlays. In *Proceedings ICDE Workshop on Ranking in Databases (DBRank'07)*, pages 285–288, Istanbul, Turkey, 2007.

[KSHS06] Marcel Karnstedt, Kai-Uwe Sattler, Manfred Hauswirth, and Roman Schmidt. Similarity queries on structured data in structured overlays. In *Proceedings of the 22nd International Conference on Data Engineering Workshops (ICDEW'06): Proceedings of the 2nd IEEE International Workshop on Networking Meets Databases (NetDB'06)*, page 32, Atlanta, GA, USA, April 2006. IEEE Computer Society.

[KSR+07] Marcel Karnstedt, Kai-Uwe Sattler, Martin Richtarsky, Jessica Müller, Manfred Hauswirth, Roman Schmidt, and Renault John. Unistore: Querying a dht-based universal storage. In *Proceddings of the 23rd International Conference on Data Engineering (ICDE 2007)*, Istanbul, Turkey, April 16-20 2007.

[LCP+04] Eng Keong Lua, Jon Crowcroft, Marcelo Pias, Ravi Sharma, and Steven Lim. A survey and comparison of peer-to-peer overlay network schemes. *IEEE Communications Surveys & Tutorials*, 7(2):72–93, March 2004.

[Lev66] Vladimir Levenshtein. Binary codes capable of correcting deletions, insertions, and reversals. *Soviet Physics Doklady*, 10(8):707–710, 1966.

[LNS93] Witold Litwin, Marie-Anne Neimat, and Donovan A. Schneider. Lh*: Linear hashing for distributed files. In *Proceedings of the 1993 ACM SIGMOD international conference on Management of data (SIGMOD '93)*, pages 327–336, New York, NY, USA, 1993. ACM.

[LNS94] Witold Litwin, Marie-Anne Neimat, and Donovan A. Schneider. Rp*: A family of order preserving scalable distributed data structures. In *Proceedings of the 20th International Conference on Very Large Data Bases (VLDB '94)*, pages 342–353, San Francisco, CA, USA, 1994. Morgan Kaufmann Publishers Inc.

[LNS+04] Chu Yee Liau, Wee Siong Ng, Yanfeng Shu, Stéphane Bressan, and Kian-Lee Tan. Efficient range queries and fast lookup services for scalable p2p networks. In *Proceedings of the International Workshop on Databases, Information Systems, and Peer-to-Peer Computing (DBISP2P)*, pages 93–106, 2004.

[Man04] Gurmeet Singh Manku. Balanced binary trees for id management and load balance in distributed hash tables. In *Proceedings of the twenty-third annual ACM symposium on Principles of distributed computing (PODC '04)*, pages 197–205. ACM Press, 2004.

[MBN+06] Sebastian Michel, Matthias Bender, Nikos Ntarmos, Peter Triantafillou, Gerhard Weikum, and Christian Zimmer. Discovering and exploiting keyword and attribute-value co-occurrences to improve p2p routing indices. In *CIKM '06: Proceedings of the 15th ACM international conference on Information and knowledge management*, pages 172–181, New York, NY, USA, 2006. ACM.

[MM02] Petar Maymounkov and David Mazières. Kademlia: A peer-to-peer information system based on the xor metric. In *In Proceedings of 1st International Workshop on Peer-to-Peer Systems (IPTPS '02)*, pages 53–65, Cambridge, MA, USA, March 7-8 2002.

[MTW05] Sebastian Michel, Peter Triantafillou, and Gerhard Weikum. Klee: a framework for distributed top-k query algorithms. In *Proceedings of the 31st international conference on Very large data bases (VLDB '05)*, pages 637–648. VLDB Endowment, 2005.

[MUV84] David Maier, Jeffrey D. Ullman, and Moshe Y. Vardi. On the foundations of the universal relation model. *ACM Trans. Database Syst.*, 9(2):283–308, 1984.

[Nap] Napster website. Online. http://www.napster.com/.

[NBY98] Gonzalo Navarro and Ricardo Baeza-Yates. A practical q-gram index for text retrieval allowing errors. *CLEI Electron Journal*, 1(2):31–88, 1998.

[NCWD84] Shamkant Navathe, Stefano Ceri, Gio Wiederhold, and Jinglie Dou. Vertical partitioning algorithms for database design. *ACM Trans. Database Syst.*, 9(4):680–710, 1984.

[NDLR00] Yakham Ndiaye, Aly Wane Diene, Witold Litwin, and Tore Risch. Scalable distributed data structures for high-performance databases. In *Proceedings of Workshop on Distributed Data and Structures*, 2000.

[NOT02] Wee Siong Ng, Beng Chin Ooi, and Kian-Lee Tan. Bestpeer: A self-configurable peer-to-peer system. In *Proceedings of the 18th International Conference on Data Engineering (ICDE '02)*, page 272, Washington, DC, USA, 2002. IEEE Computer Society.

[NOTZ03] Wee Siong Ng, Beng Chin Ooi., Kian-Lee Tan, and Aoying Zhou. Peerdb: a p2p-based system for distributed data sharing. *Proceedings of the 19th International Conference on Data Engineering (ICDE'03)*, pages 633–644, 5-8 March 2003.

[OTZ$^+$03] Beng Chin Ooi, Kian-Lee Tan, Aoying Zhou, Chin Hong Goh, Yingguang Li, Chu Yee Liau, Bo Ling, Wee Siong Ng, Yanfeng Shu, Xiaoyu Wang, and Ming Zhang. Peerdb: peering into personal databases. In *SIGMOD '03: Proceedings of the 2003 ACM SIGMOD international conference on Management of data*, pages 659–659, New York, NY, USA, 2003. ACM.

[OV91] M. Tamer Ozsu and P. Valduriez. *Principles of distributed database systems*. Prentice-Hall, Inc., Upper Saddle River, NJ, USA, 1991.

[PACR02] Larry Peterson, Tom Anderson, David Culler, and Timothy Roscoe. A blueprint for introducing disruptive technology into the internet. In *Proceedings of HotNets–I*, Princeton, New Jersey, October 2002.

[Pea88] Judea Pearl. *Probabilistic Reasoning in Intelligent Systems: Networks of Plausible Inference*. Morgan Kaufmann, San Francisco, CA, USA, 1988.

[PGM05] Mark Paskin, Carlos Guestrin, and Jim McFadden. A robust architecture for distributed inference in sensor networks. In *Proceedings of the 4th international symposium on Information processing in sensor networks (IPSN '05)*, page 8, Piscataway, NJ, USA, 2005. IEEE Press.

[PLR$^+$06] Ivana Podnar, Toan Luu, Martin Rajman, Fabius Klemm, and Karl Aberer. A Peer-to-Peer Architecture for Information Retrieval Across Digital Library Collections. In *European conference on research and advanced technology for digital libraries (ECDL'06)*, Lecture Notes in Computer Science, pages 14–25, 2006.

[PM02] Vassilis Papadimos and David Maier. Mutant query plans. *Information and Software Technology*, 44(4):197–206, April 2002.

[PRR97] C. Greg Plaxton, Rajmohan Rajaraman, and Andréa W. Richa. Accessing nearby copies of replicated objects in a distributed environment. In *Proceedings of the ninth annual ACM symposium on Parallel algorithms and architectures (SPAA '97)*, pages 311–320, New York, NY, USA, 1997. ACM Press.

[PS06] Eric Prud'hommeaux and Andy Seaborne. SPARQl query language for RDF. Online, April 2006. http://www.w3.org/TR/rdf-sparql-query/.

[PSW+04] Peter Pietzuch, Jeffrey Shneidman, Matt Welsh, Margo Seltzer, and Mema Roussopoulos. Path optimization in stream-based overlay networks. Technical Report TR26-04, Harvard University, Cambridge, Massachusetts, 2004.

[Pug90] William Pugh. Skip lists: a probabilistic alternative to balanced trees. *Communications of the ACM*, 33(6):668–676, 1990.

[RB01] Erhard Rahm and Philip A. Bernstein. A survey of approaches to automatic schema matching. *The VLDB Journal*, 10(4):334–350, 2001.

[RD01] Antony Rowstron and Peter Druschel. Pastry: Scalable, decentralized object location and routing for large-scale peer-to-peer systems. In *Proceedings of the IFIP/ACM International Conference on Distributed Systems Platforms (Middleware)*, pages 329–350, November 2001.

[REG+03] Sean Rhea, Patrick Eaton, Dennis Geels, Hakim Weatherspoon, Ben Zhao, and John Kubiatowicz. Pond: The oceanstore prototype. In *Proceedings of the 2nd USENIX Conference on File and Storage Technologies (FAST '03)*, pages 1–14, Berkeley, CA, USA, 2003. USENIX Association.

[RFH+01] Sylvia Ratnasamy, Paul Francis, Mark Handley, Richard Karp, and Scott Schenker. A scalable content-addressable network. In *Proceedings of the 2001 conference on Applications, technologies, architectures, and protocols for computer communications (SIGCOMM '01)*, pages 161–172, New York, NY, USA, 2001. ACM Press.

[RGRK04] Sean Rhea, Dennis Geels, Timothy Roscoe, and John Kubiatowicz. Handling churn in a dht. In *Proceedings of the USENIX Annual Technical Conference 2004 on USENIX Annual Technical Conference (ATEC'04)*, pages 10–10, Berkeley, CA, USA, 2004. USENIX Association.

[Rit01] Jordan Ritter. Why gnutella can't scale. no, really. Online, February 2001. http://www.cs.ucsb.edu/~ravenben/classes/290F/papers/GnutellaScale.html.

[RM04] John Risson and Tim Moors. Survey of Research towards Robust Peer-to-Peer Networks: Search Methods. Technical Report UNSW-EE-P2P-1-1, University of New South Wales, Sydney, Australia, September 2004. http://www.ee.unsw.edu.au/~timm/pubs/robust_p2p/submitted.pdf.

[RRHS04] Sriram Ramabhadran, Sylvia Ratnasamy, Joseph M. Hellerstein, and Scott Shenker. Brief announcement: Prefix Hash Tree. In *Proceedings of the twenty-third annual ACM symposium on Principles of distributed computing (PODC '04)*, pages 368–368, New York, NY, USA, 2004. ACM Press.

[SA06] Gleb Skobeltsyn and Karl Aberer. Distributed Cache Table: Efficient Query-Driven Processing of Multi-Term Queries in P2P Networks. In *P2PIR*, 2006.

[SGAE04] Ozgur D. Sahin, Abhishek Gupta, Divyakant Agrawal, and Amr El Abbadi. A peer-to-peer framework for caching range queries. In *Proceedings of the 20th International Conference on Data Engineering (ICDE'04)*, page 165, Washington, DC, USA, 2004. IEEE Computer Society.

[SGS04] Eike Schallehn, Ingolf Geist, and Kai-Uwe Sattler. Supporting similarity operations based on approximate string matching on the web. In *Proceedings of the 12th International Conference on Cooperative Information Systems (CoopIS '04)*, Agia Napa, Cyprus, 2004.

[Sky] Skype website. Online. http://www.skype.com/.

[SLP+07a] Gleb Skobeltsyn, Toan Luu, Ivana Podnar Žarko, Martin Rajman, and Karl Aberer. Query-Driven Indexing for Scalable Peer-to-Peer Text Retrieval. In *Proceedings of the 2nd International Conference on Scalable Information Systems (Infoscale'07)*, 2007.

[SLP+07b] Gleb Skobeltsyn, Toan Luu, Ivana Podnar Žarko, Martin Rajman, and Karl Aberer. Web Text Retrieval with a P2P Query-Driven Index. In *Proceedings of The 30th Annual International ACM SIGIR Conference (SIGIR'07)*, 2007.

[SMK+01] Ion Stoica, Robert Morris, David Karger, M. Frans Kaashoek, and Hari Balakrishnan. Chord: A scalable peer-to-peer lookup service for internet applications. In *Proceedings of the 2001 conference on Applications, technologies, architectures, and protocols for computer communications (SIGCOMM '01)*, pages 149–160, New York, NY, USA, 2001. ACM Press.

[Tra05] Duc A. Tran. Hierarchical semantic overlay approach to p2p similarity search. In *Proceedings of the USENIX Annual Technical Conference 2005 on USENIX*

Annual Technical Conference (ATEC'05), pages 16–16, Berkeley, CA, USA, 2005. USENIX Association.

[UGMW01] Jeffrey D. Ullman, Hector Garcia-Molina, and Jennifer Widom. *Database Systems: The Complete Book*. Prentice Hall PTR, Upper Saddle River, NJ, USA, 2001.

[W3C] W3C. Resource description framework (rdf). Online. http://www.w3.org/RDF/.

[Wei00] Yair Weiss. Correctness of local probability propagation in graphical models with loops. *Neural Computation*, 12(1):1–41, 2000.

[Wie83] Gio C. Wiederhold. *Database Design*. McGraw-Hill, Inc., New York, NY, USA, 1983.

[Yam97] Kenji Yamanishi. Distributed cooperative bayesian learning strategies. In *Proceedings of the tenth annual conference on Computational learning theory (COLT '97)*, pages 250–262, New York, NY, USA, 1997. ACM Press.

[YFW00] Jonathan S. Yedidia, William T. Freeman, and Yair Weiss. Generalized belief propagation. In *Advances in Neural Information Processing Systems (NIPS)*, volume 13, pages 689–695. MIT Press, 2000.

[ZHS+04] Ben Y. Zhao, Ling Huang, Jeremy Stribling, Sean C. Rhea, Anthony D. Joseph, and John Kubiatowicz. Tapestry: A resilient global-scale overlay for service deployment. *IEEE Journal on Selected Areas in Communications*, 22(1):41–53, January 2004.

[ZS05] Jiangong Zhang and Torsten Suel. Efficient query evaluation on large textual collections in a peer-to-peer environment. In *Proceedings of the Fifth IEEE International Conference on Peer-to-Peer Computing (P2P'05)*, pages 225–233, Washington, DC, USA, 2005. IEEE Computer Society.

[ZTZ07] Keping Zhao, Yufei Tao, and Shuigeng Zhou. Efficient top-k processing in large-scaled distributed environments. *Data Knowledge Engineering*, 63(2):315–335, 2007.

Die VDM Verlagsservicegesellschaft sucht für wissenschaftliche Verlage abgeschlossene und herausragende

Dissertationen, Habilitationen, Diplomarbeiten, Master Theses, Magisterarbeiten usw.

für die kostenlose Publikation als Fachbuch.

Sie verfügen über eine Arbeit, die hohen inhaltlichen und formalen Ansprüchen genügt, und haben Interesse an einer honorarvergüteten Publikation?

Dann senden Sie bitte erste Informationen über sich und Ihre Arbeit per Email an *info@vdm-vsg.de*.

Sie erhalten kurzfristig unser Feedback!

VDM Verlagsservicegesellschaft mbH
Dudweiler Landstr. 99
D - 66123 Saarbrücken

Telefon +49 681 3720 174
Fax +49 681 3720 1749

www.vdm-vsg.de

Die VDM Verlagsservicegesellschaft mbH vertritt

Printed by Books on Demand GmbH, Norderstedt / Germany